DATE DUE

AUG 18 1992

Professional French Pastry Series

Volume 3: Petits Fours, Chocolate,
Frozen Desserts, and Sugar Work

Professional French Pastry Series

Volume 3: Petits Fours, Chocolate, Frozen Desserts, and Sugar Work

Roland Bilheux and Alain Escoffier

Under the direction of

Pierre Michalet

Translated by Rhona Poritzky-Lauvand and James Peterson

cicem

A co-publication of
CICEM (Compagnie Internationale
de Consultation *Éducation* et *Media)*
Paris

and

Van Nostrand Reinhold
New York

First published as *Traite de pâtisserie artisanale—Four secs, chocolaterie, glacerie, sucres d'art* by Editions St-Honoré, France; copyright © 1985

English translation copyright © 1988 by Van Nostrand Reinhold for the United States and Canada; by CICEM (Compagnie Internationale de Consultation Education et Media) for the rest of the world

Library of Congress Catalog Card Number 88-5537
ISBN 0-442-20568-6

Printed in the United States of America

Van Nostrand Reinhold
115 Fifth Avenue
New York, NY 10003

Macmillan of Canada
Division of Canada Publishing Corporation
164 Commander Boulevard
Agincourt, Ontario M1S 3C7 Canada

16 15 14 13 12 11 10 9 8 7 6 5 4 3 2 1

Library of Congress Cataloging-in-Publication Data
(Revised for vol. 3)

Bilheux, Roland, 1944–
   The professional French pastry series.

   Translation of: Traité de pâtisserie artisanale.
   Includes index.
   Contents: v. 1. Doughs, batters, and meringues.
v. 2. Creams, confections, and finished desserts. v. 3. Petits fours, chocolate, frozen desserts, and sugar work.
v. 4. Decorations, borders and letters, marzipan, and modern desserts.
   1. Pastry.   2. Confectionery.   3. Cookery, French.
I. Escoffier, Alain, 1947–   . II. Michalet, Pierre. III. Title.
TX773.B49813   1988   641.8'65'0944   88-5537
ISBN 0-442-20565-1 (v. 1)
        0-442-20567-8 (v. 2)
        0-442-20569-4 (v. 4)

Forewords

The *Professional French Pastry Series* consists of four volumes that I would have liked to have owned when I began my training as a professional pastry chef. Now that they are available, they are a resource that I will refer to often. These books are the first available to the serious pastry chef that contain clear and easy-to-follow instructions, which apprentice bakers will also appreciate.

To become a master pastry chef, you need a fine hand, patience, and knowledge. It takes a lot of hard work and perserverance, but the results are well worth the effort. These books show you how to prepare fine pastries using classical methods while allowing the freedom to develop your own ideas, styles, and techniques. Each volume builds upon the skills mastered in the preceding volumes; methods and recipes serve as a continuous source of ideas.

The art of French pastry making is like any art—it is done out of love. Achievements such as the publication of this series help bring respect to pastry making by demonstrating the seriousness of the technique. That's what I particularly like about these volumes—they take you through a precise body of knowledge, step by step, and build your appreciation for it.

I have always hoped that a reference like the *Professional French Pastry Series* would become available to the English-speaking pastry chef as a source to rely on during his or her day-to-day activities. These volumes carefully explain the chemistry of pastry making and include detailed timetables for the recipes. The volumes cover virtually every detail you would need to know in order to learn classical French pastry making. Until now, the only sources available were either in another language or were large collections of recipes without explanations of the methods and techniques. The experience and knowledge of the authors, Roland Bilheux and Alain Escoffier, are apparent throughout all four volumes. The fine abilities of the translators, Rhona Poritzky-Lauvand and Jim Peterson, are also evident.

No one volume or series of volumes can ensure the success of a professional pastry chef. A good resource, however, can help one to develop both the technical and the creative abilities needed for a successful career as a pastry chef. The *Professional French Pastry Series* can assist the chef throughout his or her career. This is truly an encyclopedic work, based on years of professional and teaching experience. To all who are endeavoring to learn the art of French pastry making, as either a professional or a serious amateur, I offer my best wishes for success. It is a wonderful and rewarding experience.

MARKUS FARBINGER
Executive Pastry Chef
Le Cirque Restaurant
New York

When pastry chefs come upon a new book about their craft, their first response is to look for new recipes that can improve their work and inspiring photographs that will enable the creation of more innovative products. The *Professional French Pastry Series* provides both. More important, however, it includes material essential to the day-to-day work of the pastry chef: information about raw ingredients, without which there would be no creation; new and traditional techniques for both making and using pastry; and a historical look at pastry products that enables us to recognize and be a part of the traditions of French pastry making.

In my position as a teacher, I have found this series to be a precious helper; in my position as a chef, an indispensable working tool.

JEAN-MARIE GUICHARD
Director of Instruction
Cacao Barry Training Center
Pennsauken, New Jersey

Contents

From apprentice to master chef . . .

Assorted cookies

Chocolate work

The authors: "To know and to teach"

This phrase perhaps best characterizes the authors,
Roland Bilheux
and
Alain Escoffier

Professional pastry making *refers not only to the preparation of pastry per se, but to the areas of chocolate and sugar work, ice-cream making, cream fillings, and special preparations for catering.*

Only a complete series such as the Professional French Pastry Series can cover the wide range of skills and techniques that the modern pastry chef must master. Mastery of these skills allows the pastry chef to fill a wide variety of positions and functions.

Not only professional pastry chefs, but other food service professionals, are eager to learn the diverse skills involved in French pastry making. Professional restaurant chefs often need to prepare pastries for pâtés, bouchées à la reine, vol-au-vents, and other dishes that are part of classic French cuisine. Mastery of, or at least familiarity with, basic pastry-making techniques is imperative.

Pastry making is also important to the caterer, who is often called upon to prepare special hors d'oeuvre and petits fours served at teas and cocktail parties.

Regardless of their level of experience, food service professionals will find answers to their questions in the Professional French Pastry Series.

. . . the professional's tool

Ice-cream making

Sugar work

The Professional French Pastry Series

Roland Bilheux and Alain Escoffier, both trained professional pastry chefs, now teach those wishing to become professionals. After eight years of dedicated work, they have completed the *Professional French Pastry Series*.

The editing and layout of this series originated in France under the direction of Pierre Michalet, who is the director of Editions St-Honoré, a French publishing house specializing in educational and training media.

Diagram of Contents

Basic Pastry Preparations

Basic batters and dough	Basic creams	Basic confectionery	Finished cakes
Vol. 1	Vol. 2	Vol. 2	Vol. 2

Assembly of Finished Pastries

Finished pastries	Finished cakes	Petits fours	Decorating techniques
Based on pâte brisée, pâte feuilletée, and pâte levée Vol. 1	Vols. 2 and 4	Vol. 3	Vol. 4

Specialties

Chocolate work	Ice-cream making	Sugar work	Modern specialties
Techniques Vol. 3	Sorbets, ice creams, frozen desserts Vol. 3	All techniques Vol. 3	

〜〜〜〜〜〜〜〜〜〜〜

Basic instructions

These instructions are relevant to the preparation of all petits fours.

Following Recipes

The recipes given for petits fours have been precisely calculated and should be closely adhered to. It is imperative that the ingredients be carefully weighed. This is especially true with small quantities, where a few grams or teaspoons might throw off the entire recipe.

Selecting the Raw Ingredients

Because petits fours are usually served plain, the quality of the raw ingredients is extremely important.

When preparing any kind of pastry, use only the best ingredients. This is especially true for petits fours, because the quality of the pastry cannot be masked with elaborate creams or decoration.

Preparing the Raw Ingredients

It is important to be sure that all the raw ingredients are at the same temperature before they are combined for a recipe. This is especially true for cream fillings.

To make sure the ingredients are at the same temperature, it is best to assemble the ingredients several hours or the day before preparation. This is particularly important for such ingredients as butter, almond paste, and egg whites, which should be taken out of the refrigerator and brought to room temperature.

Preparing the Equipment

It is extremely important that the equipment used for the preparation be assembled and washed if necessary.

a. *To prepare the recipe mixture:* select utensils, bowls, and sheet pans that are the appropriate size. Be sure they have been made ready to use. For example, if a copper bowl is needed for beating egg whites, make sure that it has been thoroughly cleaned with salt and vinegar, rinsed, and dried. If a pastry bag is to be used, make sure that is clean and of the right size.

b. *To bake petits fours*

Selecting Molds and Sheet Pans

Make sure that all sheet pans or molds are the same size and thickness and that they are made of the same material.

Prepare enough molds or sheet pans to ensure that an entire batch of petits fours can be baked at once.

Always prepare an extra sheet pan or mold in the same way as the others so that the petit four mixture can be tested.

Testing the Mixture

It is always a good idea to test the petit four dough or batter by baking a small sample before baking the whole batch. The recipe or oven temperature can then be adjusted if necessary without danger of ruining many of the cookies. Testing also allows a check to see if the sheet pans have been correctly buttered or if the petits fours are sticking.

Preparing the Sheet Pans and Molds

The correct preparation of the molds and sheet pans is essential to the success of petits fours. If the sheet pans and molds are not perfectly clean or have been incorrectly buttered, the petits fours are liable to stick and tear when they are removed from them.

Sheet pans that are excessively or insufficiently buttered will adversely affect the petits fours in different ways. For example, when making cigarettes:

- If the sheet pans have too much butter, the batter tends to spread too thinly over the surface. Because they are too thin, the cigarettes dry out quickly and become very difficult to roll.
- If the sheet pans do not have enough butter, the batter stays in a lump rather than spreading. If this happens, the edges of the batter brown too quickly while the center remains raw.

If the sheet pans are irregularly buttered, the problem is compounded. Some petits fours will cook correctly, others will remain raw, and some will brown too quickly (see *Buttering Techniques,* volume 1, pages 32 to 33).

Types of petits fours

Definition

Petits fours are miniature pastries or cookies that can be eaten in a bite or two. In France they are often served with coffee or with dessert. They are almost invariably served with desserts that contain no flour, such as crème renversée, ice cream, bavarians, or fruit salads.

Petits fours are also served as an accompaniment to tea or coffee in the afternoon.

In pastry shops petits fours are usually sold by weight. Most people allow from six to ten petits fours per serving.

In France, petits fours are sometimes divided into two categories: "secs," which are dry and crunchy, and "frais," which have some kind of filling. Petits fours frais are often what Americans think of when they use the term petit four.

Some petits fours fit between the two categories. Macaroons, which are considered "sec," usually have a fruit or hazelnut filling, and punches, which are also categorized as "sec," should have soft, moist centers.

Petit Four Assortments

There are many different varieties of petits fours. The mastery of a few classic types, however, will allow the pastry chef to present a pleasing and varied assortment.

Types of petits fours

Petits fours are grouped into four categories, based on the method of preparation:

A. Simple mixtures
B. Creamy mixtures
C. Beaten egg whites folded with powdered ingredients
D. Beaten egg whites folded with liquids or semisolid ingredients

---

A. Simple Mixtures

(tuiles, sablés, diamants, etc.)

The preparation of the batters for these petits fours involves a simple combination of ingredients. No special techniques or experience is required. The mixture should, however, be placed on the sheet pans and baked following the same precautions as with other types of petits fours.

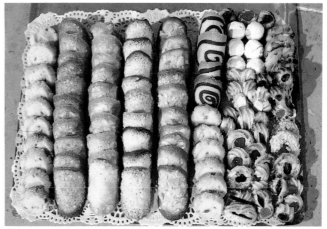

(Page 14)

B. Creamy Mixtures

(cigarettes, copeaux, etc.)

Creamy mixtures require combining a creamy element with other ingredients. Certain precautions should be taken, as described in the recipes.

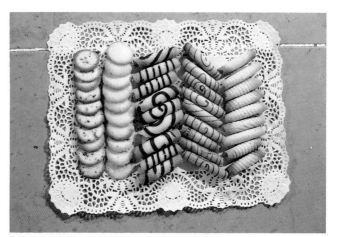

(Page 22)

C. Beaten Egg Whites Folded with Powdered Ingredients

(rochers, doigts de fée, etc.)

These batters are prepared by folding dry, powdered ingredients such as sugar, almond powder, or hazelnut powder into beaten egg whites.

Certain precautions need to be followed for beating the egg whites, folding in the powdered ingredients, and piping the mixture onto the sheet pans.

(Page 28)

D. Beaten Egg Whites Folded with Liquids or Semisolid Ingredients

(macaroons, punches, etc.)

These batters are prepared by folding beaten egg whites into cream and semisolid bases.

Because some of the mixtures are quite stiff, folding them with the beaten egg whites can be a delicate procedure.

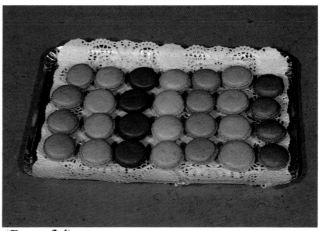

(Page 34)

Group A: Simple mixtures

This is the simplest group of petits fours to prepare.

For these mixtures, no complicated techniques are required to combine the ingredients. There are no unstable emulsions to worry about, and there is no need to incorporate air or work the mixtures to develop creaminess or lightness.

It is important, however, to add the raw ingredients in the correct order and to combine them completely so the mixture is smooth and homogeneous. This is especially true with tuiles and diamants.

Even though the preparation of these mixtures is simpler than that for the other groups, the choice of raw ingredients and the execution of certain techniques must be carried out very carefully. This is particularly true with the preparation of beurre noisette.

Preparation

Some mixtures must be baked immediately once they are prepared. When preparing these recipes, make sure the oven is available and preheated to the correct temperature. Make sure that all sheet pans are clean and buttered.

Piping or Spooning the Batter onto the Sheet Pans

Make sure the sheet pans are properly buttered or covered with parchment paper. Remember to test the mixture before piping or spooning out a large batch.

Recommendations

Each recipe differs from the others in the number and type of raw ingredients used in its preparation.

Even though recipes given here list the ingredients in the order they are used, it is sometimes necessary to adjust the consistency of a batter by adding more of one or more of the ingredients. Do not hesitate to make these adjustments several times if necessary.

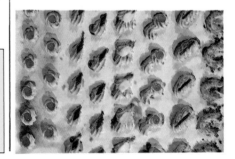

    The preparation of these petit four batters is straightforward and easy to accomplish. The preparation of the sheet pans and the baking of the petits fours requires careful attention, however.

Mixing: Combine the dry ingredients (such as almond powder, sugar, flour) in a clean, dry mixing bowl using a wooden spatula.

Optional: Brush the surface of the mixture with melted butter. This butter should not be incorporated into the mixture until the last minute. Its purpose is to prevent the formation of a crust on the mixture's surface.

Test the mixture: Bake a sample batch of the cookies on a sheet pan.

Then:

Adjust the recipe if necessary

Pipe or spoon the batter onto the sheet pans

Bake

Store

Adding liquids: Add the liquids (such as eggs or egg whites) all at once and combine them with the dry ingredients using a wooden spatula.

Flavoring: Add the flavorings and food coloring if they are being used.

Simple Mixtures
(Petits Fours Sec/Assorted Cookies)

PREPARATION	**0** min	
Assemble the Equipment Prepare, Weigh, and Measure the Raw Ingredients		• Select the correct sheet pans or molds. • Carefully butter the sheet pans or molds. • Precisely weigh and measure the raw ingredients. • Use only the best-quality raw ingredients.
PROCEDURE	**10** min	
Combine the Dry Ingredients		• Use a clean mixing bowl and a wooden spatula. • Combine powdered almonds, sugar, flour, and other dry ingredients.
Add the Liquid Ingredients	**12** min	• Add all at once. • Incorporate, using a wooden spatula.
Add the Flavoring and Food Coloring		• Add the flavorings and food coloring if they are being used. • A simple mixing of the ingredients is sufficient.
Add the Melted Butter	**15** min	• The butter should be melted and cooled. • Do not incorporate the butter until the last minute.
TESTING THE MIXTURE		• Bake a small batch of petits fours to test the batter.
PIPING OUT OR SPOONING		• Pipe or spoon the remaining batter onto sheet pans once the test has been successfully completed.
BAKING		• Adjust the oven temperature according to the type and size of petits fours being baked.
STORING:		• The petits fours may be stored for up to 1 week at room temperature if protected from air and for several weeks in the freezer.

Les fours poches (Piped petits fours)

Recipe

for 2 sheet pans

1 kg raw almond paste (35 oz.)
50 to 100 g trimoline or honey (1.5 to 3.5 oz.)
Kirsch, to flavor
50 g apricot preserves (1.5 oz.), optional
10 egg whites, approximately

Procedure

See *Basic Procedure*, page 15.

It is easier to pipe out a stiff mixture because it will hold its shape and the designs and decorations will stay in place during baking.

If the mixture is too thin, distinctive and decorative shapes will run together during baking.

Piping the Mixture onto Sheet Pans

Use buttered and floured sheet pans or cover them with parchment paper.

Pipe the mixture onto the sheet pans the night before baking so that a crust will form on the surfaces of the petits fours. The mixture can be piped out in a variety of shapes, such as rosettes, horseshoes, flames, teardrops, hearts, and fleurs-de-lys.

The piped-out petits fours should be held for at least 24 hours at room temperature or in a proof box before baking.

Baking

Bake the petits fours at 250°C (475°F) on doubled or tripled sheet pans. The petits fours should be baked quickly so the centers remain soft and do not dry out.

The surfaces of the petits fours should be lightly colored on the edges.

As soon as the petits fours come out of the oven, brush them with sugar syrup at 1260 D that contains an additional 500 g (17.5 oz.) glucose. The glucose should be

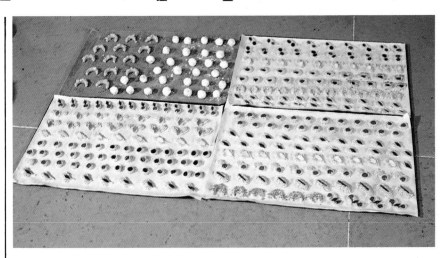

added to the syrup and the mixture brought to a boil ahead of time. The petits fours can also be glazed as soon as they come out of the oven with gum arabic that has been melted in a bain-marie.

Storage

These petits fours can be stored at room temperature for 6 to 8 days or frozen for 5 to 6 weeks.

Variations on Piped Petits Fours

Croissants

Make a stiffer petit four batter by cutting the quantity of egg whites in half, to about 5.

Form the mixture into small sausage shapes. Bend these into croissant (crescent) shapes.

Sprinkle the croissants with slivered almonds and bake in the same way as regular piped petits fours.

Moon Rocks

Make a stiffer petit four batter by cutting the quantity of egg whites in half.

Form the batter into balls the size of walnuts. Roll half a candied cherry into the center of each one.

As soon as the balls are formed, roll them in confectioners' sugar and bake them in the same way as piped petits fours.

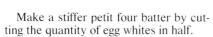

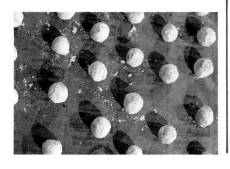

Petits fours made from simple mixtures

Les sablés diamants (Raisin shortbread cookies)

Recipe

for 4 sheet pans

1 kg all-purpose flour (35 oz.)
400 g confectioners' sugar (14 oz.)
750 g butter (26.5 oz.)
vanilla extract
150 g chopped dark raisins (5 oz.)

Procedure

Fraise the dough and roll it into cylinders with diameters of 2 to 3 cm (about 1

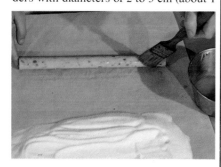

inch). Chill the dough in the refrigerator, 5°C (40°F), for at least an hour.

Cutting the Petits Fours

Brush the cylinders of dough with egg wash and roll them in crystallized or

granulated sugar. Cut the cylinder into 1-cm-thick (⅜-in.) rounds.

Put the rounds of dough on lightly buttered sheet pans.

Baking

Bake the cookies on lightly buttered doubled sheet pans in a 200° to 220°C (400° to 425°F) oven.

Storage

Raisin shortbread cookies can be stored at room temperature from 8 to 10 days in sealed containers. They can be frozen for 3 to 4 weeks.

Les Montmorency

Recipe

for 2 sheet pans

125 g flour (4.5 oz.)
1 kg raw almond paste (35 oz.)
250 g honey (9 oz.)
50 ml Kirsch (1.5 fl. oz.)
(Soften the mixture by working it with raw egg whites, as for piped petits fours; see page 16).

Procedure

See *Basic Procedure*, page 15.

Piping Out

Pipe the mixture onto sheet pans covered with parchment paper. Use a medium-sized fluted tip.

Place half a candied cherry in the center of each rosette.

Let a crust form for 24 hours before baking. Bake and glaze the Montmorency using the same method as for piped petits fours.

Les visitandines (Almond butter cookies)

Recipe

for 3 sheet pans

Grind together 300 g dry raw almonds (10.5 oz.) with 600 g granulated sugar (21 oz.), 50 g invert sugar such as honey or trimoline (1.5 oz.), and 200 g flour (7 oz.)
18 raw egg whites
500 g beurre noisette—butter cooked until golden brown (17.5 oz.)
vanilla extract

These proportions are for three special sheet molds used specifically for visitandines.

Procedure

See *Basic Procedure*, page 15.

Be careful that the beurre noisette is at the right stage, because the final flavor of the visitandines depends on its correct preparation.

Strain the butter through a fine strainer before adding it to the mixture.

Buttering the Molds

Butter the molds thoroughly with creamed butter using a pastry brush.

Filling the Molds

Let the batter relax and firm up slightly before piping it into the molds. Use a pastry bag with a plain no. 5 tip or a small fluted tip with the prongs pinched together to keep the mixture from running out.

Fill the molds three-fourths of the way up.

A slivered almond can be placed on top of each visitandine.

Baking

Bake in a 200°C (400°F) oven with the vents open (if available) or the door slightly ajar.

Check if the visitandines are done by unmolding one and checking its color. It should be pale brown. The bottom of the visitandines should be slightly darker than the sides.

Storage

The visitandines will keep from 3 to 4 days in a sealed container at room temperature or 3 to 4 weeks in the freezer if well protected from frost.

When this same recipe is baked in rectangular (financier) or barquette molds, the petits fours are called, respectively, *financiers* or *friands*.

The visitandine mixture can also be baked in savarin or miniature brioche molds for larger individual-sized portions. Bake these in a 190°C (375°F) oven.

Petits fours made from simple mixtures

Les tuiles (Tiles)

Recipe

for 6 sheet pans

300 g slivered almonds (10.5 oz.)
250 g confectioners' sugar (9 oz.)
100 g flour (3.5 oz.)
3 egg whites
3 whole eggs
vanilla extract
orange flower water (optional)
75 g melted butter (2.5 oz.)

Procedure

See *Basic Procedure*, page 15.

Spooning Out the Mixture

Butter the sheet pans and spoon 20 to 24 dollops of batter about the size of walnuts on each.

Flatten each dollop of batter with the back of a fork that has been dipped in cold water.

Baking

Bake the tuiles in a 220°C (425°F) oven until they are pale brown with a dark brown rim around the edges.

The tuiles can also be baked in two stages—a preliminary stage during which they are cooked halfway and then cooled, followed by the final cooking, during which they are cooked normally. This method improves the texture of the tuiles and gives them an appealing crunchy texture.

Shaping

As soon as the tuiles come out of the oven, place them in special tuile molds to give them their curved shape. (If no

molds are available, wrap them around rolling pins.) Use a metal spatula. Work quickly, as they must be warm when molded or they will break.

Storage

Tuiles can be stored from 3 to 4 days in sealed containers at room temperature or from 3 to 4 weeks in the freezer.

Note

Tuiles can also be prepared with slivered hazelnuts or a mixture of chopped almonds and hazelnuts instead of the slivered almonds.

If chopped nuts are used, the mixture can be piped onto the sheet pans rather than being spooned. The dollops of batter can also be flattened with the bottom of a wet tumbler rather than a fork.

Variations

for 12 sheet pans of 24 tuiles each

Orange Tuiles (Version A)

500 g confectioners' sugar (17.5 oz.)
5 eggs
5 egg whites
175 g flour (6 oz.)
350 g slivered almonds (12.5 oz.)
200 g candied orange rind (7 oz.), finely chopped
red food coloring

Orange Tuiles (Version B)

500 g granulated sugar (17.5 oz.)
160 g flour (5.5 oz.)
150 g chopped almonds (5 oz.)
10 egg whites
400 g candied orange rind (14 oz.), finely chopped
150 g melted butter (5 oz.)

Coconut Tuiles

600 g confectioners' sugar (21 oz.)
7 eggs
160 g flour (5.5 oz.)
600 g chopped almonds (21 oz.)
250 g grated coconut (9 oz.)
vanilla extract

Lemon Tuiles

500 g granulated sugar (17.5 oz.)
150 g flour (5 oz.)
150 g chopped almonds (5 oz.)
8 egg whites
350 g candied lemon rinds (12.5 oz.), finely chopped
130 g melted butter (4.5 oz.)

Les copeaux (Corkscrews)

Recipe

for 2 sheet pans

250 g confectioners' sugar (9 oz.)
250 g flour (9 oz.)
30 g finely ground almonds (1 oz.)
2 eggs
2 egg whites
vanilla extract

Procedure

See *Basic Procedure*, page 15.

Pipe the batter onto buttered sheet pans in strips 15 cm (6 in.) long. Use a no. 5 plain tip.

Baking

Bake the strips in a 220°C (425°F) oven until they are pale brown with a dark brown rim around the edge.

As soon as the strips come out of the oven, roll them around a small tube or thin wooden dowel. The cookies should be about 1 cm (½ in.) in diameter.

Storage

The copeaux will keep for 10 to 15 days in tightly sealed containers at room temperature.

They can also be frozen for several weeks if well protected from frost.

Les macarons craquelés (Almond macaroons)

Recipe

for 3 sheet pans

1 kg raw almond paste (35 oz.)
egg whites
50 g honey (1.5 oz.)
small amount of water
vanilla extract

Preparing the Batter

Soften the almond paste by hand after putting it through the grinder (if necessary).

Work the egg whites into the almond paste a bit at a time until it has a creamy consistency. It must be malleable enough to work with a wooden spatula.

At this stage add the honey, the vanilla, and a few teaspoons of water. These ingredients help give the macaroons a crunchy texture once baked.

Finish adjusting the consistency of the batter with the egg whites. The batter should be somewhat firm yet soft enough so that it can be piped using a no. 7 plain tip.

Piping Out

Cover the sheet pans with parchment paper and pipe the batter out into dollops in the same way as piping out chouquettes (see volume 2, page 135).

Once the batter is piped onto the sheet pans, let it rest for 30 minutes.

Baking

Moisten the tops of the raw macaroons with a pastry brush or a damp towel. Bake the macaroons in a medium oven, 220°C (425°F), until they are pale brown. Use doubled sheet pans.

Removing the Macaroons from the Sheet Pans

As soon as the macaroons come out of the oven, sprinkle water between the parchment paper and the sheet pan.

Remove the macaroons from the paper. Gently sandwich the macaroons together in pairs, with a filling in the center of each pair (see vanilla macaroons, page 34).

Storage

These macaroons will keep for up to 48 hours stored at room temperature in sealed containers or up to 3 weeks, well wrapped, in the freezer.

Group B: Creamy mixtures

Introduction

All the creamy petit four mixtures are prepared in the same way. The methods described in this chapter are applicable to all the recipes that follow.

Preparation

Check the temperature of the raw ingredients to make sure they are all the same.

Make sure an oven is available and preheated to the correct temperature.

Preparing the Sheet Pans and Raw Ingredients

Carefully clean and butter the sheet pans or molds appropriate for the particular recipe.

Carefully weigh and measure the raw ingredients. Use the highest-quality ingredients available since they will directly influence the quality of the petits fours.

Tips

When preparing creamy mixtures, it is advisable to prepare the raw ingredients several hours in advance so they will all be at the same temperature when they are combined. This helps the batter to hold together and improves the quality of the finished petits fours.

The butter used for petits fours should be worked until it is creamy and malleable. Be sure to use the best-quality sweet butter available. The final flavor and texture of the petits fours depends more on the quality of the butter than anything else.

Be sure that the sugar is at the same temperature as the butter before combining the ingredients. It is best to use confectioners' sugar, which gives the batter the correct consistency and helps it hold together.

The liquid ingredients, such as the eggs, egg whites, or milk, should be slightly warmer than the butter/sugar mixture. Always use extremely fresh eggs. Eggs give the petits fours their firmness and texture and help them to coagulate during baking. They also contribute to the taste.

The flour used for making petits fours should not contain too high a percentage of gluten. Otherwise, the mixture might become elastic, and the petits fours will be hard and tough. Use a brand of all-purpose flour with a relatively low gluten content or use pastry or cake flour. Sift the flour before combining it with the other ingredients.

Make sure that the batter is smooth and homogeneous. If it breaks apart and separates, it will affect the finished petits fours and give them an unpleasant crumbly texture.

Do not overwork these mixtures. If they are overworked, they will become elastic and the resulting petits fours will be hard.

Certain precautions should be followed when preparing these mixtures. Be certain that the sheet pans are carefully buttered. Skill with a pastry bag is necessary, as is great care during and immediately after baking.

Basic Procedure for All Recipes

1. Soften the butter by working it with a whisk. If necessary, the butter can be heated until soft (but not melted) in a bain-marie or directly over a flame. Do not overwork it. In no case should the butter be worked to a froth.

2. Add the sugar to the creamed butter.

It is best to use confectioners' sugar.

3. Add the liquid ingredients to the sugar/butter mixture a bit at a time. The liquid ingredients should be tepid, 40°C

(104°F). Completely stir in the liquids after each addition.

Remember that the mixture must be kept smooth at all times.

If the mixture starts to become grainy, stop adding liquid and start stirring in the flour. When the flour has been incorporated, add the rest of the liquid.

Add the flavoring (for example, vanilla extract). Thoroughly combine the

flavoring without overworking the batter. The flavoring can be added before or after the addition of the flour.

4. Add the rest of the flour and stir it in

thoroughly with a wooden spatula.

5. Add any additional ingredients such as raisins, chopped walnuts or hazelnuts, or grated coconut.

If the mixture is allowed to rest or not used immediately, it should be held in a warm place or at room temperature, 20° to 25°C (68° to 75°F).

Testing the Mixture

Place several dollops of the batter on buttered sheet pans. Bake them at the recommended temperature. Carefully examine the petits fours after baking.

Adjust the recipe if necessary:

1. **If the petits fours do not spread enough on the surface of the sheet pan:**
- Either the sheet pans have not been sufficiently buttered, or they need to be tapped firmly onto a hard surface to make the batter spread out before baking.
- The batter might be too stiff. It can be thinned by adding a small amount of melted butter or vegetable oil.

2. **If the petits fours spread too much over the surface of the sheet pan:**
- The sheet pans might be covered with too thick a layer of butter. Either wipe off some of the butter with a clean towel or sprinkle the surface of the sheet pan with a thin layer of flour.
- The batter may be too thin, in which case a small amount of flour should be added. It may also be helpful to let the mixture stiffen for a few minutes in the refrigerator.

Creamy Mixtures
(Petits Fours/Assorted Cookies)

PREPARATION	0 min	
Assemble the Equipment Prepare, Weigh, and Measure the Raw Ingredients		• Gather the molds or sheet pans. • Carefully butter the sheet pans or molds. • Select the highest-quality raw ingredients. • Make sure that all the raw ingredients are at the same temperature. • Weigh and measure the raw ingredients very carefully.
PROCEDURE	10 min	
Soften the Butter		• Gently heat the butter if necessary. • Combine the almonds, sugar and the butter. • Work the butter to a creamy consistency. • Do not overwork.
Add the Sugar	14 min	• Use confectioners' sugar. • Combine the sugar without overworking the mixture.
Add the Liquids	15 min	• The liquid ingredients should be tepid, 40°C (105° F). • Add a little bit at a time. • Carefully stir the mixture after each addition. • Do not overwork the mixture.
Add the Flavoring and Food Coloring	20 min	• Add the flavoring after the addition of the liquids.
Add the Flour		• Add the flour all at once. • Thoroughly incorporate the flour with a wooden spatula.
Add Additional Ingredients		• Combine any additional ingredients with a wooden spatula. • Add additional ingredients all at once.
TESTING THE MIXTURE	22 min	• Test some of the mixture on buttered sheet pans. • Bake a sample of the mixture; adjust the batter if necessary.
PIPING OUT OR SPOONING		• Bake the petits fours only after having tested a sample and adjusting the recipe accordingly.
STORAGE:		• Petits fours made from creamy mixtures can be kept for up to a week in a sealed container protected from moisture. They can also be frozen for several weeks if protected from frost.

Les cigarettes (Cigarettes)

Recipe

for 12 sheet pans

350 g butter (12.5 oz.), worked until creamy
500 g confectioners' sugar (17.5 oz.)
10 egg whites
vanilla extract
300 g all-purpose flour (10.5 oz.) plus 100 g almond powder (3.5 oz.)

Variation

300 g butter (10.5 oz.), worked until creamy
450 g confectioners' sugar (16 oz.)
10 egg whites
vanilla extract
300 g all-purpose flour (10.5 oz.)

Procedure

See *Basic Procedure*, page 22.

Piping Out

Coat the sheet pans with a medium-thick layer of butter. Pipe out the cigarette batter using a pastry bag with a no. 7 plain tip into 4 × 5 or 4 × 6 rows for a total of 20 to 24 per sheet pan.

Tap the sheet pans against a hard surface so that the mixture spreads out thinly and evenly.

Baking

Bake the cigarettes in a 220°C (425°F) oven. They should be golden with a somewhat darker brown rim.

As soon as the cigarettes come out of the oven, roll them up onto wooden or metal dowels or rods.

Start by rolling the cigarettes that are the most done (often those at the cor-

ners of the sheet pans). Roll the metal or wooden dowel, with the cigarette around it, over the work surface or the opened door to the oven. Once the cigarettes have been completely rolled, press the seams firmly with the dowel so that they are well sealed.

Once the cigarettes have been completely rolled and sealed, slide them off onto a cooling rack. Spiral-shaped indentations can be added to the cigarettes by rolling them over the circular cake rack with the dowel.

Variation

Add cocoa powder to some of the cigarette batter and place it in a paper cone. Once the cigarettes are piped onto the sheet pans, place them in the oven for about 1 minute, until the mixture softens. Pipe the chocolate cigarette mixture in a spiral over the heated and softened cigarettes and continue baking.

Storage

Cigarettes can be stored at room temperature in tightly sealed containers for 4 to 5 days. They can be frozen for 4 to 5 weeks.

Les langues-de-chat (Cats' tongues)

Recipe

for 6 sheet pans

375 g butter (13 oz.), worked until creamy
500 g confectioners' sugar (17.5 oz.)
14 egg whites
vanilla extract
500 g flour (17.5 oz.)

Procedure

See *Basic Procedure*, page 22.

Piping Out

Pipe the mixture in strips of 5 to 6 cm (2 to 2.5 in.) on buttered sheet pans using a plain no. 7 pastry tip. Do not tap the sheet pans on a surface.

Baking

Bake the langues-de-chat in a 220°C (425°F) oven until they are light brown with a dark brown rim. Quickly remove them from the sheet pans as soon as they come out of the oven and transfer to cool baking sheets.

Storage

Langues-de-chat can be stored from 10 to 15 days in sealed containers or from 6 to 8 weeks in the freezer.

Les palets aux raisins (Raisin cookies)

Recipe

for 6 sheet pans

250 g butter (9 oz.), worked until creamy
250 g confectioners' sugar (9 oz.)
5 eggs (250 g/9 oz.)
125 g raisins (4.5 oz.), finely chopped and macerated in rum
325 g all-purpose flour (11.5 oz.)

Procedure

See *Basic Procedure*, page 22.

Piping Out

Pipe the mixture onto lightly buttered sheet pans using a pastry bag with a #10 plain tip. Pipe dollops of the mixture about the size of the tops of religieuses.

If the mixture seems stiff, give the sheet pans a light tap on a hard surface before baking.

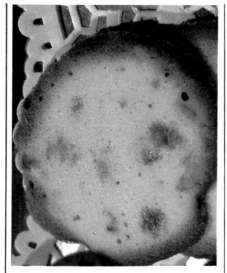

Baking

Bake the cookies in a 220°C (425°F) oven until they are golden with a dark brown rim.

Transfer the cookies to cool sheet pans as soon as they come out of the oven.

Note: These cookies can be glazed when they come out of the oven by brushing them with rum-flavored sugar syrup. After brushing with the syrup, put them back in the oven for a few seconds to set the glaze.

Storage

The raisin cookies can be stored in well-sealed containers at room temperature for 10 to 15 days or from 6 to 8 weeks in the freezer.

Les palets fondants (Butter cookies)

Recipe

for 6 sheet pans

250 g butter (9 oz.), worked until creamy
250 g confectioners' sugar (9 oz.)
250 g egg whites (9 oz.)
400 g flour (14 oz.)

Procedure

See *Basic Procedure*, page 22.

Piping Out

Pipe the mixture in small dollops onto lightly buttered sheet pans using a no. 8 or no. 10 plain tip.

Baking

Bake the cookies in a medium oven, 200°C (400°F), until they are pale brown with a dark brown rim.

Glazing

Brush the surface of the cookies with

hot apricot glaze. Brush a second time with Kirsch- or Grand Marnier–flavored sugar syrup.

Put the cookies back in the oven for a few seconds to set the glaze.

Storage

The butter cookies can be stored for 5 to 10 days at room temperature in sealed containers or from 4 to 6 weeks in the freezer.

Les sablés pochés (Piped shortbread cookies)

Recipe

for 3 sheet pans

200 g softened butter (7 oz.)
170 g confectioners' or granulated sugar (6 oz.)
1 egg
1 egg yolk
vanilla or lemon extract
60 ml milk (2 fl. oz.)
370 g flour (13 oz.)
60 g cornstarch (2 oz.)
7 g baking powder (¼ oz. or 1 heaping tsp.)

Procedure

See *Basic Procedure*, page 22.

Piping Out

Pipe the mixture onto lightly buttered sheet pans using a no. 7 fluted tip. The mixture can be piped into different shapes, including rosettes, crescents, or stars.

A candied cherry half or other candied fruit can be placed in the center of each cookie before baking.

Baking

Once the mixture has been piped, let

it rest on the sheet pans for 20 minutes before baking. Bake the cookies on doubled sheet pans in a 220°C (425°F) oven.

Decoration

If appropriate to their shape, the cookies can be dipped in melted couverture chocolate.

Storage

These butter cookies can be stored at room temperature in sealed containers for 6 to 8 days or frozen for 3 to 4 weeks.

Group C: Beaten egg whites folded with powdered ingredients

Introduction

All the petits fours in this group are based on beaten egg whites.

In order to prepare these mixtures correctly, the chef must have mastered the proper beating of egg whites (see *Beating Egg Whites,* volume 1, pages 78 to 80).

The folding of the dry ingredients with the beaten egg whites and the piping of the mixture onto the sheet pans must be done very carefully.

Preparation

Prepare the equipment, including the copper bowl for the egg whites, which should be thoroughly cleaned with salt and vinegar and then rinsed. Select the appropriate pastry bag and tip.

Make sure an oven is available and that it is preheated to the right temperature. This is especially important for beaten egg white mixtures, which must not be kept waiting once they are piped onto the sheet pans.

Make sure that all the sheet pans have been properly cleaned and prepared before beginning to pipe out the mixture.

Weigh and Measure the Raw Ingredients

Note: Remember when preparing small quantities of batter that it is always preferable to beat the egg whites by hand. Whether the whites are beaten by hand or in the electric mixer, it is essential that they not become grainy. This is best prevented by beating a small amount of sugar into the whites before the final folding with the powders. Remember also to sift together the dry ingredients if several types are being used, for example, almond powder, flour, and hazelnut powder.

Once the powders have been incorporated into the beaten egg whites, the mixture should not be kept waiting before being piped onto the sheet pans.

Always use fresh egg whites.

It is always better to use confectioners' sugar for beaten egg white mixtures. It dissolves more quickly into the whites and results in a smoother, more homogeneous mixture. If the sugar is being cooked in a syrup, however, it is better to use granulated sugar.

Because beaten egg white mixtures cannot be kept waiting before baking, careful organization is important. The beating of the egg whites and the folding with the dry ingredients must be done carefully. Correct preparation of the sheet pans is also important.

All powdered ingredients, including powdered almonds, cocoa powder, and flour, must be sifted together before being folded into the egg whites.

Basic Procedure for All Recipes

1. Beating the Egg Whites

Follow the usual procedure and precautions (see volume 1).

2. Adding Sugar to the Egg Whites

Add part or all of the sugar called for in the recipe to the beaten egg whites. Continue beating until they become stiff, like meringue.

3. Adding the Flavoring

If flavoring or food coloring is being used, it should be added after the whites are completely beaten.

4. Folding in the Powdered Ingredients

Carefully fold the powdered ingredients

into the whites by pouring them in a steady stream into the center of the bowl. Fold with a rubber spatula or a skimmer.

5. Piping Out the Mixture

A small amount of the mixture should be tested, and then the rest of the mixture piped out and baked as soon as possible.

Testing the Mixture

Pipe some sample petits fours onto a sheet pan and bake them to make sure the mixture has the right consistency and that the oven temperature is correct.

Correcting Problems

When using beaten egg white mixtures, the mixture itself cannot be adjusted, but problems are sometimes caused by incorrect buttering of the sheet pans.

If the petits fours spread too much:

There may be too much butter on the sheet pans. If this is so, coat the sheet pans with a thin layer of cornstarch or flour.

If the petits fours stick to the sheet pans:

This problem can sometimes be corrected by buttering the sheet pans more thickly with a cloth or paper towel. Using clarified butter will sometimes prevent sticking.

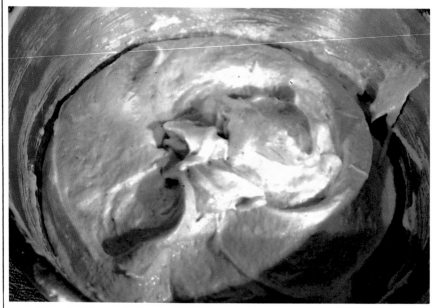

Beaten Egg White/Powder Mixtures
(Petits Fours/Assorted Cookies)

PREPARATION	0 min	
Assemble the Equipment Prepare, Weigh, and Measure the Raw Ingredients		• Make sure an oven is available and preheated to the correct temperature. • Weigh and measure precisely. • Sift together the dry ingredients. • Carefully butter the sheet pans.
PROCEDURE	**10** min	
Beat the Egg Whites		• The egg whites should preferably be beaten by hand, with the usual precautions.
Add Sugar to the Whites		• Add sugar to the whites when they form stiff peaks, to stiffen them further. • The beaten whites should be firm and smooth.
Add Flavoring (optional)		• Add the flavoring and food coloring if either is being used.
Fold in the Powdered Ingredients		• Pour the sifted powders in a steady stream into the beaten whites. • Fold the mixture carefully without overworking it.
TESTING THE MIXTURE		• Bake a small amount of the mixture.
PIPING OUT THE MIXTURE	**20** min	
Use a Pastry Bag		• Pipe the mixture onto sheet pans as soon as possible after it is prepared. • Do not keep the mixture waiting before baking.
STORAGE:		• The finished petits fours can be kept for a week in sealed containers away from heat and humidity, or they can be frozen for several weeks.

Les éponges (Sponges)

Recipe

for 3 sheet pans

8 egg whites, beaten to stiff peaks
125 g confectioners' sugar (4.5 oz.), to stiffen the whites
250 g finely ground almonds (9 oz.) plus 125 g confectioners' or granulated sugar (4.5 oz.) plus 50 g flour (1.5 oz.), sifted together

Procedure

See *Basic Procedure*, page 28.

Spooning or Piping Out

Either spoon or pipe out the mixture onto three sheet pans that have been lightly buttered and coated with flour or cornstarch.

a. Spoon the mixture in balls about the size of walnuts onto the sheet pans.

Sprinkle them lightly with confectioners' sugar.

b. Pipe the mixture into round shapes about the size of the top of a religieuse. Use a pastry bag with a no. 7 plain tip.

The sponges can be coated with different ingredients such as chopped almonds, slivered almonds, chopped or slivered hazelnuts, grated coconut, or chocolate or colored sprinkles.

Baking

Bake the sponges as soon as they have been piped or spooned onto doubled sheet pans in a 200°C (400°F) oven. Leave the vents open if available.

Remove the sponges from sheet pans after they have been out of the oven for 4 to 5 minutes. Use a triangle or metal spatula.

Filling

The flat sides of the sponges should be coated with raspberry preserves, chocolate ganache, or other filling. The sponges should then be sandwiched together in pairs.

Storage

The sponges can be stored for 4 to 5 days at room temperature as long as they are well sealed and protected from moisture.

They can also be frozen for several weeks if well protected from frost.

Les bâtons maréchaux (Marshall's batons)

Recipe

for 3 sheet pans

8 egg whites, beaten to stiff peaks
125 g confectioners' sugar (4.5 oz.), to stiffen the whites
250 g finely ground almonds (9 oz.) plus 125 g confectioners' sugar (4.5 oz.) plus 50 g flour (1.5 oz.), sifted together

Procedure

See *Basic Procedure*, page 28.

Piping Out

Pipe the mixture out in strips onto lightly buttered and floured sheet pans using a pastry bag with a no. 7 plain tip.

The batons can be coated with different ingredients in the same way as sponges.

Baking

Bake the batons as soon as they have been piped onto doubled sheet pans in a 200°C (400°F) oven. Leave the vents open if available.

Remove the batons from sheet pans after they have been out of the oven for 4 to 5 minutes. Use a triangle or metal spatula.

Filling

Coat the flat side of each of the batons with tempered couverture chocolate or coating chocolate. They can also be sandwiched together in twos with ganache or praline-flavored couverture chocolate.

Storage

The batons can be kept for 4 to 5 days at room temperature if well sealed and protected from humidity.

They can also be frozen for several weeks if well protected from frost.

Les miroirs (Mirrors)

Recipe

sponge batter (see page 29)
almond cream
stiff apricot preserves or red currant jelly
fondant or water glaze

Procedure

See *Basic Procedure*, page 28.

Piping Out

Pipe the mixture out in small circles or ovals onto lightly buttered and floured sheet pans. Use a no. 5 plain tip.

Sprinkle the mirrors with chopped almonds. Turn the sheet pan sideways to

shake off the excess almonds.

Fill the center of each of the mirrors with the almond cream, using a pastry bag with a no. 5 or no. 7 tip.

Baking

Bake the mirrors in a 220°C (425°F) oven on doubled sheet pans until they are pale brown.

Let the mirrors cool on the sheet pans before removing them.

Finishing the Mirrors

Coat the center of each of the mirrors with the fruit preserves or jelly, which should first be heated. This coating can be applied with a paper cone, the end of a pastry brush, or a special funnel used specifically for this purpose.

Let the fruit coating cool and then par-

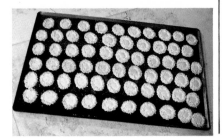

tially cover it with a dollop of rum fondant or glaze. Make sure the fondant is warm and has a fluid consistency before applying it to the cookies.

Once the cookies have been coated with the fruit and fondant, put them back in the oven for a few seconds to set the glaze.

Remove the cookies from the sheet pans as soon as they come out of the oven.

Note: The final glazing with fondant is sometimes omitted in the preparation of mirrors.

Storage

The mirrors will keep for 4 to 5 days at room temperature or from 4 to 5 weeks in the freezer.

Les rochers (Meringue rocks)

Recipe

for 3 sheet pans

With Italian Meringue

8 egg whites, beaten to stiff peaks
150 g confectioners' sugar (5 oz.), to stiffen the whites
350 g sugar (12.5 oz.), cooked to soft ball stage
250 g chopped walnuts, grated coconut, or slivered almonds (9 oz.)

With Swiss Meringue

8 egg whites
500 g sugar (17.5 oz.)
100 g confectioners' sugar (3.5 oz.)
250 g slivered almonds (9 oz.)

See volume 1, pages 82 to 85, for instructions on preparing Italian and Swiss meringues.

Piping Out

Lightly butter and flour the sheet pans. Pipe out the meringue with a fluted tip

into walnut-sized balls or rosettes. The meringue can also be spooned onto the sheet pans.

The top of each rocher can be decorated with half a walnut, half an almond, or grated coconut.

Let the meringues dry in a proof box for 24 hours at 70°C (160°F). Be sure to protect them from moisture.

When the meringues have dried, place them in a hot oven, 250°C (475°F), just long enough to color them lightly.

Storage

The rochers can be stored for up to a week at room temperature if protected from humidity.

Les doigts de fée (Fairy fingers)

Recipe

for 4 sheet pans

8 egg whites plus 600 to 700 g confectioners' sugar (21 to 24.5 oz.), stirred together and warmed in a bain-marie

Flavoring possibilities include:

- vanilla extract
- coffee extract, instant coffee
- melted chocolate
- fruit extracts such as strawberry, raspberry, or currant
- anise (color the cookies yellow)
- mint (color the cookies green)

Procedure

See Swiss meringue, volume 1, pages 84 to 85.

Piping Out

Make sure that the sheet pans are perfectly clean. Wipe them with a buttered

cloth to coat them with a very thin film of butter. Pipe out the meringue using a pastry bag with a no. 7 plain tip into strips about 5 cm (2 in.) long.

Dry the meringues in a proof box set at from 80° to 100°C (175° to 210°F). Be sure to protect them from humidity. They can also be dried in a 100° to 120°C (210° to 250°F) oven with the door left ajar or with the vents left open.

Storage

Fairy fingers can be stored for 10 to 15 days if protected from humidity.

Les macarons (Macaroons)

Chocolate Macaroons

Recipe

for 5 sheet pans

18 egg whites, beaten to stiff peaks
1 kg sugar (35 oz.), cooked to soft ball stage
400 g confectioners' sugar (14 oz.) sifted with 300 g cocoa powder (10.5 oz.)

Procedure

See Italian meringue, volume 1, pages 82 to 83.

Piping Out

Pipe the mixture out in walnut-size balls onto well-buttered and floured sheet pans. Use a plain no. 7 pastry tip.

Baking

Bake the macaroons on double sheet pans in a 160°C (325°F) oven with the vents open if available.

Take the macaroons out of the oven while they are still a little soft in the center.

Finishing

Place a small dollop of chocolate ganache on the flat sides of the macaroons and sandwich them together, two by two.

Storage

Chocolate macaroons will keep for 3 to 4 days if protected from humidity or from 3 to 4 weeks in the freezer.

Strawberry, Raspberry, Black Currant, and Red Currant Macaroons

Recipe

for 5 sheet pans

350 g almond powder (12.5 oz.), sifted with 650 g confectioners' sugar (23 oz.)
10 egg whites, beaten to stiff peaks
50 g confectioners' sugar (1.5 oz.), to stiffen the whites
fruit extract for color and flavor

Procedure
See Basic Procedure, page 28.

It is extremely important that all the equipment used for preparing the macaroons be perfectly dry. When baking fruit-flavored macaroons, cover the sheet pans with parchment paper.

Piping Out and Baking

See vanilla macaroons, page 34. Use doubled sheet pans.

Finishing the Macaroons

Put a dollop of fruit jam thinned with a little Kirsch on the flat sides of the cookies and sandwich together, two by two.

Storage

Fruit macaroons can be stored for up to 24 hours at room temperature or for 48 hours in the refrigerator. They will keep frozen for up to a week if protected from frost.

Group D: Beaten egg whites folded with liquids or semisolid ingredients

Introduction

This group of petits fours is similar to Group C, beaten egg whites folded with powdered ingredients. The same precautions should be taken for beating the egg whites and folding the mixture (see volume 1, pages 78 to 80).

Preparation

Preparation is the same as for beaten egg whites folded with powdered ingredients; see page 27.

The preparation of the various recipes for egg whites folded with liquid and semisolid ingredients requires careful organization of the work station because it is often necessary to prepare the base mixture and beat the egg whites at the same time.

Precautions

The same precautions recommended for the preparation of group C petits fours should be followed here. It is helpful if two people are available to fold the beaten whites with the liquid or semisolid base. Quick and careful folding is necessary to obtain a smooth and homogeneous mixture.

Basic Procedure for All Recipes

Preparing the Base Mixture

Combine the ingredients for the base mixture in a stainless steel bowl. The bowl should be large enough to hold the beaten egg whites later. Use a wooden spatula to combine the ingredients until a smooth paste is obtained. When preparing these mixtures, the finished base should have the consistency of raw pâte à choux (cream puff pastry).

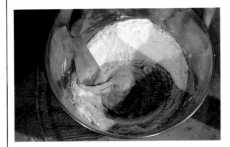

Flavoring and Coloring

Some recipes have additional flavoring or food coloring added. The flavoring and coloring of these mixtures can be accomplished in two ways. The base mixture can be flavored and colored before being folded with the whites, or the whites can be flavored and colored after they are beaten. In either case, remember to add enough flavor and food coloring so that it will remain pronounced enough after the two mixtures are combined.

   Careful weighing of the raw ingredients and correct preparation of the equipment is essential. The work station must be carefully organized so that the mixture is not kept waiting at any stage.

Beating the Egg Whites

Take the usual precautions for beating the egg whites. Beating the whites by

hand is strongly recommended for these petits fours.

Note: At this stage it is imperative that the mixture be folded, piped, and baked without being held at any stage.

Stiffening the Whites

Add a small quantity of confectioners' or granulated sugar to the egg whites when they have stiff peaks. Continue beating until the whites become stiff and shiny.

Folding the Beaten Whites with Base

It is best to perform this operation with two people:

- the first person continues beating the whites so they remain stiff and do not become grainy, and then adds the whites to the base mixture
- the second person folds the whites into the base mixture

This is the most difficult stage in the preparation of the petits fours and requires experience so that the resulting mixture is smooth and homogeneous and does not lose its airiness.

Proceed as follows:

a. Combine one-fourth of the beaten

whites with the base mixture. Do not try to fold the mixture at this point. The whites are added to lighten the mixture before the final folding.

b. Add the second quarter of the beaten egg whites to the lightened mixture. Gently fold the two together by lifting the mixture up from the bottom with a rubber spatula and folding it over itself.

Do not try to obtain a perfectly smooth mixture at this point.

c. Add the remaining egg whites and carefully fold them together in the same way is in step b. At this point, the mixture should be folded until it is smooth and regular, but avoid overworking it or it will lose volume.

Piping Out or Spooning

As soon as the mixture is folded, it should be spooned or piped out onto sheet pans.

![chef hats]				**Beaten Egg White/Liquid Mixtures** *(Petits Fours/Assorted Cookies)*
PREPARATION Assemble the Equipment Prepare, Weigh, and Measure the Raw Ingredients	**0** min			• Make sure an oven is available and preheated to the correct temperature. • Carefully weigh and measure the raw ingredients. • Be careful buttering the sheet pans or molds.
PROCEDURE Prepare the Base Mixture	**10** min			• Use a large stainless steel bowl and a wooden spatula. • Combine the ingredients until the mixture is smooth and homogeneous. • The base mixture should have the consistency of raw pâte à choux (cream puff pastry).
Flavor and Color the Mixture (optional)				• Add the flavoring and coloring to the finished base mixture or to the beaten whites.
Beat the Egg Whites	**15** min			• It is best to beat the whites by hand. • Take the usual precautions.
Stiffen the Whites				• Add the sugar to the whites after they have been beaten to stiff peaks. • Continue beating the whites until they are stiff and shiny.
Fold the Beaten Whites with the Base Mixture	**20** min			• Two people should work together if possible. • Use one-fourth of the beaten whites to lighten the base mixture before folding. • Fold in the second quarter of the whites. • Gently fold in the rest of the whites. • Fold until the mixture is smooth and homogeneous. • Do not overwork the mixture.
TESTING THE MIXTURE	**22** min			• Quickly bake a few sample petits fours.
PIPING OUT OR SPOONING	**30** min			• Work quickly. Put the mixture on the sheet pans as soon as possible after the final folding. • Bake immediately.
STORAGE:				• The shelf life of each recipe varies depending on the ingredients and the type of garniture or decoration that is used. See individual recipes.

Petits fours made from beaten egg whites folded with liquids or semiliquid ingredients

Les macarons vanille (fraise) (Vanilla and strawberry macaroons)

Recipe

500 g almond powder (17.5 oz.)
500 g confectioners' sugar (17.5 oz.)
10 g powdered vanilla or vanilla extract (2 tsp.)
200 g egg whites (7 oz.)
200 g egg whites (7 oz.), beaten to stiff peaks
350 g confectioners' sugar (12.5 oz.), to stiffen the whites

Procedure

See *Basic Procedure*, page 32.

Note: Make sure that all the pastry equipment is perfectly dry. The slightest trace of moisture either on the equipment or in the dry ingredients can compromise the final result.

Be especially careful when folding the beaten whites with the base mixture.

Piping Out

Cover the sheet pans with parchment paper and pipe the mixture out into

small rounds (about the size of the top of a religieuse) with a pastry bag using a plain no. 10 tip.

Baking

Bake the macaroons for 2 minutes in a 250°C (475°F) oven and then double or triple the sheet pans and transfer them to another oven, preheated to 200°C (400°F) to finish the baking. Bake until golden. Leave the door ajar and, if available, the vents open on the second oven.

Remove the macaroons from the second oven while the centers are still slightly soft.

Pour about 250 ml (8.5 fl. oz.) of water between the parchment paper and

the sheet pan. Make sure the water spreads under the entire sheet of parchment paper. It is also possible to slide the sheet of paper containing the macaroons onto a moistened work surface.

As soon as the macaroons have cooled, remove them from the parchment paper with a metal spatula and sandwich them together two by two. Be careful not to touch the smooth surface of the macaroons at any point, as this will leave fingerprints.

The macaroons can also be stuck together with a small dollop of strawberry preserves.

Storage

The macaroons will keep for up to 24 hours at room temperature or for 48 hours in the refrigerator. They can also be frozen for up to a week.

Smooth Macaroons

Recipe

750 g powdered almonds (26.5 oz.) plus 750 g confectioners' sugar (26.5 oz.), sifted together
8 egg whites
25 g powdered vanilla (1 oz.)
8 egg whites, beaten to stiff peaks
750 g sugar (26.5 oz.), cooked to soft ball stage, 117°C (243°F).

Procedure

The procedure is similar to that given for vanilla macaroons except that in this case, Italian meringue is used (see Italian meringue, volume 1, pages 82 to 83).

Baking

The baking method is the same as for vanilla macaroons. Begin baking at 250°C (475°F), double the sheet pans, and finish in a 200°C (400°F) oven.

Hazelnut Macaroons

Recipe

380 g whole hazelnuts (13.5 oz.), ground with 600 g confectioners' sugar (21 oz.)
80 g egg whites (3 oz.)
200 g egg whites (7 oz.), beaten to stiff peaks
70 g confectioners' sugar (3 oz.), to stiffen the whites

Procedure

The procedure is the same as for vanilla macaroons.

Recipe

for 14 sheet pans

350 g hazelnuts (12.5 oz.), with the dark skin removed, ground with 350 g sugar (12.5 oz.)
4 egg whites
100 ml milk (3.5 fl. oz.)
vanilla extract
100 g butter (3.5 oz.), melted
12 egg whites, beaten to stiff peaks
50 g sugar (1.5 oz.), to stiffen the whites

Alternative Recipe

400 g almonds (14 oz.) ground with 400 g sugar (14 oz.)
3 whole eggs
100 ml milk (3.5 fl. oz.)
vanilla extract
100 g butter (3.5 oz.), melted
10 egg whites, beaten to stiff peaks
50 g sugar (1.5 oz.), to stiffen the whites

Procedure

See *Basic Procedure,* page 32.

Piping Out

Pipe the mixture out into small round

Les duchesses (Duchesses)

shapes on buttered and lightly floured sheet pans. Use a plain no. 7 tip or a medium-size fluted tip.

Baking

Bake the duchesses in a 190° to 200°C (375° to 400°F) oven until they are golden with a slightly darker rim.

Remove the duchesses from the sheet pans as soon as they come out of the oven, using a triangle or a pastry cutter. Let them cool on clean sheet pans.

Filling

Sandwich the duchesses together two by two using a mixture of equal parts melted couverture chocolate and pra-line paste. Praline paste alone can also be used.

Storage

The duchesses will keep for up to 1 week in the refrigerator and for several weeks in the freezer.

Note

Duchesses can also be made with a simple mixture of:

500 g sugar (17.5 oz.)
400 g almond powder (14 oz.)
100 g flour (3.5 oz.)
6 whole eggs
100 g beurre noisette (3.5 oz.)

Les biarritz
(Chocolate-covered almond cookies)

Recipe

for 10 sheet pans

1 kg raw almond paste (35 oz.), worked
    and softened in the grinder
100 g cake or all-purpose flour (3.5 oz.)
milk—enough to soften the mixture
    until it has the consistency of raw
    pâte à choux (cream puff pastry) be-
    fore adding the egg whites
12 egg whites, beaten to stiff peaks
50 g confectioners' sugar (1.5 oz.), to
    stiffen the whites

Alternative Recipe

450 g sugar (16 oz.)
500 g almond powder (17.5 oz.)
100 g flour (3.5 oz.)
4 whole eggs
8 egg whites, beaten to stiff peaks
50 g sugar (1.5 oz.), to stiffen the whites

Procedure

See *Basic Procedure*, page 32.

Piping Out

Pipe the mixture onto well-buttered
and floured sheet pans into small round
shapes. Use a plain no. 7 pastry tip.

Baking

Bake the biarritz until they are golden
with a slightly darker rim in a 200°C
(400°F) oven.

Let the biarritz cool before removing
them from the sheet pans.

Glazing

Glaze the flat surface of the biarritz
with tempered dark couverture chocolate using a small metal spatula or a serrated knife.

Storage

The biarritz will keep for 10 to 15
days at room temperature and from 4 to
5 weeks in the freezer.

Les punchs orange ou ananas
(Orange and pineapple punches)

Recipe

350 g raw almond paste (12.5 oz.), soft-
    ened with Cointreau
200 g ground candied orange rind (7 oz.)
25 g flour (1 oz.) sifted with 5 g baking
    powder (1 tsp.)
6 egg whites, beaten to stiff peaks
50 g sugar (1.5 oz.), to stiffen the whites
red food coloring

Procedure

See *Basic Procedure*, page 32.

Piping Out

Completely fill miniature paper cups
with the punch mixture using a pastry
bag with a no. 7 plain tip.

Baking

Bake the punches in a 180°C (350°F)
oven on doubled sheet pans. If the oven
is equipped with vents, leave them
open.

Remove the punches from the oven
while they are still slightly soft in the
center.

Pineapple Punches

These are the same as the orange
punches except that:

• the Cointreau is replaced with Kirsch
• the candied orange rind is replaced
  with candied pineapple
• the red food coloring is replaced with
  yellow food coloring

Storage

The punches will keep for 4 to 5 days
at room temperature if protected from
moisture. They can be frozen for several weeks.

Chapter 2
Chocolate

Basic professional techniques

Chocolate work is a profession unto itself. It is a large field that is entirely based on one product, derived from the cacao bean, that can be formed into various types of chocolate used by a chocolate maker.

Chocolate is a well-known, widely used product that can be studied as a raw material historically, botanically, culturally, economically, and technologically.

Different products derived from the cacao bean, such as cocoa butter and cocoa liquor, are combined to form chocolate that is used for chocolate making.

Composition and Regulations of Various Products Derived from the Cacao Bean

The following definitions are based on French regulations, where the standards

for chocolate and chocolate products are among the highest in the world. Each country has its own standards.

Chocolate Liquor or Unsweetened Chocolate (Pâte de Cacao)

Chocolate liquor, also called unsweetened chocolate, is obtained by crushing the cacao bean after it has been shelled. It should not contain more than 2 percent residue of the shell. Chocolate liquor contains cocoa butter unless otherwise treated.

Cocoa Butter

Cocoa butter is a fat extracted from the cocoa beans.

Cocoa butter is most commonly made by pressing the chocolate liquor.

It contains more than 1.75 percent of fatty acids.

Cocoa Powder

Cocoa powder is obtained by first removing a large percentage of cocoa butter from the chocolate liquor, then grinding and sifting the resulting paste into a powder. Cocoa powder must contain at least 20 percent cocoa butter and a maximum 9 percent water.

Low-Fat Cocoa Powder

Cocoa powder with a range of only 8 to 12 percent cocoa butter is, according to regulations in France, called *cacao maigre,* low-fat cocoa powder.

Soluble Cocoa Powder (Dutch Process)

Cocoa powder can be obtained by treating the chocolate liquor with an alkaline solution such as ammonium carbonate or potassium carbonate to raise the pH level, thereby lowering the acidity.

Sweetened Cocoa Powder

Sweetened cocoa powder is mixed with a minimum of 32 g (1 oz.) sucrose per 100 g (3.5 oz.) of cocoa powder.

Sweetened, Low-Fat Cocoa Powder

Low-fat cocoa powder can be sweetened by mixing it with a minimum of 32 g (1 oz.) of sucrose per 100 g (3.5 oz.) of low-fat cocoa powder.

Sweetened Cocoa Powder for Household Use

For household use every 100 g (3.5 oz.) of cocoa powder contains at least 25 g (.8 oz.) of sugar. Low-fat cocoa powder is also made with the same percentage of sugar per 100 g (3.5 oz.) of powder. In this case the powder is marked as being low in fat.

Baking or Household Chocolate

In general, chocolate made for household use will consist of a minimum of 30 g (1 oz.) of chocolate containing 18 g (½ oz.) of cocoa butter and the rest sugar to equal 100 g (3.5 oz.) total.

"Eating" or Laboratory Chocolate

Laboratory chocolate is made of 38 to 57 g (1.5 to 2 oz.) of chocolate liquor con-

taining 26 g (10 oz.) of cocoa butter per 100 g (3.5 oz.) chocolate.

Fondant Chocolate

For fondant chocolate (do not confuse this with the cooked, worked sugar that is also called fondant), cocoa butter is added to the chocolate at the end of conching. Conching is a process whereby the chocolate is worked in a machine that mixes, rolls, and warms it to make it smooth and homogeneous. Fondant chocolate is made up of a maximum of 57 g (2 oz.) of sugar, a minimum of 48 g (1.5 oz.) of chocolate liquor containing a maximum of 26 g (10 oz.) of cocoa butter per 100 g (3.5 oz.) of chocolate.

Milk Chocolate

Milk chocolate is made by adding milk solids (with a minimum of 24 percent milk fat) to the chocolate. Every 100 g (3.5 oz.) of milk chocolate contains a minimum of 2.5 g (¹⁄₁₀ oz.) of defatted cocoa, a maximum of 14 g (½ oz.) of milk solids, a minimum 25 g (1 oz.) of cocoa butter, and a maximum of 55 g (2 oz.) of sugar.

Couverture Chocolate

Couverture chocolate, the highest-quality chocolate, must contain at least 31 percent cocoa butter. Couverture can be translated as covering chocolate, but do not confuse it with cake coating, which uses other fats than cocoa butter and is a product of lesser quality.

When a product is marked "chocolate" or "cocoa," it must contain at least 35 percent chocolate liquor or cocoa powder if it is solid; 32 percent if it is powdered; and 6 percent if it is liquid.

If a product contains less than 20 percent chocolate liquor or powder, it is labeled chocolate- or cocoa-flavored.

The quality of chocolate is directly related to the caliber and amount of cocoa butter used. Cocoa butter contributes greatly to the richness, smoothness, and melting quality of chocolate.

It is also because of cocoa butter that chocolate must be *tempered* to an exact temperature when working with and molding it, so that it will be shiny and appealing.

It is important to understand the role of cocoa butter in chocolate making. Cocoa butter is composed of six different fat molecules that do not melt or solidify at the same temperature. Once heated beyond a certain temperature, cocoa butter melts and separates.

To make the chocolate homogeneous again, for molding and dipping, the chocolate must be worked until the cocoa butter reaches a temperature close to its point of fusion. Otherwise, once melted, the chocolate will either never become firm again or if incorrectly tempered, will harden with white streaks and a dull appearance.

The temperature to which the cocoa butter must be brought can vary depending on the percentage of cocoa butter in the chocolate used. This makes it imperative to use couverture chocolate that is "à point" or tempered to a specific temperature.

Note: The point at which the molecules fuse cannot be seen with the naked eye or felt by touching.

Before beginning to attempt to temper chocolate, it is important to prepare the work area and all necessary equipment as well as follow all precautions discussed below.

The Work Area

The area reserved for working with chocolate should be cool, between 18° and 25°C (65° and 77°F). Below this range, the chocolate will become too firm too quickly and the equipment too cold, making it difficult to work with the chocolate. Above the given range of temperatures, the chocolate will take too long to become firm and the marble or other work surface will be too warm for procedures such as making chocolate cigarettes or shavings, and dipping. Avoid working in drafts, which will cool the chocolate unevenly.

It is important that no moisture come in contact with the chocolate. Be careful of the steam and hot water from the water bath and humidity from the marble or other equipment, which must be completely dry before use.

If water comes in contact with the chocolate, the chocolate can no longer be used. This is because water penetrates the cocoa butter, causing it to coagulate and "seize" (making it very

firm and grainy), thus rendering the chocolate unusable for chocolate work. If more liquid such as cream or milk is added, it is possible to use the chocolate for sauces.

It is not always possible to have a separate area for chocolate work. In this case choose an area in the kitchen as close to the requirements mentioned as possible.

Equipment

Various types and shapes of metal chocolate molds are available, some of which are very expensive. In place of these types of molds, firm plastic molds can be used; although more fragile, they are considerably less costly.

Making chocolates (outside of large commercial establishments) does not require special equipment:
Stainless steel bowls, saucepans (for water baths), wooden spatulas, plastic scrapers, cutting boards, knives, metal triangles, pastry combs, dipping forks, plastic and aluminum sheets, rulers, sheet pans, high-sided sheet pans or cake sheets for candy making, molds for making imprints in cornstarch, cutters.

This list includes the most important equipment for chocolate work.

For making large amounts of chocolates, it is possible to add the following equipment: tempéreuse (a machine for tempering chocolate), a machine for covering large amounts of chocolates at a time, a mandoline (a cutter), and a machine to form balls for rochers.

Tempering couverture chocolate

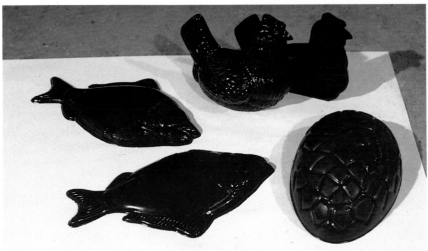

As indicated in the introduction on chocolate, couverture chocolate is rich in cocoa butter, 31 percent minimum. Couverture chocolate is the highest-quality chocolate (there are various brands and grades of it). For this reason couverture chocolate is usually called for in most of the recipes in this series.

Tempering couverture chocolate is the first and most important phase for working with chocolate.

Two Methods of Tempering

With both methods, the couverture is chopped into small pieces, about the size of walnuts, and placed in a dry, clean bowl.

First Method

The couverture is slowly melted in a proof box or in a tempéreuse (an electric machine that tempers chocolate through temperature controls). The couverture should not be heated beyond the ''mise à point'' or final temperature, between 30° and 32°C (86° and 89°F) for dark chocolate, and 29° and 30°C (84° and 86°F) for milk or white chocolate.

The couverture will slowly soften, then melt, without separating or turning grainy.

Once brought to the final temperature, the couverture is ready to use.

This method takes a long time; allow 4 to 6 hours for a piece of couverture weighing 2.5 kg (5.5 lb.) to reach the proper temperature. It is also very important to be able to regulate the heat source precisely, which can be difficult, as thermometers and thermostats are not always completely accurate.

Second Method

Melting

The chopped couverture is quickly melted in one of three ways: in a proof

box at 50° to 55°C (122° to 131°F); by placing it in an oven, removing to stir it often with a dry wooden spatula; or

over a hot water bath, stirring constantly while being careful not to allow any steam or water to get into the couverture.

Regardless of the method used for melting the couverture, never allow it to become warmer than 55°C (131°F) for dark chocolate and 50°C (122°F) for milk or white chocolate.

If the couverture is heated above these temperatures, the sugar will crystallize, causing the chocolate to become grainy and thick, affecting its final appearance.

Tempering

Once the couverture is melted, it is ready to be reblended. To do this, the couverture is cooled by pouring most of it, about three-quarters, onto a dry, clean marble. The couverture should now be spread and smoothed out on the

marble with a metal triangle or scraper and a metal spatula so it will cool evenly.

 To temper chocolate couverture, it is necessary to follow precisely the temperatures indicated. Tempering chocolate, especially in small amounts, requires professional experience.

Once the couverture is on the marble it will cool quickly. Therefore, after spreading out the couverture, bring it back together with a metal triangle and

then spread it out again with a metal spatula. Repeat as necessary until it begins to thicken and is cool to the touch (test with the top of the index finger); this technique of spreading will help it cool evenly. The temperature of the couverture after it is cooled should be:

- 27° to 29°C (80° to 84°F) for dark couverture
- 26° to 28°C (78° to 82°F) for milk and white chocolate couverture

The temperature can be tested using the top side of a finger or the lower lip (it

should feel cool); these methods require some experience. It is also possible to use a thermometer, placing it in the middle of the couverture and holding it still until the temperature registers.

Once the couverture has reached the right temperature, quickly lift it off the marble and mix it with the remaining couverture in the bowl. Blend the two well. The couverture that was kept in the bowl will be slightly warmer than that which was worked on the marble, so that the chocolate will warm to the proper final temperatures—between 30° and 32°C (86° and 89°F) for dark couverture and 29° and 30°C (84° and 86°F) for milk or white couverture.

If the couverture is too warm, pour a small amount on the marble and repeat the process.

Note: Remember that the first time the couverture is tempered, about three-quarters of it should be poured onto the marble.

If a second tempering is needed to cool it to the correct final temperature, pour out only one-quarter of the couverture so that it cools by only a few degrees. Otherwise it may become too cool, start to solidify, and form small lumps.

Tempering couverture (2nd method)

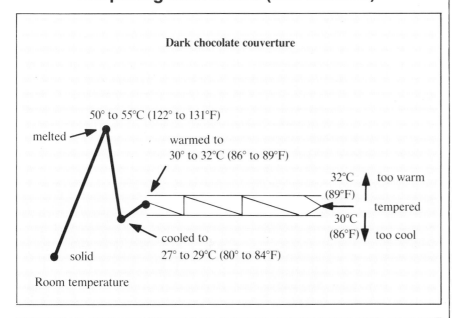

Dark chocolate couverture

melted — 50° to 55°C (122° to 131°F)

warmed to 30° to 32°C (86° to 89°F)

32°C (89°F) — too warm

tempered

30°C (86°F) — too cool

cooled to 27° to 29°C (80° to 84°F)

solid

Room temperature

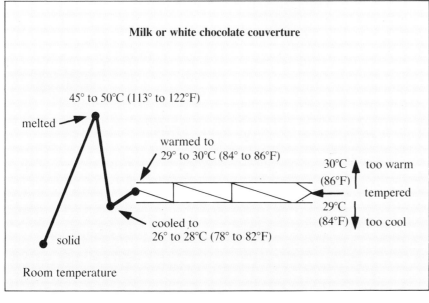

Milk or white chocolate couverture

melted — 45° to 50°C (113° to 122°F)

warmed to 29° to 30°C (84° to 86°F)

30°C (86°F) — too warm

tempered

29°C (84°F) — too cool

cooled to 26° to 28°C (78° to 82°F)

solid

Room temperature

Warming

If the couverture is too cool, it can be warmed slightly (a few degrees) so that it is brought to:
- 30° to 32°C (86° to 89°F) for dark chocolate couverture
- 29° to 30°C (84° to 86°F) for milk and white chocolate couverture

It is very important to keep the couverture from exceeding the temperatures given. The chocolate should be warmed only 1° to 3°C (2° to 6°F) after it is cooled.

If the couverture is overheated, the cocoa butter will break down again and the couverture will have to be retempered (melted, cooled, and rewarmed).

Testing

Before molding or working with the chocolate, it is best to test it to see if it has been properly tempered. This can be done by spreading a bit of the couverture on a piece of parchment paper, a metal spatula, or a triangle, and allowing the couverture to cool at room temperature, 18° to 22°C (64° to 71°F).

Within 5 minutes, the couverture should evenly thicken. If it is scraped with the back of a knife, it should roll up like a cigarette. If so, the couverture has been properly tempered and is ready to be used.

The couverture will slowly cool as it is used because the temperatures of the room, molds, and candies dipped are cooler than couverture itself.

It is therefore occasionally necessary to warm the couverture slightly to prevent it from becoming too firm. If it does become too firm, the couverture should be reheated and retempered.

To help maintain the proper temperature of the couverture while working with it, place the bowl of couverture over a heat source, preferably in an oven at 200°C (400°F) for a few seconds. Repeat this procedure for warming the chocolate each time it begins to harden around the sides of the bowl.

Do not stir the couverture while it is being warmed, or it may become too warm and would then require retempering.

Cigarettes

Chocolate cigarettes are a classic garnish, used for decorating large and individual cakes for special occasions and holidays.

They are often made with dark chocolate couverture but can also be made with milk, white, and other colored chocolate couverture.

Equipment

The work surface should be flat and smooth (marble, Formica) and have a constant, even temperature.

It is best to work on a nonrefrigerated surface, so that the couverture will harden less quickly. If the marble is re- frigerated, try to work in a section that is the least cool—at the edge of the marble, for example.

Use a large metal spatula to smooth out the couverture, a large knife or triangle for rolling the cigarettes, and an airtight container for storing the pieces.

Simple Chocolate Cigarettes

Procedure

Spread a band of tempered couverture on the work surface so that it is even in thickness—approximately 2 mm (1/16 in.)—and width. Spread the couverture thinner for smaller cigarettes.

Even out the band of couverture to the desired width by trimming it with the back of a chef's knife.

At this point the couverture should begin to cool and start to become evenly firm over the entire band.

Use a clean, dry knife or triangle to roll the cigarettes. It is important that the couverture be at the proper stage, firm enough not to stick to the knife, yet soft enough to roll without breaking. The consistency of the couverture can be tested by pressing it with a fingertip: it should feel firm but not hard.

Try rolling one cigarette as a test at one end of the band.

Hold the knife or triangle firmly with both hands, at a 45-degree angle, and place it 4 to 5 cm (1.5 to 2 in.) from the end of the band. Holding the knife or triangle, maintaining the 45-degree angle, scrape the chocolate with a clean stroke forward toward the end of the band.

The cigarette should not stick to the knife or triangle as it is rolled. Without lifting the triangle, quickly repeat the movement further back on the band of couverture.

The cigarettes can be used immediately or as needed.

Storage

Cigarettes can be stored for several months in airtight containers free from humidity and heat.

Two-toned Cigarettes

Cigarettes made with two colors are attractive and can be combined with other chocolate work for decorating.

Two different colors of tempered couvertures are needed for this procedure.

The same equipment is required as for simple cigarettes, plus a pastry comb or large serrated palette knife.

Procedure

Two-toned cigarettes are made very much like simple cigarettes are.

Pour out a band of tempered white or orange-flavored couverture. Spread the chocolate with a pastry comb, making thin, even grooves in the couverture while smoothing it out on the marble.

The grooves should be approximately 1 mm ($\frac{1}{16}$ in.) apart. Diagonal grooves can also be made by drawing the pastry comb through the chocolate diagonally after spreading it evenly on the marble.

Trim and even out the sides and ends of the band of couverture as it begins to set.

Pour approximately the same quantity of a second color of tempered couverture

over the combed band. Spread it quickly and evenly over the band, using a metal

spatula or triangle. This thin layer of couverture should cover the entire band, filling in the grooves.

Trim the sides and ends of the band of the two couvertures as the second layer starts to set.

Form the cigarettes in the same way as for the simple cigarettes.

The storage is the same as for the simple cigarettes.

Pour two different colors of tempered couverture on the marble next to each other. As they are spread out on the mar-

ble, they will blend into each other. They now form one strip of two colors and can be rolled into cigarettes in the same way

as for simple cigarettes. The proportion of the two colors can be adjusted as desired.

Copeaux
(Shavings)

Chocolate shavings are made in a variety of sizes and used, like cigarettes, to decorate and finish various chocolate-based cakes.

Several procedures can be used to make chocolate shavings; they can be classified into two categories:

1. Shavings made in advance so they can be stored, like cigarettes.
2. Shavings that are made and used immediately.

1. Shavings Made in Advance
(on a marble surface)

Classic shaped shavings are made from a band of tempered couverture smoothed out onto the work surface as for cigarettes. Using the tip of a metal spatula, scrape a diamond or diagonal pattern in the couverture. Then roll up the shavings as for making cigarettes using a scraper.

Large, wide shavings can also be used to decorate cakes. Cover the cakes entirely with the shavings, forming a flower around the cake (see photo on the next page).

Small, delicate shavings can be made by scraping a piece of chocolate with the blade of a knife held at a 90-degree angle or by peeling shavings from the side of a piece of couverture with a vegetable peeler.

Very small shavings are made like two-toned cigarettes. Spread a band of couverture on the marble. Comb and scrape away small shavings. Several colors of couverture can be mixed together to create multicolored shavings.

Spread a layer of tempered couverture 2 mm (1/16 in.) thick on the marble. Wait until it starts to firm up slightly, as for making cigarettes.

With a medium-size plain cutter held in both hands at a 30-degree angle, scrape the couverture by pulling the cutter backward (toward yourself), in a curve or a straight line, depending on the desired shape of the shavings.

Carefully place the shavings in airtight containers, where they can be stored for several months if protected from moisture and heat.

2. Chocolate Shavings Made on Sheet Pans

Shavings made on sheet pans must be placed immediately on the cake they are decorating.

There are two methods for this technique:

1. Using warm sheet pans
2. Using cold sheet pans

1. Using Warm Sheet Pans

Use a flat (not warped), clean blue steel sheet pan. Turn it over, and spread a layer of untempered, melted couverture approximately 1 mm (1/16 in.) thick on the bottom side of the sheet pan. Place the sheet pan in the refrigerator at 5°C (40°F).

It is also possible to heat the sheet pan to between 40° and 50°C (105° and 120°F) and rub a piece of solid couverture on the back of the sheet pan. The couverture should melt, leaving a layer on the sheet pan. Place the sheet pan in the refrigerator.

The remaining procedure is the same, regardless of how the layer of couverture was made.

Once the chocolate is firm, remove the sheet pan from the refrigerator and allow to come to room temperature.

Procedure

Remove any trace of moisture from the back of the sheet pan by wiping it with a clean, dry cloth.

Using a metal spatula, quickly spread a thin layer of melted couverture on the back of the sheet pan.

The couverture will instantly harden. Cut to size and lift off strips of couverture using a metal spatula or triangle. Shape the strips and immediately place them on the cakes to be decorated.

With this method, the couverture is malleable for only a few seconds, making it necessary to work quickly to shape it.

With a metal spatula, scrape off the couverture. By holding the spatula at different angles, shavings of various

All the types of shavings and strips prepared on sheet pans can be made with all types of couverture, including dark, milk, white, and different-colored couvertures.

It is also possible to mix two colors of couverture before spreading them on the sheet pans to create various effects, such as autumn leaves.

Note

With the method using cold sheet pans, it is easy to make ribbons out of strips of chocolate couverture. They are shaped like ribbons of pulled sugar (see pulled-sugar ribbons, pages 200 to 203).

sizes can be obtained. Smaller angles yield larger pieces. The larger strips can be shaped as needed before placing them on cakes.

2. Using Cold Sheet Pans

Place blue steel sheet pans (marble boards can be substituted) in the freezer at −30°C (−20°F) for several hours before they are to be used.

Organizing the Work Station

It is important to work quickly when making chocolate shavings on cold sheet pans. Before starting the procedure, the work station as well as the equipment, couverture, and cakes to be decorated should be available and ready.

To prevent the sheet pans from warming up too quickly, place them on cutting boards or make a stack of three to five cold sheet pans.

Chocolate cutouts

Using cutouts of tempered couverture that have been smoothed out on paper offers a wide range of possibilities for creating shapes, such as

- cutouts lifted by hand, to make small pieces for hatchets, saws, stars, and evergreens used to decorate bûches de Noël (yule logs)
- three-dimensional cutouts, using a model or template to build pieces such as small houses, churches, angels, and hearts
- using a preshaped cutter, for such shapes as crescents, flowers, and leaves

Procedure

Spread an even layer of tempered couverture on a piece of parchment paper. Depending on the piece to be made, the thickness of the couverture can vary from 1 to 3 mm (1/16 to 1/8 in.).

The top side of the couverture can be decorated by gently running a serrated knife or pastry comb over the strip in a wavy motion and then piping out a thin strip of couverture of a different color with a paper cone over it. Place a second piece of paper on top of the couvertures to create a marbled effect (good for making autumn leaves).

Cutting Out the Pieces

Cut the couverture with the tip of a small paring knife, using a template as a

guide, or use a cutter. Work quickly, as the couverture will become firm fast and crack when cut if hard.

Lifting the Pieces

Place a thin metal spatula or a knife with a thin blade (such as a fish knife) between the couverture and paper. The pieces should lift off easily. Remove the pieces as soon as the couverture is firm enough, as it shrinks when cold and may buckle and warp, which can be a problem, especially when constructing three-dimensional pieces.

Sticking the Pieces Together

The cut pieces can be attached together with tempered chocolate piped from a paper cone.

Note

The leftover trimmings of couverture can be melted down and tempered again for further use.

Tips

Prepare the templates or cutters before spreading out the couverture to prevent it from hardening too much before cutting.

If possible, it is best to use a thick paper (butcher paper), rather than parchment paper, as this will stay smoother, with less tendency to buckle.

Sketches for models of flowers, butterflies, birds and other figures are given in volume 4.

Raised chocolate decorations using a paper cone

Chocolate decorations piped out with a paper cone can be used to complement pieces decorated with chocolate cutouts or other types of chocolate decorations.

Attractive pieces made to stand upright can be made by tracing over sketches. The pieces can be made in advance and stored to be used as needed.

Procedure

Laboratory chocolate (chocolate lower in cocoa butter than couverture) is recommended for this procedure because it is less fluid than couverture chocolate and easier to work with. The tip of the paper cone should be cut to a medium-size opening. If cut too large, the chocolate will smear; too small, and the piece will be overly delicate and will break easily when lifted.

Piping Out the Decorations

Two methods can be used:
1. For those good at drawing, the chocolate can be piped out freehand with a paper cone, to create words and small figures such as birds and butterflies.

2. For those more comfortable drawing from models or to learn a new pattern, it is possible to trace over a design. Place a sketch under a sheet of transparent plastic.

Tips

The lines of chocolate cannot be broken when piped out: they must all connect.

For tracing with the paper cone, use the appliqué technique (see volume 4, *The Three Methods of Decorating with a Paper Cone,* pages 56 to 57).

Before piping out the chocolate, be sure that the plastic sheet is perfectly clean and dry so that the chocolate will lift off easily.

Place the decoration in a cold area, such as the refrigerator, for a few minutes to make it easier to remove the decoration.

Remove the decorations by passing a thin knife blade or spatula between the decorations and the plastic sheet to pick them up gently.

They can either be used immediately or stored flat on the plastic sheet in an

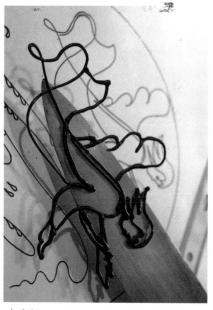

airtight container in a refrigerator at 5°C (40°F), free from humidity.

Note

This technique, piping tempered chocolate with a paper cone, can be used with different colors of chocolate such as white and orange. Two or more colors can also be used for the same decoration, such as for a heart traced in orange that is interlaced with a second heart in white chocolate.

Dipping candies in chocolate

Candies are coated with chocolate by submerging fillings previously cut to shape in tempered chocolate.

Dipping forks and rings are the tools used for dipping individual fillings. The dipping fork comes with two, three, or four prongs. The prongs are used to decorate the chocolates after they have been dipped by making lines on top of the candies. Dipping rings come in a variety of sizes. Dipping rings are usually used for coating round fillings such as truffles.

Preparing the Fillings

The fillings to be dipped should be previously cut to size, have smooth surfaces, and be fairly firm. The fillings should be brought to room temperature, approximately 18° to 20°C (65° to 68°F) before dipping.

Very soft fillings that might stick to the dipping fork, such as soft caramels, pralines, and Montélimar nougats, are dipped twice. For the first coating, soft fillings are kept cold so they will be as firm as possible. They are held on the fork during the first dipping, instead of being dropped into the chocolate as firm fillings are.

The first coating can also be brushed on, with the same technique used for glazing pastries. For large quantities the first coating can also be sprayed on, using a paint sprayer.

The first coating can be made of a combination of tempered couverture chocolate and cocoa butter or two parts tempered couverture and one part unsweetened chocolate. This thin first coating will dry quickly and make it possible dip the chocolates a second time with excellent results.

Setting Up the Work Station

The work station should be organized so as to avoid unnecessary movement and reaching.

Place fillings to be dipped to the left for right-handed persons (reverse the positions if left-handed).

The bowl of tempered couverture chocolate should be placed on a towel to prevent it from coming directly in contact with the marble or other cold surface, which would cause it to harden quickly. Sheets of plastic or aluminum foil are placed beneath the right hand and should be prepared and cut to size before the couverture is tempered.

Dipping the Fillings

Two methods can be used to dip the fillings.

Method 1

With the left hand (if right-handed), turn the fillings over, one by one, placing them in the bowl of tempered couverture with the smoothest side up, which from now on will be considered the top side. This side is usually a bit larger because what was originally the top side (now considered the bottom) contracted slightly after being cut to size.

The top side of the fillings will have slightly straighter edges after cutting, which prevent chocolate from running down the sides and forming a puddle of chocolate around the bottoms of the candies as they dry.

Use the dipping fork to submerge the filling completely in the chocolate. Then position the fork beneath the filling and lift it out of the chocolate so it will not fall off the fork.

Gently brush the top of the candy with the index finger to remove any ex-

cess chocolate and prevent a puddle of chocolate from collecting around the bases of the candies.

Tap the fork two or three times on the edge of the bowl to even the chocolate coating. Remove any excess couverture by scraping the dipping fork on the edges of the bowl or brushing a finger under the candy.

Remove the candy from the fork by holding the fork at a slight angle and letting the candy slide off onto the sheet of plastic or aluminum. Pull the fork quickly away from the candy so the candy will stay in place.

Decorating

The candies can be decorated with the prongs of the dipping fork before the chocolate sets. Place the fork flat on top of the covered candy and slowly lift it straight up, so that the couverture rises a little with the fork. A line in relief will be made by each prong of the fork. The fork can be applied at various angles to create diagonal, lengthwise, or criss-cross patterns on the candies.

Before the chocolate becomes firm, a nut or liqueur coffee bean can be placed on top of each candy.

Once the chocolate is firm, the candies can also be decorated by piping out a different color of tempered chocolate onto them, using a paper cone.

Method 2

With this method, the fillings are not placed in the chocolate upside down; the less smooth side stays on top.

The dipping procedure is the same as for the first method: press the candy into the chocolate. Lift, brush, tap, and scrape off any excess chocolate.

The main difference between these two methods is that the candy is turned over (upside down) when placed onto the plastic sheet with the fork.

This second method is faster but requires a precise movement when turning

the candies over onto the plastic. This method can only be used when the candies are decorated with the fork, as it is not possible to obtain a smooth surface on top after turning them over.

Use this method for coating round fillings with dipping circles.

Dipping candies is repetitive, exacting work requiring good coordination and speed so the work can be completed quickly, allowing ample time for decoration.

Hand-dipping candies

Candies dipped by hand offer two advantages over using dipping tools. This method is considerably faster, and it coats the filling with a thinner, more delicate layer of chocolate.

It is important to perform this procedure with a second person for an efficient, fast organization that provides the best results. This method is most often used for coating truffles and rochers (chocolate/praline fillings).

Procedure

Prepare the fillings, shaping or cutting them to size. Temper the couverture

chocolate. Place sheets of aluminum foil on sheet pans; the coated candies will dry on them. These sheet pans should be placed to the right (for right-handed persons); they can be stacked if more than one sheet pan will be needed. Truffles to be coated with cocoa powder should be dropped and rolled around in a sheet pan

filled with cocoa powder immediately after being coated with couverture.

Coating the Candies

Cover the palm of the left hand and the fingertips of the right hand with couver-

ture. Place the rochers or truffles, two at a time, in the left hand and roll them with the fingers of the right hand until they are well covered with chocolate.

Place the two coated candies on the sheet pan to dry. The second person should, at the same time, place two more fillings in the left hand.

By following this method for coating round fillings, two people can make approximately ten sheet pans of rochers in one hour; ten sheet pans of truffles can be made in an hour if a third person is available to roll them in the cocoa powder.

Lining sheet molds with chocolate

Many types of chocolate-covered candies are made in sheet molds of various sizes and shapes.

Chocolate molds are usually made out of rigid plastic or Bakelite. Molds offer the advantages of speed, even size, and assortment, and are excellent for soft fillings and liqueur fillings. Molding is easier than dipping with forks. If the couverture is properly tempered, neat and shiny candies will result.

Procedure

1. Lining the Molds

The cleanliness of the molds is of utmost importance, as it will determine how easily the candies unmold as well as how shiny they will be. The interior of the molds should be cleaned by wiping them with cotton (for example, cotton balls) to remove any trace of chocolate, humidity, or dust.

Note: Some molds have nooks and corners that are difficult to reach and clean. These should be washed with hot water and dried in a proof box or slow oven.

The molds should be brought to room temperature, approximately 18°C (65°F), before they are filled.

Fill the molds to the rims with tempered couverture using a ladle or wooden spatula.

Tap the side of the mold with the spatula, ladle, or a knife handle to eliminate any air bubbles and ensure an even lining of the molds.

Turn the molds upside down over the bowl of tempered chocolate and again tap the side of the mold to eliminate excess couverture.

With a metal spatula or triangle, scrape off the excess couverture from the top of the molds (be careful not to remove any couverture from inside the molds).

Turn the molds upside down again and place them on top of metal rulers or wedges until the couverture firms up and will not drip down to the bottom of the molds when turned over.

Check to see if the couverture is somewhat, but not completely, firm, and scrape the molds a second time with a triangle or pastry cutter to remove any excess couverture still remaining.

Allow the couverture to become completely firm before filling.

2. Filling the Molds

Depending on the type of filling used, the molds can be filled with a pastry bag and tip (for soft fillings such as ganache and gianduja) or with a candy funnel (for liqueur fillings).

In either case, the molds are filled 2 to 3 mm (¹⁄₁₆ to ⅛ in.) from the top.

The molds are placed in the refrigerator to allow the fillings to become firm or for the liqueurs to form a crust (see liqueur-filled candies, page 74).

3. Sealing the Molds

After the fillings have firmed up or the liqueurs have acquired a crust, they are ready to be sealed with a layer of couverture.

Seal the molds by scraping a layer of tempered couverture back and forth over the tops of the molds to ensure a perfect seal.

Place the molds in the refrigerator to harden. The time can vary for each type of filling to become firm. Allow 1 hour for giandujas, 2 hours for fondant cream fillings, 3 hours for heavily liqueur-filled ganaches.

4. Unmolding the Candies

To unmold the candies, quickly turn the molds over onto a sheet of parchment paper. Sometimes it is necessary to tap the back of the molds at an angle against the marble or other surface to remove the candies.

Classic techniques for molding chocolate

Definition

Molding chocolates is a very important procedure to understand in chocolate work. The procedure for molding consists of lining the insides of molds (often specially made for this purpose) with tempered chocolate couverture to create figures of various shapes and sizes.

As the couverture cools inside the molds and becomes solid, it contracts and pulls away from the mold, making it possible to unmold the figure when solid.

Important Tips to Remember

- The couverture must be perfectly tempered.
- The molds must be perfectly clean, shiny, and ideally at 22°C (72°F).
- It is helpful to work in an area that is 19° to 23°C (66° to 74°F); the ideal temperature is 20°C (68°F).
- All equipment such as ladles, metal spatulas, and brushes should be perfectly clean and dry. Be especially careful to check the brush used.

Couverture is most successfully molded when the molds are close in temperature to the temperature of the work area.

Two basic types of molding are possible:

- classic molding
- special molding

Classic molding will be discussed here; special molding techniques will be covered later in the text.

Preparation

Preparing the Equipment

The first step is to prepare all equipment: gather the equipment for tempering the couverture, clean the molds, and

get together the remaining equipment—brushes and metal rulers.

Cleaning the Molds

As the condition of the molds greatly determines the end result of this procedure, be sure to clean them well by wiping them with cotton and shining them

with a second piece of cotton lightly dipped in melted cocoa butter.

Molds that are often used can be washed and then dried in a proof box before wiping them with cotton and cocoa butter.

Procedure

Lining the Molds with Couverture

Two methods can be used.

1. Lining Molds with Two or More Colors of Couverture

Although optional, adding more than one color can improve the appearance of a piece.

With a pastry brush, brush a thin layer of tempered couverture into the mold, starting with contours and parts in relief; for example, use red chocolate to make the crest of a rooster or white chocolate to make the fins of a fish first. Allow the chocolate to harden, and then finish filling the mold as described below for one-color molds.

2. Lining a Mold with One Color of Couverture

Using a pastry brush, brush a thin layer of tempered couverture on the inside of a mold. Throughout this part of the procedure, hold the mold by the handles between the fingers. Never rest the mold inside the hand: because the hand generates heat, the mold would have hot spots and unmolding would be difficult.

Allow this first layer of couverture to become firm before proceeding with a second layer.

Never place the mold directly on the marble or other cold surface. Instead, place it on a rack, supported on metal rulers, or on an egg carton, so that the couverture will become firm evenly.

Once the couverture is firm, fill the mold with a second layer. This time fill the mold to the rim with a ladle.

With a wooden spatula, tap the filled mold gently to break up any air bubbles.

Tap the mold with a wooden spatula to even out the layer of remaining couverture in the mold.

Immediately turn the mold upside down over the bowl of tempered couverture to eliminate the excess couverture.

Turn the mold right side up and allow the couverture to become firm, supporting it up off the marble as before.

Allow the couverture to harden for several minutes until it is somewhat, but not completely, firm.

Trim off any excess couverture from the sides of the mold with:

- a pastry scraper or triangle

- a paring knife
- a firm plastic scraper (this tool is strongly recommended for beginners as it cannot scratch the edges of the mold)

During this part of the procedure, it is again important to hold the mold only by the handles or at the edges.

Chilling and Firming the Chocolate Molds

After trimming the molds, place them in a cool area to allow the couverture to become firm. The ideal temperature is 12° to 16°C (53° to 60°F).

If the work area is too warm for chilling the molds, they can be placed in the refrigerator. Place the molds in the top of the refrigerator, not at the bottom, where it tends to be coolest.

It can take from 30 minutes to 1 hour for the couverture to completely firm up, depending on the size and shape of the mold used.

Unmolding

Unmolding is very tricky and requires careful attention throughout the procedure.

As the couverture hardens, it will contract and pull away slightly from the mold, leaving approximately 1 mm ($\frac{1}{16}$ in.) of space between the chocolate and the mold. This can be easily seen and is a good way of determining when the chocolate has become firm enough to be unmolded.

Gently press against the chocolate inside the mold with the thumb. It should release easily from the mold.

Another method for unmolding is to bend the mold gently by pressing it with both hands at opposite corners. The chocolate will immediately release from the mold.

If the chocolate was properly tempered and molded, it will fall easily out of the mold. Turn the mold upside down and let the piece drop onto a hand held underneath.

If the pieces are to be kept in the refrigerator, to keep them shiny fit the pieces back inside the mold after unmolding and store them this way until they are to be used.

To prevent any traces of moisture from forming on the pieces, it is best to bring them slowly to room temperature. This can be done by placing the pieces on a sheet of parchment paper or a cooling rack, allowing them to reach room temperature before they are handled further.

Assembling or Attaching Chocolate Molds

Two methods can be used to seal chocolate mold halves, such as eggs, bunnies, chickens, or fish, together:

- Place the two halves, flat sides down, on a warm sheet pan, and shake the pan for a few seconds. Then quickly attach the two halves together, pressing gently so the warmed edges form a seal.
- Pipe a thin thread of tempered chocolate around the entire inside edge of one of the two halves, then quickly press the two halves together until they are sealed.

Unmolding

Unmolding is very tricky and requires careful attention throughout the procedure.

As the couverture hardens, it will contract and pull away slightly from the mold, leaving approximately 1 mm ($\frac{1}{16}$ in.) of space between the chocolate and the mold. This can be easily seen and is a good way of determining when the chocolate has become firm enough to be unmolded.

Specialized molding

Introduction

Variations of molded chocolates can be made by using different colors of couverture chocolate applied in a variety of ways to create various effects, thus personalizing the pieces.

The pieces resulting from this method of molding will be exceptionally shiny and smooth. Unmolding is also fairly easy.

Preparation

Prepare All Equipment

Use the same equipment as for classic molding.

Clean the Molds

Wipe the molds with cotton. Shine them with a piece of cotton or foam rub-

ber that has been lightly soaked in melted cocoa butter. A paintbrush or even the fingers can be used for this step.

Prepare all types of molds in the same way.

Prepare the Chocolate

Melt two parts unsweetened chocolate and one part couverture chocolate separately. Mix and temper the two chocolates together.

Basic Procedure for Specialized Molding

Brush a thin layer of the combined tempered chocolates on the mold with a pastry brush, holding the mold by the handles or edges as for classic molding.

After the chocolate is set, brush on a thin layer of tempered orange or red couverture with a pastry brush or the finger

tips. It is this layer of chocolate that will be seen through the first layer and will cause the piece to be very shiny and bright after unmolding.

After the second layer of chocolate has set, brush on a thin layer of white chocolate or couverture. White chocolate is very sweet and will balance out the un-

sweetened chocolate used to line the piece.

Finish molding by adding a last layer of tempered couverture chocolate as for the classic method or by adding a last layer of the mixture of unsweetened and couverture chocolate used for the first layer. This last layer can be applied as for the classic method, or it can be brushed on with a pastry brush.

Turn the molds over so any excess couverture can drip down, tap the molds lightly, and place them on racks or between metal rulers as for classic molding.

Allow the couverture to set halfway, then trim the edges as for the classic method.

Cooling and Setting the Couverture

Follow the same procedure given for the classic method. The couverture will set more quickly with this method of molding, as thin layers have been brushed on each time and have set up before the next layer was applied.

Unmolding

To unmold, simply lift the molds up off the pieces, which should immediately release from the molds. This can be done on a rack, or the mold can be held over the fingers, which catch the molded chocolate as it falls from the mold, a somewhat easier method.

Tips for Proper Molding

Never place cold couverture in a cold mold.	The piece will unmold but will have white streaks (marbled) and will not contract properly from the mold.
Never place cold couverture in a warm mold.	The piece will be difficult to unmold and will be very fragile and break easily.
Never place cold couverture in a hot mold.	The piece will either stick and not come out of the mold, or, if it comes out, it will be marbled with white streaks.
Never place hot couverture in a cold mold.	The piece will probably not unmold; if it does, it will be shiny at first, then mat and grainy the next day.
Never place hot couverture in a warm mold.	The piece will probably not unmold; if it does, it will be dull and marbled.
Never place hot couverture in a hot mold.	The piece will probably not unmold; if it does, it will be very dull.
Never place tempered couverture in a cold mold.	The piece will unmold but will be dull and contract poorly from the mold.
Never place tempered couverture in a hot mold.	The piece will stick to the mold and be marbled with white streaks.
Never place hot, cold, or tempered couverture in a mold that is not perfectly clean.	The piece will be difficult to unmold, will contract poorly from the mold, and will be dull and unattractive.
Always place tempered couverture in a mold at room temperature, 22°C (72°F).	The piece will unmold easily, contract from the mold properly, and be very shiny.

Decorative Ways of Molding Chocolate

To obtain nuances of color on molded pieces, brush on a different-colored layer tempered couverture before allowing the previous layer to set.

Variations of color can be obtained by brushing on layers of varying thickness or allowing the previous layer to set to various degrees or not at all before the next is applied.

To achieve red highlights, brush on a thin layer, very thin in some places, of red tempered couverture as the first layer.

By lining the mold with cocoa butter, a white veil effect can be obtained. This highlight or layer of white can be altered by varying the thickness and length of time the cocoa butter is allowed to set.

Chocolate lace eggs

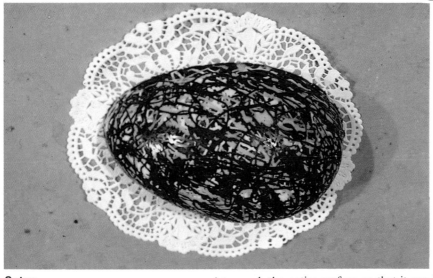

Setup

Tempered couverture chocolate, or a mixture of tempered unsweetened and couverture chocolate, plus tempered couvertures of various colors (optional).

Procedure

Clean the mold as for classic molding.

Make a separate paper cone for each color of couverture to be used. Cut the tip of each paper cone and test to see how the thickly the couverture pipes out.

Hold the cone straight up, perpendicular to the mold, and pipe out an even,

steady stream of couverture. Interlace and crisscross the lines of couverture inside the mold. Place the mold at an angle

to reach the entire surface so that it can be evenly covered with lines of couverture.

Follow the same procedures for all colors of couvertures.

Using a paper cone, pipe a thicker line of couverture around the edges of the mold to reinforce the piece and facilitate attaching two halves together.

Allow the piece to set partially, and trim the edges.

Chill, set, and unmold the piece as for the classic method of molding.

Caution: Chocolate lace eggs (or other pieces made with this technique) are very fragile.

Using the pastry bag to mold

Molding Small Pieces

Setup

Tempered couverture chocolate, any color

Equipment

Plastic sheet molds of small figures, pastry bag with a fluted tip, a bottle, and a small piece of tart dough.

Procedure

Wipe the molds carefully with cotton. Place a piece of tart dough in a bottle.

Place the pastry bag inside the bottle with the tip resting on the dough. The dough acts as a stopper to prevent the couverture from spilling out when the bag is filled. Turn the sides of the pastry bag over the sides of the bottle and fill only halfway with couverture.

Remove the pastry bag from the bottle with the dough attached, remove the dough, and fill the molds to the rims with the couverture, or mound slightly. Tap the sheet molds to eliminate any air bubbles and even out the pieces.

Place the molds in a cold area to set the couverture, as for classic molding.

Unmold the pieces by placing the sheet on its side with a sheet of parchment paper underneath for the pieces to fall onto. The pieces should release easily.

Molding larger figures

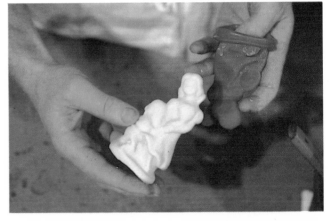

Support the mold, upside down, to fill it.

Fill the mold using a pastry bag and tip or ladle. Allow the couverture to set.

Unmold, according to the type of mold used, and decorate as desired.

Chocolate Cups

Setup

Tempered couverture chocolate

Equipment

Rolling pin, sheets of aluminum foil or silk paper, parchment paper or plastic sheets, and a paper cone.

Procedure

Cover the end of a rolling pin with aluminum foil or silk paper to a depth of about 6 to 8 cm (2.5 to 3 in.), forming a cup shape.

Dip the rolling pin with the cup into a bowl of tempered couverture; the coating should cover 4 to 5 cm (1.5 to 2 in.) of the foil or paper. The protruding foil or paper will make it easier to remove the cup when the couverture sets.

Carefully lift the piece out of the couverture and allow the excess couverture to drip off.

Place the cup on a sheet of plastic or parchment paper, and let it set.

Once set, carefully remove the foil or paper from the cup by rolling the cup around the index finger, drawing the foil or paper away from the cup.

Make handles, to be attached to the sides, for cups, or to the tops, for baskets, by piping out tempered couverture with a paper cone onto the sheets of plastic or parchment paper.

Attach the handles on the sides with more tempered chocolate, or place the handles on top after the cups are filled.

The cups can be decorated and filled in a variety of ways.

Making an Opening in an Egg

Cutting an opening in a chocolate egg for decoration is fairly simple but delicate work and requires careful attention throughout the procedure.

Heat the tip of a thin knife. Carefully and slowly cut into the egg, allowing the heat of the knife to melt the chocolate. Be careful: forcing the knife can cause the egg to crack or break.

Decorating an Egg or Other Small Piece

Chocolate eggs are often decorated with a royal icing or different colors of tempered couverture chocolate piped from a paper cone.

The following can be used to decorate small molded chocolate pieces:

- rock sugar, colored candied almonds
- figures made of marzipan, such as flower and animals
- different colors of chocolate shavings
- tinted, grated coconut
- flowers, leaves, and branches made from pulled sugar

Examples of classically molded chocolate pieces

Examples of figures made from egg molds

Figures Made from Various Molds

The following can be used to mold chocolate in different shapes:

- Egg molds
- Baba molds
- Tartlet molds
- Ladles
- Pastry tips
- Pithiviers cutters
- Cutouts from paper
- Molds made from marzipan
- White chocolate piped from a paper cone

Examples of large decorative chocolate pieces

Building large chocolate pieces

Building large decorative chocolate pieces is a fairly simple procedure if the key points are followed.

It is important that the work station be set up before proceeding. No special equipment is required.

The following discussion describes an example of *montage,* the construction of a large, classic, chocolate piece based mostly on molded chocolate eggs.

Setup

Tempered fondant chocolate

Chocolate molded in a round-bottomed stainless steel bowl to be used as the base

Various sizes of molded chocolate eggs

Chocolate molded in savarin molds

Large paper cones filled with tempered couverture chocolate

Various chocolate designs piped out on plastic sheets or parchment paper with a paper cone

Chocolate cigarettes, shavings, and cut-outs

Equipment

Metal spatula, paring knife, wooden spatula, pastry brush, scissors, metal triangle

Procedure

An unlimited number of configurations can be built, although the balance of the piece must be considered, or it may topple over after being constructed.

Place all the parts in their final positions without attaching to get an idea of the presentation. With a knife, mark where different parts will be attached.

The size of the base will vary according to the size, weight, and construction of the piece.

To help the pieces stick together, small eggs can simply be scratched with a knife

where they will be attached. Larger pieces require an opening cut, using the technique for opening an egg, with a hot knife.

Before permanently attaching the piece together, hold it up in place to check that each piece will fit together.

Pipe tempered couverture as needed where the pieces are joined and hold the larger pieces (eggs) in place with supports such as bottles until the piped-out couverture has set.

When the couverture has set, remove the supports. Trim and clean the piece with a paring knife, gently scraping as necessary.

Continue to build upon the piece, paying careful attention to the equilibrium as

more pieces are added, so that the final piece will stand up on its own when finished.

Attach the smaller pieces, and cut openings of various sizes and shapes to decorate the piece.

Place the whole piece in the freezer before covering it with couverture chocolate using a spray gun.

Decorating with a spray gun

- Be sure to strain the couverture before using it.
- Adjust the aperture of the spray tip to the size needed. Cakes should be covered with a very fine spray. Display pieces can be covered with a thicker spray.
- Hold the spray gun at a distance of 25 to 35 cm (10 to 14 in.) from cakes and 35 to 50 cm (14 to 20 in.) from large display pieces.
- Keep the spray gun in constant motion while spraying. Do not tilt the spray gun; always try to hold it perpendicular to the piece. If left stationary or tilted, the couverture will drip. An uneven, overly thick layer will also form on the piece, especially at the joints where pieces connect.
- Allow the couverture to set after spraying, and before handling the piece. Handle the finished piece very gently.

Prepare the Work Area

Protect the work area well, as the spray gun will cover the surrounding area with a fine spray of couverture.

Using a spray gun makes it possible to apply a thin layer of milk or dark chocolate couverture over an entire surface or just on certain sections of various desserts and display pieces.

Equipment

Paint spray gun, sieve, bowls, whisk, wooden spatula, plastic scraper, ladle

Setup

Milk or dark chocolate couverture and cocoa butter

Procedure

Prepare the Couverture

It is necessary to use equal amounts of cocoa butter and milk or dark couverture chocolate to obtain the consistency required to achieve a fine spray.

Melt the couverture to between 35° and 40°C (95° and 104°F). Strain it to re-move any foreign particles, so it is completely smooth.

Melt the cocoa butter and add it to the couverture, blending well. Keep the mixture at 35°C (95°F), which is the ideal temperature for spraying.

Creating a Velvety Texture

Place the dessert or display piece in the freezer for 20 to 40 minutes. Because the piece will be extremely cold, the couverture will set instantly on the piece as it is sprayed, creating a velvety texture.

Key Points to Follow

- Maintain the temperature of the couverture/cocoa butter mixture at 35°C (95°F).
- The equipment, including the spray gun, should also be brought to 35°C (95°F). This can be done by placing it in a proof box.

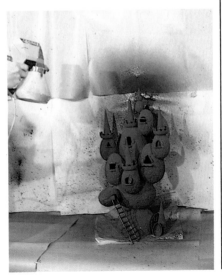

The couverture can be captured for further use if plastic sheets or parchment paper is used to catch the overspray.

The Two Textures Made with a Spray Gun

Smooth and Shiny Surfaces

It is easier to create a smooth and shiny surface on a cake by applying a classic chocolate glaze (see chocolate sauce, volume 2, pages 84 to 85), rather than by using a spray gun. Consequently, a spray gun is used primarily to apply smooth and shiny coatings to large display pieces.

Velvet Surfaces

The spray gun creates very interesting and professional results when used to cover a surface or parts of a surface with a velvety texture. It can be used to decorate cakes, frozen desserts, and chocolate candies, as well as display pieces.

Chocolate bonbons

Definition

Chocolate bonbons (sometimes simply called chocolates) contain a variety of fillings of different textures and flavors; they all share one common trait: all are covered with chocolate. This chocolate covering, the type and flavor of which can vary, serves to protect and preserve the filling as well as decorate and flavor the bonbon.

Chocolate bonbons are judged by how evenly the fillings are cut and how carefully they are molded or dipped in chocolate.

Making chocolate bonbons requires careful attention, cleanliness, precision, and organization throughout the procedure. If the filling is poorly cut or badly dipped or handled, there is no way of improving or correcting the final results.

Classification

Chocolate bonbons can be grouped into two categories:

1. Based on how the chocolates are covered or made

- fillings rolled in chocolate
- chocolates piped out of a pastry bag
- fillings dipped with a fork or hand dipped.

2. Based on the type of filling used

An unlimited variety of fillings can be used for chocolate bonbons. Some of these fillings are discussed in detail in the text that follows, and some can be found in volume 2.

Cut or Shaped Fillings

Instructions for making the following fillings, which can be cut or shaped to size, are found in volume 2: almond or hazelnut praline paste (pages 114 to 117), gianduja (pages 118 to 119), ganache (page 124 to 125), almond paste (pages 94 to 95), marzipan (pages 96 to 98), walnut paste (page 99), nougat, soft and firm (pages 105 to 107), caramel (pages 102 to 104), jellied fruits (pages 86 to 89), and nougatine (pages 108 to 111).

Creamy Fillings

These can be based on ganache, fon-

dant cream filling (volume 2, pages 120 to 121), gianduja.

Fondant-based Fillings

Fondant can be flavored with natural flavorings, such as coffee, chocolate, or vanilla; with fruit, such as strawberry, raspberry, black currant, or red currant; with herbs or plants such as mint or tea; with liquor or liqueur.

Liquor- and Liqueur-filled Chocolates

Cointreau, Grand Marnier, rum, Marie-Brizard, Kirsch, or whiskey can be used.

Fillings of Candied Fruit Rinds

Orange or lemon rinds can be cut in strips and candied.

Fruit and Nut Fillings

Candied cherries, pieces of glazed chestnuts, walnuts, or peeled, lightly roasted hazelnuts or almonds are all possibilities.

Chocolate-covered Cherries Soaked in Brandy

Truffles

Decorated Fruits (crystallized or candied marzipan-filled fruits).

Shaped or cut fillings

Gianduja

Procedure

Cool the gianduja by spreading it on a cool surface such as a pastry marble. Then put it between metal rulers, forming a square layer that is approximately 1 cm (½ in.) thick.

Allow the mixture to set. The gianduja can be spread between the rulers on a sheet pan and chilled in the refrigerator to speed the setting.

The filling is now ready to spread with a thin layer of couverture chocolate (either milk or dark chocolate). This thin coating will prevent the dipped bonbons from sticking to the dipping fork.

The slab of gianduja can be turned over and coated with a thin layer of couverture before cutting, but this is not necessary.

Cut the gianduja into the shapes and sizes as needed:

- squares, 20 to 22 mm (¾ to ⅞ in.) per side
- diamonds, 20 to 22 mm (¾ to ⅞ in.) per side
- triangles, 22 to 24 mm (⅞ to 1 in.) per side
- rectangles, 30 by 20 mm (1¼ × ¾ in.)

These shapes are cut with a knife or in a cutter (called a "guitar") with rows of adjustable fine wires that are drawn over the entire layer of gianduja.

Other shapes can be made with special cutters, such as rounds 22 to 24 mm (⅞ to 1 in.) in diameter, or rounds 30 to 32 mm (approximately 1 in.) in diameter that are then cut in half to form half-moon shapes. Oval, hexagonal, and a variety of other differently shaped cutters can also be used.

Balls of gianduja can be formed by rolling equal-sized pieces of filling in the palms of the hands. This is a common shape used to make rochers (bonbons of gianduja covered with chopped pralines).

Marzipan and Walnut Marzipan

Almond and walnut marzipan can be flavored to taste and colored if desired to create a variety of candies.

It is also possible to place macerated dried fruits or candied fruits or craquelin (nut brittle) in the centers of almond or walnut marzipan bonbons. Some examples are: raisins and rum, walnuts and coffee, candied fruits and Kirsch.

Cutting and shaping is done as for gianduja.

The possibilities of matching flavors and colors to form an assortment of candies are endless.

For example, gianduja and marzipan can be combined by coating a 5-mm (¼-in.) layer of rum-flavored white or green marzipan with a 5-mm (¼-in.) layer of gianduja. Another possibility is to combine marzipan and ganache. The possibilities with this combination are unlimited.

Ganache Fillings

Cut Shapes

Place a 10-mm-thick (½-in.) layer of filling between metal rulers or in a square form, such as a sheet pan, to cool. Chill the filling in the refrigerator to speed up the process.

Coat with a thin layer of couverture and let the couverture set. Turn the entire piece over and cut to the desired shape as for gianduja.

Logs

Pipe out the filling into strips with a pastry bag and plain no. 9 or no. 10 tip onto parchment paper set in a sheet pan. Allow the filling to cool in the refrigerator.

Cut the logs into even-sized pieces approximately 4 cm (1.5 in.) long.

Variations

Pipe out the filling with a pastry bag and fluted tip onto parchment paper over a sheet pan. Cover the fluted logs with couverture using a spray gun.

Place the filling in the refrigerator to set before dipping.

Nougat, Caramel, Nougatine, Jellied Fruits

Nougat

Cut 35 × 20 mm (1¼ × ¾ in.) rectangles that are approximately 10 mm (about ½ in.) thick.

Caramel

Cut squares of approximately 20 mm (¾ in.) that are about 10 mm (½ in.) thick.

Nougatine

Classically, nougatine is used to accompany or support other fillings such as ganache or gianduja, or it is sandwiched between two layers of different fillings.

Nougatine can also be rolled to be very thin, so that it can be eaten easily.

Jellied Fruits

Do not cover the jellied fruits with sugar when using them as a filling. Instead, cut them to size as explained for gianduja and cover them with a thin layer of couverture using a spray gun. Allow the couverture to set before dipping.

Chocolates with liquid centers

A. Liqueur-filled Chocolates

Presentation

Although liqueur-filled chocolates are very much appreciated, they are not often made.

Two procedures can be used to make liqueur-filled chocolates, both using the same filling.

1. Molded in colored aluminum cups or plastic molds, lined with couverture chocolate (see *Lining Sheet Molds with Chocolate,* page 52)
2. Poured fillings molded in cornstarch imprints

Preparation

Before the liqueur syrup can be made, it is necessary to prepare the molds or frames of cornstarch.

It is important to prepare the frame that will hold the cornstarch properly. The frame (often made out of wood, although a high-sided sheet pan or hotel pan can be substituted) should be 4 cm (1.5 in.) high. It is important to have a cover the same size as the frame that rests approximately 1 cm (½ in.) above the cornstarch.

Fill the frame with sifted, dried cornstarch. The cornstarch can be dried by placing it in a proof box or oven set at 60°C (140°F) for several days. Set aside enough dried cornstarch to cover the imprints, after they are filled with liqueur syrup, with a layer of cornstarch 1 cm (½ in.) thick. Warm the frame filled with cornstarch to 150°C (302°F) for 30 minutes just before making the liqueur syrup.

Preparing the Liqueur Syrup

Recipe

For 1 container 40 × 60 cm (16 × 24 in.)

750 g sugar (26.5 oz.)
250 ml water (8.5 fl. oz.)
5 g glucose (1 tsp.)
liqueur or liquor

Place the water, sugar, and glucose in a copper sugar pan or saucepan. Heat over a high flame, brushing down any crystals that form on the sides of the pan, until the mixture reaches 110° to 112°C (230° to 234°F). Cover the copper sugar pan or saucepan with a clean, damp towel and then place a cover over the towel. This will prevent the syrup from crystallizing as it cools. Let the mixture cool for 5 minutes.

Place the liqueur or liquor in a clean bowl. Slowly pour the syrup (after it has rested for 5 minutes) over the liquor or liqueur.

To be certain the mixture is well combined, pour it into a second container and back into the first.

Adding the Syrup

1. Using Chocolate-lined Cups or Molds

After combining the syrup with the liquor or liqueur, cover it again with a damp towel and let it cool to a temperature of about 35°C (95°F).

Once the syrup has reached the proper temperature, pour it into the chocolate-lined cups or molds using either a special large funnel reserved for this purpose that has a stopper or stick to control the amount poured or a small spoon or cup with a small spout. Fill the cups or molds to 2 mm (1/16 in.) from the top.

Place the cups or molds in the refrigerator until the syrup is completely cool.

Liquors and Liqueurs (per recipe)	
Armagnac	250 ml (8.5 fl. oz.)
Grand Marnier	250 ml (8.5 fl. oz.)
Calvados	250 ml (8.5 fl. oz.)
Cognac	250 ml (8.5 fl. oz.)
Kirsch	250 ml (8.5 fl. oz.)
Rum	250 ml (8.5 fl. oz.)
Cherry brandy	300 ml (10 fl. oz.)
Curaçao	300 ml (10 fl. oz.)
Chartreuse	300 ml (10 fl. oz.)
Bénédictine	300 ml (10 fl. oz.)
Anisette	325 ml (11 fl. oz.)
Marie-Brizard	325 ml (11 fl. oz.)
Cointreau	325 ml (11 fl. oz.)

Warm the reserved dried cornstarch, place it in a fine-mesh drum sieve, and gently sift it over the filled candies until they are covered with a layer 1 mm (1/16 in.) thick.

Set the cups or molds in a dry, warm area, approximately 30°C (86°F), that is free from drafts, for 24 hours. The cups or molds should be kept still to avoid disturbing the thin layer of crust that must form on top of the syrup.

2. Using Cornstarch Imprints

While the syrup is cooling, remove the container of cornstarch from the 150°C (300°F) oven. Stir the cornstarch in the container with a dry wooden spatula or whisk; then smooth the surface so it is level with the sides of the container, using a metal ruler as shown in the photo at the lower left on page 74.

Make imprints in the cornstarch using a mold. It is possible to have a stick with several molds attached to it to speed up this step (see photo at lower right on page 74).

Fill the imprints with the liquor syrup. In this case the syrup must still be hot. A funnel with a stop or a cup with a spout can be used to fill the imprints. Regardless how the syrup is poured, it must be done gently so as to not disturb the imprints, which are very delicate.

Sift the reserved cornstarch through a drum sieve directly over the imprints until they are covered with a layer 1 cm (½ in.) thick.

Allow the filled imprints to rest undisturbed for 3 to 4 hours.

After 3 to 4 hours, place the cover over the container and, holding it on securely, turn the container over in a quick motion. Turning the container over will enable the crystallization to be even throughout the candy.

Set the container aside for 26 to 48 hours so the syrup can crystallize.

Turn the container over and remove the cover. Gently remove the candies.

Brush the candies gently with a very soft brush to remove as much cornstarch as possible. Brush each candy, lifting them up one by one, using a small paintbrush with very soft, long bristles.

Finishing the Candies

1. Chocolate-lined Molds

This procedure can be started after the liquor or liqueur syrup has rested for 24 hours and a crust has begun to form.

Using a small, soft paintbrush, gently brush off as much of the cornstarch as possible from the tops of the candies.

Cover the tops of the molded candies with a layer of tempered couverture, using the same procedure as for covering all molded fillings. Cover the tops of candies made in aluminum cups with tempered couverture using a small

paintbrush. A small, decorative label with the name of the liquor or liqueur used in the filling can be placed on top.

Place the candies in the refrigerator at 5°C (40°F) for 2 hours. As it chills, the chocolate will contract, making it easier to unmold the candies. Once the chocolate has set, the candies should be unmolded over a clean kitchen towel. Candies made in aluminum cups are served in the cups.

Molds with the names of various liquors and liqueurs imprinted on them are available.

2. Fillings Made in Cornstarch

Lift each piece very carefully and gently brush all the cornstarch off the candies using a soft paintbrush. These candies are very fragile. Carefully dip them in tempered couverture.

After the couverture has set, wrap them in colored foil candy wrappers, and place stickers with the name of the liquor or liqueur used on top. This is especially important for candies sold commercially.

Note

All liquor- or liqueur-filled candies should be stored in a dry area at 20°C (68°F).

It is best to wait 10 to 15 days before eating these types of chocolates, as the crystallized layer around the fillings will have dissolved in this time, resulting in a purely liquid filling.

B. Fondant-filled Candies

Fondant fillings can be made using a variety of flavors and colors. They are relatively inexpensive to make and so have a low food cost.

Fondant candies are molded in imprints made in cornstarch and are not very difficult to make.

Preparation

Prepare the frames filled with cornstarch as described on the previous page for liquor-filled candies. Be sure the cornstarch is dry and sifted in an even layer in the frame. The major difference between preparing the cornstarch for the two fillings is that fondant fillings require cornstarch to be at room temperature, not warm as for liquor-filled candies.

Allow 750 g fondant (26.5 oz.) per 40 × 60 cm (16 × 24 in.) frame of cornstarch, which will yield approximately 1 kg (35 oz.) of candies.

Equipment

Cornstarch-filled frames, candy funnel, saucepan, wooden spatula, plastic container, and equipment for dipping candies in chocolate, including a dipping fork

Recipe

750 g white fondant (26.5 oz.)
liquor or sugar syrup at 1260 D, plus flavoring and coloring

Procedure

Work white fondant with the hands to soften it and place it in a bowl over a bain-marie (warm water bath) or in a saucepan directly over a very low flame. Stir constantly with a wooden spatula until it reaches 60°C (140°F).

Add desired flavoring to taste (liquor, liqueur, or extract, such as lemon, strawberry, black currant, raspberry, or pistachio). A few drops of food coloring that corresponds to the flavor can be added.

The fondant should be smooth and malleable, as when used for glazing. It can be thinned with sugar syrup at 1260 D if necessary. The fondant must be 60°C (140°F) throughout the procedure.

Warm the candy funnel over a low flame and fill it with the fondant. Carefully fill the imprints made in cornstarch to the rims.

Allow the fondant to cool and form a crust at room temperature. After the fillings are completely cool, in approximately 1 hour, place the fillings in a drum sieve and gently shake the sieve to remove any excess cornstarch. The fillings can be carefully brushed as for the liquor fillings before dipping them in tempered couverture.

Note

When dipping fondant fillings in chocolate, cover them only halfway or just below the rims so the different colors of the filling can be seen.

Fondant candies can be stored for 2 to 3 weeks in the refrigerator at 5°C (40°F). They are served at room temperature.

Creamy centers

Ganache Fillings

Candies Made in Sheet Molds

After lining a sheet mold with tempered couverture, fill each mold with ganache (see volume 2, pages 124 to 125), using a pastry bag and tip. Be careful not to overfill the molds, as overfilling might make it difficult to attach the other half of the molded candy as well as cause the filling to ooze out of the candy.

Candies Formed with a Pastry Bag and Fluted Tip

Rosettes of ganache can be piped out, using a pastry bag and fluted tip, onto sheet pans covered with parchment paper. Garnish the centers of the rosettes with walnut halves, almonds, or other nuts before placing them in the refrigerator to set.

Spray the candies with a layer of couverture using a paint spray gun before dipping them in tempered couverture.

Rosettes of ganache can also be piped over bases of marzipan or gianduja. Again place them in the refrigerator to set before dipping them in tempered couverture.

Aluminum candy cups can be filled with ganache using a pastry bag and fluted tip, finishing with a rosette on top.

Fondant Cream Fillings

Candies Made in Chocolate-lined Molds

Prepare the filling (see volume 2, pages 116 to 117), line the molds with tempered couverture (see page 52 of this volume), and fill the lined molds with fondant using a pastry bag and tip. Candies consisting of two separately molded sides, such as eggs, chickens, and seashells,

can be attached together with a small amount of tempered couverture or filling. This work requires a delicate hand.

Giandujas

After lining molds or aluminum candy cups with tempered couverture, fill with gianduja using a pastry bag. A fluted tip can be used to form rosettes on the tops when aluminum cups are used.

Rosettes of gianduja can also be piped out of a pastry bag over bases of marzipan or nougatine, as for ganache fillings.

Truffle Fillings

Truffle fillings are frequently used in other types of candies. They can be used in the same way as ganache, fondant cream, and gianduja fillings.

Les Truffes (Truffles)

Truffles are perhaps the most popular chocolate candy in France.

The filling, a type of ganache, is the most important part of the truffle. It is not very difficult to prepare, requiring no special equipment.

Although there are many different recipes for truffle fillings, all fillings are usually covered in tempered couverture and rolled in cocoa powder.

Truffles can be stored for 8 to 15 days, depending on the recipe. Because of this short storage time, they are usually prepared as needed.

Truffles are stored in the refrigerator and served at room temperature.

Basic Recipe

1 L crème fraîche or heavy cream (34 fl. oz.)
250 g invert sugar (9 oz.)
500 g butter (17.5 oz.)
1.5 kg chocolate couverture (53 oz.)
500 g milk-chocolate couverture (17.5 oz.)
250 ml liquor (8.5 fl. oz.)

For alternative recipes see volume 2, ganache fillings, pages 124 to 125.

Equipment

Saucepan, bowls, whisk, pastry scraper, knife and cutting board, pastry bag and no. 7 tip, sheet pans, parchment paper, plastic pastry scraper, equipment for tempering chocolate, high-sided sheet pan or other container for the cocoa powder, dipping fork, small rack, drum sieve, airtight container for storing truffles

Procedure

Make the ganache truffle filling. For truffles, the ganache is usually not whipped or is whipped only slightly. Stir the filling occasionally as it cools so it will cool evenly.

When the ganache is the consistency of soft butter, it can be piped out onto sheet pans covered with parchment paper. Place the fillings in the refrigerator to set.

If the fillings are very flat on the bottom after they have set, two pieces can be pressed together to obtain a round ball or the pieces can be rolled betweens the palms of the hands to obtain round balls. They can also be left as is, in half ovals. Some pastry chefs can pipe out the ganache so as to form round balls, but this requires practice and experience with the pastry bag.

Dipping

Truffles are dipped either by hand or with a dipping fork (see Dipping Candies in Chocolate, page 51).

Immediately after the truffles are dipped, they are rolled in cocoa powder that is either unsweetened or has been lightly sweetened by sifting approximately 250 g (9 oz.) sugar with 750 g (26.5 oz.) cocoa powder.

After the truffles are covered with cocoa powder, they are lifted with a small cooling rack or rake and placed in a drum sieve, where they are gently shaken to remove excess cocoa powder.

Storage

Truffles can be stored in the refrigerator for 8 to 15 days.

Chocolate-covered fruit and fruit candies

Shown in the above photograph is an assortment of candies, including candied fruit and fruit macerated in liquor and dipped in fondant, cooked sugar, or chocolate.

Sugar-covered Fruit

The liquor cherries are dipped in sugar cooked to the hard crack stage and colored pink.

Recipe

1 kg sugar (35 oz.)
400 ml water (13.5 fl. oz.)
200 g glucose (7 oz.)
several drops of red coloring

Combine all the ingredients except the coloring and cook to 150°C (302°F). Add the coloring. To make a coating for candied pineapples, follow the same recipe without coloring.

Candied chestnuts can be dipped in the following recipe:

1 kg sugar (35 oz.)
300 ml water (10 fl. oz.)
100 g glucose (3.5 oz.)
100 g unsweetened chocolate (3.5 oz.), melted

Combine all ingredients except the chocolate and cook to the hard crack stage, 150°C (302°F). Add the chocolate.

Cherries Dipped in Chocolate and Kirsch Fondant

Liquor-macerated cherries dipped in chocolate are a popular, classic confection.

Composition

Cherries macerated in Kirsch, warmed fondant, tempered couverture

Preparation

Carefully, so the fruit is not bruised, drain the macerated cherries on a clean towel for 2 to 3 hours. It is best to use cherries with stems firmly attached so they can be easily dipped.

Procedure

Dipping in Fondant

Slowly warm firm, white fondant to 65° to 70°C (149° to 158°F) and flavor with Kirsch.

Dip the cherries in the Kirsch-flavored fondant while it is hot.

Important: Do not dip the cherries all the way up to their stems, but leave the tops around the stems uncovered. Doing this will prevent the flesh of the cherry from getting too hot, which could cause the stem to fall off, and will also prevent the formation of small air pockets between the skin and fondant.

Place the dipped cherries one by one on a sheet pan covered with confectioners' sugar or on a sheet of plastic. Allow the cherries to cool.

Dipping in Couverture

1. *Classic Technique*

The cherries are dipped twice in tempered couverture to give a stronger base to the cherry and prevent the fondant, which becomes liquid during the time it rests, from running out.

The first dipping can be made with a bittersweet chocolate to add to the depth of flavor.

Dip the cherries so they are entirely covered in the tempered couverture, and place them on a sheet of plastic to set.

Once the chocolate has set, dip the cherries a second time, repeating the first procedure.

Once the chocolate has set, place the cherries in little paper candy cups.

2. *Technique with Chocolate Bases*

In this second method, the cherries are placed on small bases of couverture. With this method, the cherries need be dipped in couverture only once.

The bases are made by piping out balls of tempered couverture about the size of hazelnuts onto a sheet of plastic using a paper cone. Place the fondant-coated

cherries onto the bases before the couverture sets.

Once the couverture has set, dip the cherries and their attached chocolate bases in tempered couverture once, as for the first procedure.

Settling

Liquor cherries should not be eaten immediately after being made. They should be allowed to settle for 15 days to 3 weeks. During this time the fondant will liquefy as the cherries release the liquor in which they were macerated.

Chocolate-covered Candied Orange Rinds

Strips

Cut strips of candied orange rind approximately 4 to 6 cm (1.5 to 2.5 in.) long and 5 mm (¼ in.) thick. Dip the strips in tempered couverture with a dipping fork.

Triangles

Cut pieces of candied orange rind into triangles 4 to 6 cm (1.5 to 2.5 in.) long with bases at least 1 cm (⅜ in.) wide.

Dip the triangles in white fondant flavored with Grand Marnier that is hot, approximately 65°C (149°F).

Allow the fondant to set before dipping the candies in tempered couverture.

Chestnut Fillings

Roll scraps of glazed chestnuts into a ball the size of a cherry (use tempered couverture to stick them together if necessary).

Wrap the pieces with a 5-mm-thick (¼-in.) layer of white marzipan flavored with rum. Wrap the piece a second time with rum-flavored marzipan tinted pale green; this layer should be slightly thinner than the first layer.

Dip the candies in tempered couverture and roll them on a rack to give them a textured look.

Once set, cut a small section out of each candy, remove the layer of green-tinted marzipan, and paint the opening with melted cocoa butter (see photograph at bottom on page 78).

Candied Cherries

Cover candied cherries with white marzipan flavored with Kirsch. The marzipan may also be tinted pale green or yellow.

Dip the covered cherries in tempered couverture and roll them in small chocolate sprinkles.

The same procedure can be followed to wrap whole walnuts in coffee- or rum-flavored marzipan or to wrap walnut pieces worked into walnut marzipan. The candies are then dipped in tempered couverture and rolled in lightly roasted, chopped almonds.

Whole Almonds

Wrap lightly roasted, peeled almonds in Kirsch-flavored pale green marzipan, maintaining an almond shape. Dip the candies in tempered couverture and roll them on a rack. Finish by placing an almond slice on top of each before the couverture has set.

Macerated Raisins or Roasted Hazelnuts

Fill an aluminum candy cup half full with one of the creamy fillings, such as ganache or fondant cream. Place a roasted hazelnut or several raisins macerated in rum in the cup. Finish by piping out tempered couverture to seal the cup, using a pastry bag and tip.

Chocolates piped from a pastry bag

The pastry bag and tip are often used to fill previously lined chocolate molds. They can also be used to fill chocolate-lined aluminum candy cups quickly; for example, cups with roasted hazelnuts are filled with a creamy gianduja, using a fluted pastry tip to form a rosette on top.

The same technique can be used with macerated raisins and various colored and flavored ganaches.

Other candies can be made with the pastry bag and plain no. 5 tip or small to medium fluted tip. Pipe out a mixture of tempered couverture and praline paste (ranging from equal amounts of each to two parts couverture and one part praline paste) onto a perfectly clean, flat sheet of aluminum or plastic.

Usually this technique is used for small chocolates, such as rounds topped with roasted hazelnuts or ovals topped with

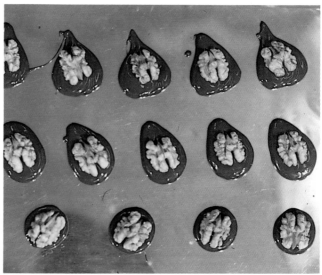

two roasted hazelnuts or walnuts; other shapes can be made, including pretzels, circles, and figure eights, and can be covered with raisins, chopped roasted almonds, or toasted grated coconut.

In France these assorted chocolates are often sold by weight and wrapped in colored cellophane bags.

The simplicity of these chocolates makes them particularly appropriate for tea time, and they are often available in salons de thé (tea parlors) in France.

Les rochers au praliné (Praline-filled chocolates)

Praline-flavored rochers (*rochers* literally translates as "rocks"; these candies are made with a creamy hazelnut filling and have a rough exterior) are very popular in France.

Composition

Filling

Praline paste and chocolate, or gianduja, craquelin (chopped hazelnut brittle) or diced almond craquelées

Covering

Chocolate couverture (dark or milk), roasted diced almonds or almond craquelées

Recipe for Filling

300 g couverture (10.5 oz.), melted
900 g almond/hazelnut praline paste (31.5 oz.)
200 g almond brittle (7 oz.), optional

Alternative Recipe

1 kg almond/hazelnut praline paste (35 oz.)
50 g unsweetened chocolate (1.5 oz.), melted
150 g cocoa butter (5 oz.), melted

Covering

1 kg milk- or dark-chocolate couverture (35 oz.)

250 g roasted, diced almonds or almond craquelées (9 oz.)

Procedure

Mix the melted couverture with the praline paste. Add diced almond craquelées (see volume 2, page 112) or diced, roasted almonds to the mixture.

Cool the mixture by spreading it on a marble.

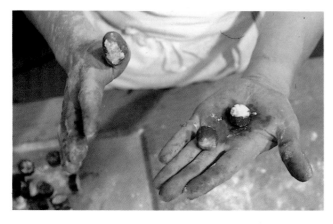

Shaping

Method A

Sprinkle the surface of the marble and the filling with confectioners' sugar and roll out the filling between two metal rulers until it is approximately 1 cm (⅜ in.) thick.

Allow the filling to become somewhat firm and cut 2-cm (¾-in.) squares or use a round cutter 2 to 2.5 cm (¾ to 1 in.) in diameter.

Roll the pieces between the palms of the hands to form small, even balls, and place them on a sheet pan that is covered with confectioners' sugar to prevent them from sticking.

Allow the filling to set before dipping.

Method B

Pipe out the filling into a cylindrical shape with a pastry bag fitted with a large plain tip (no. 10).

Allow the filling to become firm enough to handle. Slice small pieces off the cylinder, rolling the pieces into balls as for method A.

Method C

Roll out cylinders of the filling when it has become firm enough to handle. Finish by cutting off even pieces and shaping them into balls as in methods A and B.

Prepare the Covering

Temper the milk or dark couverture. Then add the diced almond craquelées, which should be at room temperature, and thoroughly mix them into the couverture.

Dip the rochers in the couverture as for truffles, either by hand or using a dipping ring.

Rochers can also be made rather large and sold individually. Small rochers are usually sold by weight or as part of an assortment of chocolates.

Individual large candies

Large chocolates, which can be thought of as high-quality candy bars, are made in a variety of ways. They can be plain or filled, piped from a pastry bag or cut from a sheet. Some are then covered with couverture chocolate and decorated with nuts or dried fruits such as raisins. The shapes that can be formed are endless. The candies in the photographs on these two pages are just a few examples of the many types of chocolates that can be made.

Simple Individual Chocolates

Composition

Tempered couverture (dark or milk chocolate), walnuts, hazelnuts, or almonds for decoration

Variations

Tempered couverture (dark or milk chocolate), diced roasted almonds or almond craquelées

Large Filled Chocolates

Composition

Nougatine, sweetened tart dough, or tempered couverture to create bases; gianduja, ganaches, marzipan, or walnut marzipan for fillings; walnuts, hazelnuts, or almonds for decoration

Les fruits déguisés (Decorated fruit)

Although chocolate is not used for this type of candy, decorated fruits are discussed in this section because they are usually sold in candy shops along with chocolates. Les fruits déguisés are so named because these dried or candied fruits are filled with marzipan or attached to marzipan bases in a decorative fashion (*déguisé* meaning "disguised").

They are often sold by the pound but can also be used to decorate a cake or presentation piece.

Preparation

Preparing the Fruits

Carefully sort through the fruit, checking for quality and looking for even size.

Peel almonds or hazelnuts, pick over walnuts (removing broken pieces), and roast the nuts to bring out their flavor.

Cut the candied fruit to be used, such as cherries, melons, pears, or pineapples.

Pit prunes and dates by cutting them lengthwise and carefully pulling the flesh of the fruit away from the pit before removing it, to help maintain the shape of the fruit. Be careful not to cut or pull the fruit in half. Pick over raisins and dried apricots and discard stems.

Preparing the Marzipan

Divide a fresh, high-quality marzipan into batches, adding colors appropriate to the flavoring used.

The color should indicate the flavor, as it does for all pastry preparations.

Below are examples of matching colors and flavors:

Flavor	Color
Rum	Pink
Grand Marnier	Salmon
Cointreau	Yellow
Kirsch	Pale green
Coffee	Light brown

The following list gives examples of matching colors with fruits:

Fruit	Colors
Prunes	Green/yellow/white
Dates	Pink/green/yellow
Cherries	White/green/yellow/pink
Almonds	Green
Hazelnuts	Yellow/green/white
Apricots	White/green
Pineapples	White/green
Walnuts	Light brown

Marzipan is usually left white when used with slices of candied melon and pear.

Procedure

Filling and Shaping Candies

Approximately 10 g (⅓ oz.) of marzipan is used for each fruit. This makes it possible to weigh out the marzipan needed for the amount of fruit to be filled. For example, use 160 g (5.5 oz.) of marzipan for 16 pieces of fruit. To divide the marzipan quickly and evenly, roll it into a sausage shape and cut it in half. Then cut each half in half again, so there are four even pieces; cut each piece in half again, making eight pieces; repeat this procedure once more, and there will be sixteen even pieces. This method is easiest when working with numbers that have roots of 2, such as 4, 8, 16, 32.

Roll the pieces into the desired shapes between the palms of the hands or on a pastry marble.

Open the incisions made in the dates and prunes when they were pitted. Carefully place an oval of marzipan inside the fruit, maintaining the shape of the fruit.

For aboukirs (almonds with marzipan), shape the marzipan into triangles, and push an almond, either on its side, or flat, into the face of each triangle. Use a small amount of sugar syrup at 1260 D to hold it in place. Decorative lines can be made in the marzipan with the back of a knife or a clay-modeling tool.

For sliced candied fruits such as pineapples, make a base out of marzipan and attach it to the fruit. Then cut the whole piece, fruit and marzipan, with a knife or cutter, to be uniform in size.

Drying the Marzipan

The filled fruit or nuts and marzipan are placed on a sheet pan or rack between two sheets of parchment paper.

Allow the marzipan to form a crust for 24 hours before covering the candies with crystallizing sugar (see volume 2, crystallized candies, page 72) or rolling them in sugar as for jellied fruits (volume 2, page 89) or glazing them with cooked sugar.

Glazing with Cooked Sugar

Cook sugar with glucose (20 percent of the sugar's weight) and water (30 percent, based on the sugar) to 155°C (311°F); for example, 800 g sugar (28 oz.), 200 g glucose (7 oz.), 300 ml water (10 fl. oz.).

While the sugar is cooking, run a toothpick or small skewer (brochette) through the marzipan of the candies. Be careful not to puncture the fruit, which could cause the glaze around the candy to crack when the skewer is pulled out.

Lightly oil a section of marble or a sheet pan.

Fill a bowl with fine sugar into which the skewers can be placed so the candies can drain and cool after dipping. A loaf pan or metal rulers placed over a container can also be used, with the edges of the sticks hanging over the sides.

Dip the brochettes of decorated fruit into the hot syrup, starting with the lighter colors of marzipan.

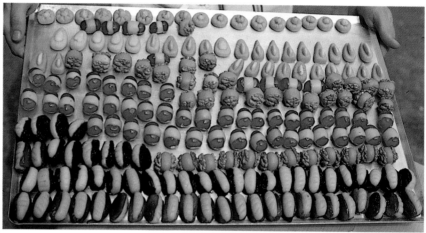

The candies should be dipped quickly, or the heat of the cooked sugar might soften the marzipan, deforming the shape and perhaps causing the fruit to fall off.

Allow the candies to cool. With a scissors, cut off any strands of cooked sugar hanging from the candies.

Once cool, remove the skewers.

Caution

These candies are very delicate and should be handled carefully. If dropped the coating of sugar will crack.

Be careful not to let the trimmings touch the candies, or they might stick to them.

Avoid handling the candies, as they easily pick up fingerprints, which can dull the surface.

Place the candies in small paper candy cups as soon as they are cool. They can then be picked up in the cups, avoiding fingerprints.

Storage

Decorated fruits can be stored for up to 48 hours in a cool, dry area.

Chapter 3
Frozen desserts

Basic preparations

History of Frozen Desserts

Even though ice creams and frozen desserts were invented over two thousand years ago, they did not become popular in Europe until the nineteenth century.

The first known description of a frozen dessert was from the court of Alexander the Great in the fourth century B.C. Fresh fruit was chopped and frozen by placing it in earthenware jars surrounded by snow.

The Romans invented a similar process for freezing sweetened drinks that were usually based on honey and fruit. According to one of the first gastronomic writers, Quintus-Maximus Gurges, the emperor Nero was the first to serve a primitive form of fruit sorbet consisting of honey, crushed fruit, and snow.

It was not until the thirteenth century that the Chinese invented a process of freezing desserts artificially rather than by using snow laboriously brought down from the mountains. The process consisted of combining saltpeter with cold water and letting it swirl around the outside of pottery jars containing different mixtures that were to be frozen. Marco Polo was the first to introduce this process in Europe.

Although the technique for freezing desserts was introduced in Italy during the Renaissance, not until the sixteenth century was it introduced to France. Catherine de Médicis, with her consort

of pastry chefs, introduced frozen desserts to the French in 1533.

By the seventeenth century, frozen desserts of various sorts were being prepared and appreciated throughout the world, but it was the English who invented the first ice cream as we know it today. The chef to Charles I, king of England, made the discovery and kept it a secret.

Not until the late nineteenth century did Auguste Escoffier perfect the modern French recipe for ice cream based on crème anglaise (see crème anglaise, volume 2, page 24).

Today frozen desserts are grouped into several categories:

- frozen drinks
- fruit ice creams
- sorbets
- ice creams
- egg-based ice creams

Frozen desserts, popular with the wealthy for centuries, were finally made available to everyone in the nineteenth century with the invention of the first version of the modern ice-cream machine, which made production on a large scale feasible.

At the end of the nineteenth century, scientists learned how to analyze the percentage of fat in dairy products. Near the beginning of the twentieth century, the

process of homogenization was discovered, making it possible to prevent the fat from separating in dairy products. Thus, richer, creamier ice creams could be made with whole milk.

Many countries have strict regulations about the ingredients, procedures, and conditions for making ice cream and other frozen desserts. The various appellations may be used only if certain conditions are met.

Basic frozen dessert mixtures

In both the United States and France, there are strict laws governing the preparation of frozen desserts. The laws are designed not only to guarantee the quality of the finished products but to ensure that they are prepared under hygienic conditions.

The recipes in this book are based on French standards; American standards are provided where appropriate, but it is important to check federal and local regulations when preparing frozen desserts for commercial sales. Classic French frozen desserts are usually grouped in five categories by the French government, which closely regulates the minimum and maximum content of the key ingredients.

a. *Ice creams:* must contain a minimum of 7 percent butter fat, 14 percent sugar, and a maximum of 31 percent additives including flavorings (in the United States, ice creams must contain a minimum of 8 to 10 percent butter fat, depending on flavoring weight, and a maximum of 0.5 percent stabilizer).
b. *Egg-based ice creams:* must contain 2 percent butter fat, 7 percent egg yolks, 16 percent sugar, plus flavorings (in the United States, egg-based ice creams have the same standards as regular ice creams and must also contain a minimum of 1.12 to 1.4 percent egg yolk solids, depending on flavoring weight).
c. *Sugar-syrup-based frozen desserts:* must contain a minimum of 25 percent sugar that is cooked into a milk- or water-based syrup and combined with fruit puree or flavoring.
d. *Fruit-flavored ice creams:* are either ice creams or egg-based ice creams flavored with fruit.
e. *Sorbets:* contain only fruit, sugar, water, and a stabilizer.
Sorbets have recently been divided into four categories under new French government regulations.

- sorbets based on acidic fruits
- sorbets based on sweet fruits
- sorbets based on wines and alcoholic beverages
- sorbets based on aromatic plants

Minimum Quantities for Flavoring

The following quantities of flavorings are the minimum amounts to be used in sorbets and ice creams:

1. Most **fruit-flavored frozen desserts** (strawberries, apricots, raspberries, blackberries, and the like) should contain at least 15 percent fresh or frozen fruit, in the form of pulp, puree, or juice. Frozen desserts with acidic fruits must contain a minimum of 10 percent fruit.

2. **Ice creams based on natural flavorings** should contain the following minimum amounts of flavorings, based on 100 g (3.5 oz.) of the mixture:

Chocolate: 2 g cocoa powder (½ tsp.)

Praline: 3 g sweet almonds or hazelnuts or a mixture of the two (½ tsp.)

Coffee: a concentrated infusion

Vanilla: 0.1 g or the equivalent amount of extract or vanilla sugar (a tiny pinch—these quantities are too small to measure, so it is best to add the vanilla to taste)

Pistachio: 3 g chopped pistachios (½ tsp.)

Malt: 10 g (2 tsp.); malt is rarely used

Caramel: 8 g caramelized sugar (2 tsp.) in addition to the sugar already included in the preparation

Churning

Old-fashioned Method

Originally, ice cream was churned by placing it in a container surrounded by ice. It was then continuously stirred with a wooden spatula until it thickened. This method is rarely used today because ice-cream machines are available that churn the mixture while simultaneously freezing it.

There are several types of ice-cream machines.

The machine used must conform to strict health laws governing both its construction and operation.

Preparation before Churning

Before churning a mixture in an ice-cream maker, it is imperative that the machine be scrupulously cleaned. Both the container designed to hold the mixture and the rotor should be soaked in a 2 percent chlorine solution. Most commercial manufacturers of ice-cream and sorbet machines provide a disinfectant for cleaning the machine. After soaking in the chlorine solution, the machine bowl and parts should be thoroughly rinsed under running water.

Churning

When ice cream and sorbet mixtures are churned in an ice-cream machine, the mixture is brought below the freezing point, usually with built-in electrical refrigeration. As the mixture is freezing, it is continually agitated by rapidly rotating blades. This constant motion prevents

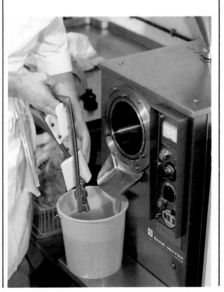

the formation of ice crystals and is responsible for the smooth textures of ice creams and sorbets. The rapid movement of the mixture also incorporates air, which helps contribute to a light texture and smoothness.

In France, government regulation limits the air that may be incorporated into

its the air that may be incorporated into an ice cream or sherbet to 100 percent. In the United States, ice cream must have a minimum weight—4.5 lbs. (about 2 kg)—per gallon (about 4 L) to ensure that the mixture is not overaerated. Sherbets and sorbets must weigh a minimum of 6 lbs. (about 2.7 kg) per gallon (about 4 L).

The ideal quantity of air that should be incorporated into an ice cream is from 35 to 40 percent. Any less and the ice cream tends to be heavy and soggy. Any more and it is too light.

Amount of Churning

It is difficult to give an ideal exact time span for churning ice creams and sorbets. The length of time necessary is a function of the ice-cream machine, the mixture, and the desired final consistency of the preparation.

An efficient ice-cream machine will usually completely freeze a mixture in 12 minutes. Some machines tend to chill the mixture too quickly and do not allow enough air to be worked into the mixture. If this is the case, let the mixture churn for a few minutes before turning on the cooling element.

Churning Temperature

The temperature of the churning varies according to the type of machine being used and the mixture being prepared. Commercial ice-cream machines usually operate at $-15°$ to $-20°C$ ($-5°$ to $+5°F$).

Once the mixture has thickened, it can be taken out of the ice-cream machine and placed in a freezer at $-18°C$ ($0°F$) until it is needed for a final preparation.

If the ice cream or sorbet is needed immediately, it can be worked as soon as it comes out of the ice-cream machine. When it comes out of the machine, it is usually rather soft and easy to work with.

Careful attention to hygiene is important not only when preparing ice creams but when storing them. Make sure that all molds and tools used with the ice cream are scrupulously cleaned. Special attention should be also given to personal hygiene. In larger establishments, gloves should be used when working with frozen desserts, especially those containing cream and milk.

Once the ice creams have been prepared and shaped into finished desserts, they should be transferred to a deep-freeze where they will harden. If the deep freeze is cold enough, $-30°$ to $-45°C$ (-20 to $-50°F$), the hardening should take place in 10 minutes to 2 hours, depending on the amount being frozen. Once the ice creams have frozen, they should be kept in freezers no warmer than $-15°C$ ($+5°F$). This is also the temperature at which they should be served.

The appropriate storage temperatures for ice creams depend on the length of time anticipated before they will be served. Following are recommended storage temperatures:

- Use a regular freezer at $-18°C$ ($0°F$) for frozen desserts that will be consumed within a week.
- Use a cold freezer at $-25°$ to $-30°C$ ($-10°$ to $-20°F$) for frozen desserts being stored for up to 3 weeks.
- Use a deep-freeze at $-30°C$ ($-20°F$) for frozen desserts that are to be stored for a month or more. Long storage, for a month or more, is in any case not recommended.

Serving

Ice creams and sorbets should be served at the proper temperature and texture. If they are either too hard or too soft, their delightful consistency and flavor will be partially lost.

Frozen desserts should be brought to a temperature of $-8°$ to $-6°C$ ($+18°$ to $+22°F$) before serving. At this temperature, they should have the perfect texture.

In order for ice creams and sorbets to be at the correct temperature and texture, they must be allowed to warm gently. This process usually takes several hours or overnight. Simply transfer the ice creams from the cold freezer or deep-freeze to a regular freezer at $-18°C$ ($0°F$) the night before the dessert is to be served.

Check the consistency of the ice cream or sorbet about an hour before serving. If it is still too hard, transfer it to the refrigerator.

Unfortunately, these precautions regarding the final consistency of frozen desserts are too often neglected.

Lining ice-cream molds

Definition

Ice-cream molds are usually lined with a 1- to 3-cm (½- to 1¼-in.) layer of ice cream or sorbet. The molds should be frozen ahead of time so the ice cream will adhere. A hollow space that can be filled with garniture or another flavor of ice cream should be left when lining the mold.

Procedure

Prepare the ice-cream molds by placing them in the deep-freeze for several minutes before lining them. This pre-

vents the ice cream from melting when it is applied to the walls of the mold.

When lining ice-cream molds, it is best to use freshly made ice cream or ice cream that has been warmed in a freezer at −15°C (+5°F). At this temperature, the ice cream is malleable enough to

cover the walls of the molds completely, so that any decorative floral patterns in the molds will remain once the dessert is removed.

Transfer the ice cream into the frozen mold using a plastic pastry scraper or a stainless steel spatula. Start by pressing the ice cream against the bottom of the mold and then gradually work up the sides. Keep pressing firmly against the sides of the mold to prevent air pockets from forming; these would spoil the appearance of the dessert once it is removed from the mold.

Continue applying the ice cream to the inside wall of the mold. Rotate the mold with the fingers of the left hand. It is sometimes helpful to hold the mold with a clean towel or to put it into another mold with the same shape and dimensions.

Continue to rotate the mold and smooth out the layer of ice cream with a metal spatula. It should be perfectly

smooth. Scrape off any excess ice cream or sorbet from the edges of the mold.

Place the lined molds in a deep-freeze to allow the ice cream to harden. Once

the first layer has hardened, it can be coated again with another layer of a different-flavored ice cream or sorbet. This process can be repeated several times. Make sure that the ice cream is put into the deep-freeze to harden after each application.

When the molds are finished, place them in the freezer.

Molding and unmolding ice creams

Molding Ice Creams and Frozen Desserts

Definition

Molding consists of filling an ice-cream mold with one or more flavors of ice cream. The ice creams can be put in the mold in layers or in sections.

Procedure

The molds should be frozen in the same way as when they are to be lined or coated with ice cream. When the molds are frozen, fill them with ice cream fresh from the ice-cream machine. Use either a plastic pastry scraper or a metal spatula to fill the molds.

Be careful to press the ice cream firmly into the molds so that no air pockets can form, which would spoil the presentation.

Continue packing the ice cream into the molds until the mold is filled all the way to the top.

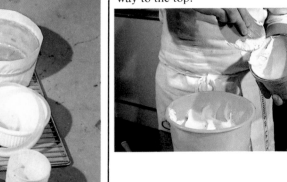

Ice-cream molds can be filled in various ways. Sometimes different flavors of ice cream are added in layers or arranged in different areas of the mold to create designs.

Finish the molding of the ice cream by smoothing off the surface of the mold with a metal spatula.

When the mold is filled, place it in a cold freezer or deep-freeze so that the ice cream quickly chills and hardens.

Unmolding Ice Creams and Frozen Desserts

It is important to remove molded desserts correctly. If the unmolding is improperly carried out, the final presentation will be spoiled.

Procedure

Before removing the dessert from the mold, prepare a plate or section of cardboard to act as a base.

Place a cutting board in the freezer for several minutes before unmolding the ice cream. This will keep the dessert from melting once out of the mold.

Dip the mold in a container of warm water up to 5 mm (¼ in.) below the top rim for several seconds.

Invert the mold and quickly shake it up and down until the ice cream loosens.

As soon as the ice cream detaches from the sides of the mold, let it slide out onto the base.

It is also possible to hold the plate or cardboard base over the bottom of the mold while shaking it. In this way, the ice cream will unmold directly onto the base. Be sure to hold the base firmly while shaking the mold and while turning it over.

As soon as the ice cream is out of the mold, place it in a cold freezer or deep-freeze to harden.

Finish the final decoration of the dessert only after it has completely hardened.

Examples of finished frozen desserts

Examples of frozen desserts

Finished Ice-Cream Desserts

Marquise, Duchesse

Base: ice-cream or bombe mixture flavored according to taste.

Bust: porcelain or molded sugar

Decoration: Chantilly cream, candied fruits

Paniers and Corbeille (Baskets and Cornucopias)

Base: braided or molded nougatine

Filling: candied fruits prepared in special fruit-shaped molds

Decoration: royal icing, flowers and leaves made from pulled sugar or marzipan

Marmite, Coupe (Candy Casserole or Coupe)

Base: molded nougatine

Filling: scoops of ice cream attached together and rolled in cocoa powder

Decoration: royal icing, leaves made from pulled sugar or marzipan

Pièce Montée (Presentation Piece)

Base: a hollow metal cone used for pieces montées (such as croquembouches) filled with water and completely frozen

Procedure: place scoops of different-flavored ice creams on sheet pans and set them in the freezer to harden

Construction: attach the scoops of ice cream on the frozen cone with Chantilly cream

Decoration: Chantilly cream, roses and leaves made from pulled sugar or marzipan

Presentation: a platter or an ice-sculpture stand

Moulin à Vent Glacé (Windmill)

Base: a stand of nougatine or sculpted ice

Filling: molded ice cream

Decoration: tuiles, piped petit four mixture for the blades and body of the mill, candied fruits, royal icing

Les crèmes glacées (Ice creams)

Definition

The terms *créme glacée* and *ice cream* apply only to frozen mixtures based on milk, cream, sugar, and flavoring. The flavor can be derived from natural ingredients, such as coffee, chocolate, and vanilla, or from fruit juices or fruit pulp. Occasionally, ice creams contain additional egg yolks to give them extra creaminess and richness.

Uses

Of all frozen desserts, ice creams are the most common. They are made in a wide variety of flavors and are produced not only in small pastry shops and restaurants, but industrially as well.

Equipment

Saucepan
Whisk
Fine-mesh strainer or cheesecloth
Plastic or stainless steel tub
Bain-marie (water bath or double boiler)

Recipes

Liquor-flavored Ice Creams

(rum, Kirsch, Calvados, Cognac, Marc, Armagnac, whiskey, vodka, gin)

1 L milk (34 fl. oz.)
250 g sugar (9 oz.)
50 g glucose (1.5 oz.)
10 g stabilizer (2 tsp.)
500 ml heavy cream (17 fl. oz.)
160 ml liquor (5 fl. oz.), for flavoring

Liqueur-flavored Ice Creams

(Cointreau, Grand Marnier, Curaçao)

1 L milk (34 fl. oz.)
250 g sugar (9 oz.)
50 g glucose (1.5 oz.)
10 g stabilizer (2 tsp.)
500 ml heavy cream (17 fl. oz.)
120 ml liqueur (4 fl. oz.)

Naturally Flavored Ice Creams

Vanilla Ice Cream

1 L milk (34 fl. oz.)
250 ml heavy cream or crème fraîche (8.5 fl. oz.)
225 g sugar (8 oz.)
10 g stabilizer (2 tsp.)
1 vanilla bean

Alternative Recipe

1 L milk (34 fl. oz.)
300 ml heavy cream or crème fraîche (10 fl. oz.)
250 g sugar (9 oz.)
15 g stabilizer (½ oz.)
1 vanilla bean
vanilla extract

Ice creams are easier to prepare than egg-based frozen desserts. Be extremely certain that all the equipment is perfectly clean. Also make sure that all the ingredients are sufficiently heated to kill bacteria. Allow about 15 minutes to prepare an ice-cream mixture. An ice-cream machine is needed.

Coffee Ice Cream

1 L milk (34 fl. oz.)
250 g sugar (9 oz.)
10 g stabilizer (2 tsp.)
100 g ground coffee (3.5 oz.)
500 ml heavy cream (17 fl. oz.)
instant coffee granules if needed

Alternative Recipe

1 L milk (34 fl. oz.)
300 g sugar (10.5 oz.)
100 g ground coffee (3.5 oz.)
250 ml heavy cream (8.5 fl. oz.)
80 g Italian meringue (2.5 oz.)
instant coffee granules if needed

Praline Ice Cream

1 L milk (34 fl. oz.)
200 ml heavy cream or crème fraîche (6.5 fl. oz.)
150 g sugar (5 oz.)
225 g praline paste (8 oz.)
10 g stabilizer (½ tsp.)

Alternative Recipe

1 L milk (34 fl. oz.)
500 ml heavy cream or crème fraîche (17 fl. oz.)

300 g sugar (10.5 oz.)
200 g almond or hazelnut paste (7 oz.)
15 g stabilizer (½ tsp.)

Chocolate Ice Cream

1 L milk (34 fl. oz.)
250 ml heavy cream or crème fraîche (8.5 fl. oz.)
300 g sugar (10.5 oz.)
50 g cocoa powder (1.5 oz.)
10 g stabilizer (½ tsp.)

Alternative Recipe

1 L milk (34 fl. oz.)
500 ml heavy cream or crème fraîche (17 fl. oz.)
250 g sugar (9 oz.)
150 g semisweet chocolate (5 oz.)
10 g stabilizer (½ tsp.)

Preparation

Before beginning the preparation of the ice cream, make sure that all the equipment is perfectly clean and that the raw ingredients are fresh and of high quality.

Procedure

Heating the Mixture

All recipes for ice cream are extremely simple. All the components should be brought to a simmer for 1 minute to sterilize them. Combine the powdered ice-cream stabilizer with the sugar and then combine this mixture with the milk. Add the cream and flavorings and bring to a simmer on top of the stove.

Straining the Mixture

Do not add liquor or liqueur to an ice-cream mixture until it is ready to go into the ice-cream machine. If alcoholic components are added before the mixture is simmering, all their flavor will evaporate.

If Italian meringue is being used as the stabilizer, do not add it until the ice cream is removed from the machine.

Make sure that the cream is combined with the milk before the mixture is brought to a simmer.

Pasteurizing the Mixture

As stated earlier, it is essential that all the ingredients for the ice cream (except spirits and Italian meringue) be boiled for at least a minute to kill bacteria. After the mixture has been simmered, it should be quickly cooled over an ice bath to 15°C (60°F) before being put in the machine.

If the mixture is not going to be used for 6 hours or more, it should be chilled to 6°C (43°F) while it is being held. In no case should ice-cream mixture be held for more than 24 hours before being churned.

Les Crèmes Glacées (Ice Creams)		
PREPARATION	**0** min	
Assemble the Equipment Prepare, Weigh, and Measure the Raw Ingredients		• Make sure that all equipment is perfectly clean. • Make sure that the raw ingredients are fresh. • Crush ice in advance for chilling the mixture.
PROCEDURE	**5** min	
Bring the Mixture to a Simmer for at Least 1 Minute		• Simmer the milk, cream, sugar, and flavoring.
Strain the Mixture	**10** min	• Strain the mixture into a clean container.
Quicky Chill the Mixture to 15° or 6°C (60° or 43°F)	**12** min	• Place the container with the mixture into the crushed ice to chill it quickly.
Churn the Mixture		• Churn within an hour after the mixture has been simmered.
STORAGE:		• The mixture can be stored for 24 hours maximum, provided it is kept below 6°C (43°F).

L'appareil à glace aux oeufs
(Egg-based ice creams)

History

Egg-based ice creams, also known in the United States as French ice creams, are often confused with crème anglaise. This is understandable because the two are very similar and originated in the same way (see crème anglaise, volume 2, pages 24 to 26). Indeed, crème anglaise was used as the base mixture for ice creams for many years.

The primary difference between crème anglaise and egg-based ice cream mixture is that the ice-cream mixture must be thoroughly pasteurized before being turned into ice cream.

Definition

In France and the United States, there are strict laws governing exactly what percentages of ingredients may go into an egg-based ice cream. In the United States, it must contain a minimum of 1.12 to 1.4 percent egg yolk solids (minimum depends on the weight of the flavoring used). A variety of dairy products may be used, including butter, cream, milk, buttermilk, evaporated milk, skim milk, condensed milk, and dry milk. In France the only ingredients that may be used in egg-based ice creams are egg yolks, cream, milk, butter, sugar, and flavoring. The French laws are used here as standards.

Uses

Egg-based ice creams come in a wide variety of flavors and can be used in the same kinds of preparations as regular ice cream.

Equipment

Saucepan, whisk, plastic pastry scrapers, thermometer, mixing bowl for the egg yolks, mixing bowl for the egg whites, metal spatula, strainer or cheesecloth, mixing bowl for cooling the mixture, plastic tub for cooling the mixture, ice-cream machine

Base Recipe (unflavored)

1 L milk (34 fl. oz.)
250 g sugar (9 oz.)
10 to 12 egg yolks
or
1 L milk (34 fl. oz.)
250 g sugar (9 oz.)
50 g trimoline (1.5 oz.)
10 egg yolks
100 g unsalted butter (3.5 oz.) or 125 ml pasteurized crème fraîche or heavy cream (4.5 fl. oz.)

Preparation

Be sure to verify the quality and freshness of the raw ingredients. It is also necessary to wash the equipment thoroughly and rinse it in chlorinated water. Hygiene is especially important when working with ice creams. The equipment should be cleaned and rinsed in the chlorinated water after each use.

Procedure for an Unflavored Egg-based Ice-Cream Mixture

Combining the Ingredients

Combine the sugar with the milk and simmer the mixture for at least 1 minute. This is necessary to kill any bacteria that might be contained in the sugar.

   Egg-based ice-cream mixtures are somewhat difficult to prepare because they require constant attention during all stages. It is especially important that all precautions regarding hygiene be closely followed. The mixture must be thoroughly pasteurized before being churned. The mixture should not be kept for over 24 hours before being frozen and in no case should be stored above 6°C (43°F). The mixture takes about 25 minutes to prepare.

While the milk/sugar mixture is coming to a simmer, separate the eggs and put the yolks into a bowl. Be sure to sniff each egg for freshness.

Whisk the yolks until they are pale yellow before adding the milk/sugar mixture.

Pour all of the milk/sugar mixture into the egg yolks while stirring with the whisk. It is important to keep stirring in order to prevent the yolks from coagulating.

When the milk has been thoroughly combined with the yolks, pour the mixture back into the saucepan and continue to stir the mixture with a whisk or a wooden spatula. Do not beat it at this stage, as this would make it too frothy.

Pasteurizing the Mixture

First Stage: Heating the Mixture

Check the temperature of the mixture with a thermometer while heating it on top of the stove. The mixture should be maintained at 80° to 85°C (175° to 185°F) for 3 minutes. The consistency of the mixture should also be checked in the

same way as when preparing crème anglaise (see volume 2, pages 24 to 26).

Second Stage: Quickly Chilling the Mixture

Once the mixture has been pasteurized and coats the spoon in the correct way, it should be quickly cooled to 6°C (43°F). Strain the mixture into a clean container and place in crushed ice until it has cooled to the correct temperature.

Stir the mixture over the crushed ice so that it cools quickly. This rapid cooling is needed to prevent the growth of bacteria.

Egg-based ice-cream mixtures can then be flavored and colored in a wide variety of ways. They can also be enriched with the addition of heavy cream or pasteurized crème fraîche. It is best to add these additional ingredients to the milk before the mixture is pasteurized in order to reduce the risk of bacterial contamination.

Summary

Preparation of the mixture: milk, sugar, flavoring, and cream brought to a simmer.

Addition of yolks: simmering mixture and egg yolks.

Les Glaces aux Oeufs
(Egg-based Ice Creams)

PREPARATION	0 min	
Assemble the Equipment Prepare, Weigh, and Measure the Raw Ingredients		• Make sure that all equipment is perfectly clean, rinsed in chlorinated water. • Make sure that all the raw ingredients are perfectly fresh. • Separate the eggs. • Prepare the crushed ice.
PROCEDURE	10 min	
Boil the Milk		• Bring the milk to the simmer with the sugar, flavoring, and crème fraîche if it is being used.
Lightly Beat the Egg Yolks.		• Use a whisk and beat until the yolks are slightly pale.
Add the Boiling Milk Mixture to the Yolks	15 min	• Add the boiling milk mixture to the egg yolks while stirring with a whisk. Return the mixture to the saucepan.
Pasteurize the Mixture		• Stir the mixture over a low flame on top of the stove.
Check the Temperature	16 min	• Use a thermometer to maintain the temperature of the mixture at 80° to 85°C (175° to 185°F) for 3 minutes.
Check the Consistency		• Use the technique for checking crème anglaise (see volume 2).
Strain the Mixture	20 min	• Chill the mixture to 6°C (43°F) by stirring over crushed ice.
Quickly Chill the Mixture	21 min	• Strain the mixture into a stainless steel bowl.
Churn the Mixture	30 to 60 min 1 hr 20	• Time required depends on the machine and mixture. • This much time is needed for an old-fashioned machine.
STORAGE:		• The mixture should be churned in the machine within 1 hour after it has been cooled to 6°C (43°F). • The mixture can be held for up to 24 hours if kept colder than 6°C (43°F).

Pasteurization of the mixture: maintain the mixture at 80° to 85°C (175° to 185°F) for 3 minutes.

Chilling the mixture stir the mixture over

crushed ice so that it is below 6°C (43°F) within an hour. The mixture should be churned in the machine within 24 hours, preferably within 6 hours. At no point should the temperature of the mixture be allowed to rise above 6°C (43°F).

When using highly efficient, rapid-cooling ice-cream machines, the preliminary cooling of the ice-cream mixture over crushed ice is not necessary, but the mixture must be put into the machine immediately after pasteurization.

Egg-based Ice-Cream Recipes

Vanilla
A. 1 L milk (34 fl. oz.)
250 g sugar (9 oz.)
250 ml crème fraîche (8.5 fl. oz.)
10 to 12 egg yolks
B. 1 L milk (34 fl. oz.)
250 g sugar (9 oz.)
50 g invert sugar (1.5 oz.)
100 g unsalted butter (3.5 oz.)
25 ml vanilla extract (1 fl. oz.)
10 to 12 egg yolks

Praline
A. 1 L milk (34 fl. oz.)
200 g sugar (7 oz.)
200 g almond or hazelnut praline paste (7 oz.)
125 ml crème fraîche (4.5 fl. oz.)
8 egg yolks
B. 1 L milk (34 fl. oz.)
250 g sugar (9 oz.)
150 g almonds or hazelnuts (5 oz.), ground to a paste
100 ml crème fraîche (3.5 fl. oz.)
10 egg yolks

Pistachio
A. 1 L milk (34 fl. oz.)
300 g sugar (10.5 oz.)
100 g pistachio paste (3.5 oz.)
100 ml crème fraîche (3.5 fl. oz.)
green food coloring, optional
30 ml Kirsch (1 fl. oz.), optional
12 egg yolks
B. 1 L milk (34 fl. oz.)
250 g sugar (9 oz.)
80 pistachio paste (3 oz.)
10 g chopped pistachios (2 tsp.)
125 ml crème fraîche (4.5 fl. oz.)
30 ml Kirsch (1 fl. oz.), optional
10 egg yolks

Chocolate
A. 1 L milk (34 fl. oz.)
300 g sugar (10.5 oz.)

50 g cocoa powder or chocolate liquor (1.5 oz.)
125 ml crème fraîche (4.5 fl. oz.)
10 egg yolks
B. 1 L milk (34 fl. oz.)
250 g sugar (9 oz.)
125 g couverture chocolate (4.5 oz.)
12 egg yolks
C. 1 L milk (34 fl. oz.)

250 g sugar (9 oz.)
350 g baking chocolate (12.5 oz.)
100 ml crème fraîche (3.5 fl. oz.)
10 egg yolks

Plombière
1 L milk (34 fl. oz.)
250 g sugar (9 oz.)
250 ml crème fraîche (8.5 fl. oz.)
50 ml Kirsch (1.5 fl. oz.)
10 egg yolks
250 g candied fruits (9 oz.), macerated in Kirsch, to fold into the ice cream after churning

Liquor or Liqueur
A. 1 L milk (34 fl. oz.)
250 g sugar (9 oz.)
50 g glucose (1.5 oz.)
250 ml crème fraîche (8.5 fl. oz.)
12 egg yolks
100 to 120 ml liquor or liqueur (3.5 to 4.5 fl. oz.)
food coloring, optional

Banana
A. 1 L milk (34 fl. oz.)
250 g sugar (9 oz.)
300 g banana pulp (10.5 oz.)—450 g (16 oz.) including the skin
250 ml crème fraîche (8.5 fl. oz.)
8 egg yolks
B. 1 L milk (34 fl. oz.)
250 g sugar (9 oz.)
300 g banana pulp (10.5 oz.)
100 g butter (3.5 oz.)
30 to 50 ml rum (1 to 1.5 fl. oz.)
8 egg yolks

Almond
A. 1 L milk (34 fl. oz.)
300 g sugar (10.5 oz.)
300 g almond powder (10.5 oz.)
250 ml crème fraîche (8.5 fl. oz.)
10 egg yolks
B. 1 L milk (34 fl. oz.)
250 g sugar (9 oz.)
almond paste, to taste
250 ml crème fraîche (8.5 fl. oz.)
10 egg yolks

Peanut
1 L milk (34 fl. oz.)
250 g sugar (9 oz.)
200 g peanut butter (7 oz.)
12 egg yolks

Honey
1 L milk (34 fl. oz.)
250 g honey (9 oz.)
100 g sugar (3.5 oz.)

250 ml crème fraîche (8.5 fl. oz.)
1 vanilla bean infused in the milk, optional
12 egg yolks

Coconut
1 L milk (34 fl. oz.)
300 g sugar (10.5 oz.)
200 g grated coconut (7 oz.)
250 ml crème fraîche (8.5 fl. oz.)
12 egg yolks

Prune
1 L milk (34 fl. oz.)
250 g sugar (9 oz.)
500 g pitted prunes (17.5 oz.)
30 to 50 ml Armagnac (1 to 1.5 fl. oz.)
12 egg yolks

Verbena
1 L milk (34 fl. oz.)
300 g sugar (10.5 oz.)
4 tea bags of verbena tea
250 ml crème fraîche (8.5 fl. oz.)
10 to 12 egg yolks

Tea
1 L milk (34 fl. oz.)
250 g sugar (9 oz.)
10 pinches of tea
100 ml crème fraîche (3.5 fl. oz.)
10 egg yolks
100 ml rum (3.5 fl. oz.)

Hazelnut
A. 1 L milk (34 fl. oz.)
200 g hazelnut pralines (7 oz.)
200 g sugar (7 oz.)
125 ml crème fraîche (4.5 fl. oz.)
8 egg yolks
B. 1 L milk (34 fl. oz.)
300 g sugar (10.5 oz.)
200 g hazelnuts (7 oz.), ground to a paste
125 ml crème fraîche (4.5 fl. oz.)
8 egg yolks

Coffee
A. 1 L milk (34 fl. oz.)
250 g sugar (9 oz.)
50 g crushed coffee beans (1.5 oz.), heated in the oven for 3 minutes
125 ml crème fraîche (4.5 fl. oz.)
coffee extract or instant coffee
12 egg yolks
B. 1 L milk (34 fl. oz.)
300 g sugar (10.5 oz.)
100 g crushed coffee beans (3.5 oz.), heated in the oven for 3 minutes
250 ml heavy cream (8.5 fl. oz.)
12 egg yolks

Caramel
1.5 L milk (50.5 fl. oz.)
600 g sugar (21 oz.), cooked to a light caramel; stop the cooking by adding 500 ml water (17 fl. oz.) to the caramel, then mix with the milk
250 ml crème fraîche (8.5 fl. oz.)
18 egg yolks
Once the ice cream is removed from the machine, chopped nougatine, craquelin, or chopped almonds can be incorporated.

Chestnut
A. 1 L milk (34 fl. oz.)
350 g sugar (12.5 oz.)
250 g peeled, canned chestnuts (9 oz.)
125 ml crème fraîche (4.5 fl. oz.)
30 to 50 ml rum (1 to 1.5 fl. oz.)
12 egg yolks
B. 1 L milk (34 fl. oz.)
300 g sugar (10.5 oz.)
125 g pureed chestnuts (4.5 oz.)
125 ml crème fraîche (4.5 fl. oz.)
75 ml whiskey (3 fl. oz.)
10 egg yolks

History

Not until the middle of the seventeenth century was fruit combined directly with eggs or milk to make fruit-flavored ice creams.

Definition

Fruit-flavored ice creams can be prepared in different ways and can be based on ice creams, egg-based ice creams, sorbets. Fruit-flavored ice creams are by definition almost identical to other types of ice creams. The essential difference is that fruit-flavored ice creams are required to contain a higher percentage of fruit than other types. In France, the government requires that only pure natural fruit be used. In the United States, only pure natural fruit may be used in products labeled with only the fruit's name (such as "strawberry ice cream"). If an artificial flavoring is added, the word *flavored* must follow the fruit name (such as "strawberry-flavored ice cream"). If more artificial than natural fruit flavor is used, the words *artificially flavored* must precede the fruit name (such as "artificially flavored strawberry ice cream").

Uses

Fruit-flavored ice creams can be presented in the same ways as other types of ice creams. They can also be molded in distinctive fruit-shaped molds.

Recipes

Les glaces aux fruits (Fruit-flavored ice creams)

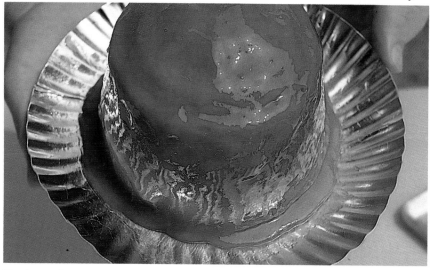

Equipment

Be sure to assemble all the necessary equipment, depending on which type of fruit-flavored ice cream is being prepared:

- fruit-flavored ice cream
- fruit-flavored egg-based ice cream
- sorbet

Preparation

Carefully select the raw ingredients. Make sure they are fresh and of excellent quality. Clean all the necessary equipment for preparing the ice cream. Use an approved disinfectant and carefully rinse all the equipment.

Fruit-flavored Sorbets

1 L fruit pulp or puree (34 fl. oz.)
1 L sugar syrup (34 fl. oz.), at 1260 D
10 g stabilizer (2 tsp.)

250 ml crème fraîche or heavy cream (8.5 fl. oz.)

This sorbet is prepared in the same way as other sorbets except that it contains cream. As for other frozen desserts containing cream, the cream should be brought to a simmer on top of the stove to pasteurize it before incorporating it into the sorbet. The mixture is then churned normally.

Fruit-flavored Egg-based Ice Creams

1 L milk (34 fl. oz.)
250 g sugar (9 oz.)
250 ml crème fraîche or heavy cream (8.5 fl. oz.)
500 g fruit puree or pulp (17.5 oz.)
10 egg yolks

Fruit-flavored egg-based ice cream is prepared in the same way as egg-based ice creams flavored in other ways. The fruit is added to the other ingredients before the final churning. The color of the ice cream can be reinforced with a little food coloring if necessary.

  Fruit-flavored ice creams and sorbets are moderately easy to prepare. The same precautions should be followed as when preparing other ice creams and sorbets. An ice-cream machine is required.

Fruit-flavored Ice Cream (without eggs)

1 L milk (34 fl. oz.)
250 g sugar (9 oz.)
10 g stabilizer (1 tsp.)
400 ml crème fraîche or heavy cream (13.5 fl. oz.)
500 g fruit pulp or puree (17.5 oz.)

Fruit-flavored ice cream is prepared in the same way as ice creams based on other flavors. The fruit is simply added to the other liquid ingredients before the ice cream is churned.

 Fruit-flavored egg-based ice creams are fairly difficult to prepare. Carefully follow the precautions for preparing egg-based ice creams.

Les sorbets (Sorbets)

Definition

Sorbets are introduced at the beginning of this chapter. Notice that French government standards for the preparation of sorbets have only recently been established. In the United States, sorbets may also be called ices or water ices. Sherbets are similar to sorbets except they contain between 1 and 2 percent milk fat; true sorbets contain no milk products. American sorbets and sherbets must weigh at least 6 lbs. per gal. (2.7 kg per 3.8 L).

Sorbets are prepared exclusively from sugar, water, and flavorings such as fruit, liqueurs, wine, or aromatic plants. These sweetened mixtures are then adjusted to the proper density (1135 D) before being churned. Sorbet mixtures usually have a thin consistency and rely on being frozen for the final dense, creamy texture.

In the United States, fruit sorbets and sherbets must contain a minimum of 2 percent citrus fruit or juice; 6 percent cherry or berry fruit or juice; or 10 percent fruit or juice if other fuits are used.

Sorbets are broken down into four categories:

Sorbets Based on Sweet Fruit: *Fresh fruits:* apricots, cherries, strawberries, melons, peaches, pears, plums, grapes. *Tropical fruits:* avocados, bananas, persimmon, lychees, papaya, loquats.

Sorbets Based on Acidic Fruits: *Fresh fruits:* cranberries, red currants, raspberries, blackberries, blueberries. *Citrus fruits:* lemons, limes, clementines, mandarin oranges, oranges, grapefruits. *Tropical fruits:* pineapples, guavas, passion fruit, kiwis, mangoes.

Sorbets Based on Wines and Alcoholic Beverages: *Wines:* Muscat, sherry, port, Madeira, Malaga, Champagne. *Spirits:* any spirits based on fruit, such as fruit brandies. *Liqueurs:* any naturally flavored liqueurs.

Sorbets Based on Aromatic Plants

These can include mint, tea, lemon verbena, lavender, linden leaves, or thyme.

Remember that sorbets must never contain eggs or milk products. They should never be flavored with artificial flavoring. If food coloring is added, make sure that it is an authorized type.

Uses

Sorbets are presented in a wide variety of ways. Occasionally, sorbets are molded in the shapes of fruits. Certain fruits, such as bananas, lemons, pineapples, and oranges, can also be filled decoratively with one or more sorbets.

Equipment

Mixing bowl, whisk, plastic pastry scraper, hydrometer (for measuring density), measuring cup, fine-mesh sieve, equipment for preparing sugar syrup

Basic recipe

1 L fruit pulp or puree (34 fl. oz.)
1 L sugar syrup containing glucose (34 fl. oz.), at 1260 D
5 g stabilizer (1 tsp.)
water to lower the mixture to 1130 to 1140 D

Preparation

If fresh fruit juice or pulp is used, it must be pasteurized. If fruit juice is being used, it should be simmered for 1 minute and then rapidly cooled. If pulp is being used, a slower method of pasteurization should be employed. The pulp should be

Frequently prepared in professional pastry kitchens, sorbets are extremely varied and relatively easy to prepare. Carefully maintain strict levels of hygiene. The success of sorbets depends on accurate measurement and adjustment of the density.

Sorbets can be prepared in 15 minutes with an efficient ice-cream machine.

heated to 60°C (140°F) for 30 minutes. The pulp should then be immediately cooled.

When pasteurizing fruit pulp, place it in a stainless steel bowl or saucepan. It is essential that the pulp be heated in a vesicle made of an inert metal. Otherwise the acids in the fruit will react with the metal and give the pulp a metallic taste. Place the bowl or saucepan containing the fruit pulp in a pan of boiling water. When the pulp reaches the desired temperature, turn the heat down so the temperature remains constant. Stir the pulp from time to time with a wooden spatula.

While pasteurizing the fruit, prepare the sugar syrup at 1260 D.

Sugar Syrup Recipe

Boil for 1 minute:
1 L water (34 fl. oz.)
1 kg sugar (35 oz.)
200 g glucose (7 oz.)

Make sure that all equipment has been carefully cleaned and that rules of hygiene have been respected.

Procedure

Pour the pasteurized fruit pulp into a bowl and add the stabilizer. Thoroughly stir the mixture.

Add the sugar syrup and whisk it with the fruit pulp until the two are thoroughly combined. Strain through a fine-mesh sieve.

Check the density of the mixture with the hydrometer. If the mixture is too dense, add water to thin it. If it is too light, add additional sugar syrup. The final density of the mixture should be

1135 D. The density of the syrup is important:

• If the density is too low (the mixture contains too little sugar), the sorbet will crystallize and become granular.

• If the density is too high (too much sugar in the mixture), the sorbet will be too sweet and will be difficult to freeze. It will also lose its refreshing quality.

Be sure to rinse off the hydrometer after each use to avoid false readings. The color of the sorbet mixture can be reinforced with authorized food coloring if necessary.

Strain the mixture through a fine-mesh sieve into a stainless steel bowl or other inert container.

Churn the sorbet mixture in the ice-cream machine as soon as possible. Sorbet is stored like other ice creams.

Sorbet Recipes

Based on Fresh Fruit Pulp

1 kg fresh fruit pulp (35 oz.)—for example, strawberries, raspberries, red currants, blueberries, blackberries

Based on Sterilized Canned Fruit

1 L fruit pulp (34 fl. oz.)—for example, strawberries, raspberries, red currants, black currants, blueberries, cherries
1 L sugar syrup (34 fl. oz.), at 1260 D
5 g stabilizer (1 tsp.)
Adjust the final density to 1135 D.

Based on Fruit Juice

800 ml sugar syrup (27 fl. oz.), at 1260 D
100 g trimoline (3.5 oz.)
juice of 1 lemon
5 g stabilizer (1 tsp.)
Adjust the final density to 1135 D.

Orange Sorbet

200 g blanched and drained orange zest (7 oz.)

1.5 L water (50.5 fl. oz.) plus 600 g sugar (21 oz.) plus 200 g glucose (7 oz.) plus 5 g stabilizer (1 tsp.), boiled with the blanched zest
700 ml orange juice (23.5 fl. oz.)
40 ml lemon juice (1.5 fl. oz.)
After the mixture has cooled, adjust the density to 1135 D.

Mandarin Sorbet

100 g blanched and drained mandarin orange zest (3.5 oz.)
1.5 L water (50.5 fl. oz.) plus 600 g sugar (21 oz.) plus 200 g glucose (7 oz.) plus 5 g stabilizer (1 tsp.), boiled with the blanched zest
700 ml mandarin orange juice (23.5 fl. oz.)
20 ml lemon juice (1 fl. oz.)
After the mixture has cooled, adjust the density to 1135 D.

Lemon Sorbet

100 g blanched and drained lemon zest (3.5 oz.)
1.5 L water (50.5 fl. oz.) plus 700 g sugar (24.5 oz.) plus 200 g glucose (7 oz.) plus 10 g stabilizer (2 tsp.), boiled with the blanched zest
600 ml lemon juice (21 fl. oz.)
After the mixture has cooled, adjust the density to 1135 D.

Grapefruit Sorbet

100 g blanched and drained grapefruit zest (3.5 oz.)
1.5 L water (50.5 fl. oz.) plus 700 g sugar (24.5 oz.) plus 200 g glucose (7 oz.) plus 5 g stabilizer (1 tsp.), boiled with the blanched zest
650 ml grapefruit juice (22 fl. oz.)
20 ml orange juice (1 fl. oz.)
After the mixture has cooled, adjust the density to 1135 D.

Pineapple Sorbet

400 g sugar (14 oz.) plus 300 ml water (10 fl. oz.), brought to a boil
1 kg strained pineapple pulp (35 oz.)
5 g stabilizer (1 tsp.)
10 ml orange juice (2 tsp.)
30 ml rum (1 fl. oz.)
After the mixture has cooled, adjust the density to 1135 D with water or pineapple juice. When the sorbet has been churned, fold it with 80 g Italian meringue (2 oz.).

Based on Wines, Liquors, and Liqueurs

Muscat Sorbet

1 L sugar syrup (34 fl. oz.), at 1260 D when cool
500 ml Muscat wine (17 fl. oz.)
20 ml lemon juice (⅔ fl. oz.)
5 g stabilizer (1 tsp.)
Adjust the density to 1110 to 1115 D. Add 60 g Italian meringue (2 oz.) after the sorbet has been churned.

Alternative Recipe
500 ml Muscat wine (17 fl. oz.)
1 L sugar syrup (34 fl. oz.), at 1260 D
125 g glucose (4.5 oz.)
juice of 1 lemon
juice of ½ orange
50 g Italian meringue (1.5 oz.)

Port Sorbet

1 L sugar syrup (34 fl. oz.), at 1260 D
500 ml port wine (17 fl. oz.)
20 ml orange juice (⅔ fl. oz.)
5 g stabilizer (1 tsp.)
Adjust the density from 1110 to 1115 D. Add 60 g Italian meringue (2 oz.) after the sorbet has been churned.

Alternative Recipe
500 ml port wine (17 fl. oz.)
1 L sugar syrup (34 fl. oz.), at 1260 D
100 g glucose (3.5 oz.)
juice of 1 lemon
5 g stabilizer (1 tsp.)

109

Kirsch Sorbet
700 ml water (23.5 fl. oz.)
350 g sugar (12.5 oz.)
5 g stabilizer (1 tsp.)
zest of 1 lemon
zest of 1 orange
20 ml lemon juice (⅔ fl. oz.)
180 ml Kirsch (6 fl. oz.)
Simmer together. Adjust the density to 1110 to 1115 D. Add 50 g Italian meringue (1.5 oz.) when the sorbet is almost completely churned (optional).

Vodka Sorbet
700 ml water (23.5 fl. oz.)
200 g sugar (7 oz.)
150 g trimoline (5 oz.)
5 g stabilizer (1 tsp.)
zest of 1 orange
zest of 1 lemon
Bring the above ingredients to a boil and cool. Add 180 ml vodka (6 fl. oz.) Add 50 g Italian meringue (1.5 oz.) after the sorbet has been churned (optional).

Alternative Recipe
750 ml water (25.5 fl. oz.)
350 g sugar (12.5 oz.)
200 g glucose (7 oz.)
5 g stabilizer (1 tsp.)
juice of 3 oranges
150 ml vodka (5 fl. oz.)
Adjust the density to 1115 D.

Rum Sorbet
750 ml water (25.5 fl. oz.)
300 g sugar (10.5 oz.)
150 g glucose (5 oz.)
200 ml rum (7 fl. oz.)
juice of 1 lime
5 g stabilizer (1 tsp.)
Adjust the density to 1115 D.

Calvados Sorbet
1 L sugar syrup (34 fl. oz.), at 1260 D
150 ml 80-proof Calvados (5 fl. oz.)
5 g stabilizer (1 tsp.)
juice from 4 green apples
juice of 1 lemon
Adjust the density to 1115 D.

Cognac Sorbet
700 ml water (23.5 fl. oz.)
300 g sugar (10.5 oz.)
200 g glucose (7 oz.)
5 g stabilizer (1 tsp.)
200 ml Cognac (6.5 fl. oz.)
juice of 1 lemon
Adjust the density to 1115 D.

Armagnac Sorbet
700 ml water (23.5 fl. oz.)
300 g sugar (10.5 oz.)
200 g glucose (7 oz.)
200 ml Armagnac (6.5 fl. oz.)
5 g stabilizer (1 tsp.)
juice of 1 lemon
Add prune juice.

Champagne Sorbet
350 ml water (12 fl. oz.)
350 g sugar (12.5 oz.)
5 g stabilizer (1 tsp.)
zest of 1 orange
zest of 1 lemon
one-half vanilla bean (not split)
750 ml Champagne (25.5 fl. oz.)
Simmer together and let cool. Adjust the density to 1115 D with water. Once the sorbet mixture has been churned, 200 g raisins (7 oz.) macerated in Cognac can be added, as can 30 g Italian meringue (1 oz.). Both of these are optional.

Orange-flavored Champagne Sorbet
750 ml Champagne (25.5 fl. oz.)
750 ml sugar syrup (25.5 fl. oz.), at 1260 D
150 g glucose (5 oz.)
juice of 2 oranges
zest from 2 oranges
5 g stabilizer (1 tsp.)

Alsatian Wine Sorbet
750 ml wine (25.5 fl. oz.)
750 ml water (25.5 fl. oz.)
200 g sugar (7 oz.)
250 g glucose (9 oz.)
juice of 2 lemons

Based on Aromatic Plants

Mint Sorbet
500 ml water (17 fl. oz.)
300 g sugar (10.5 oz.)
200 g trimoline (7 oz.)
5 g stabilizer (1 tsp.)
4 g (about 12) mint leaves (1 tsp.), infused in the simmering liquid
10 ml lemon juice (2 tsp.)
Simmer together and let cool. Adjust the density to 1140 D with water.

Verbena Sorbet
750 ml water (25.5 fl. oz.)
400 g sugar (14 oz.)
50 g glucose (1.5 oz.)
2 tea bags verbena tea
juice of ½ lemon
50 ml Chartreuse or verbena liqueur (1.5 fl. oz.)
Simmer together and let cool.

Alternative Recipe
1 L water (34 fl. oz.)
350 g sugar (12 oz.)
2 tea bags verbena tea
50 g glucose (1.5 oz.)
5 g stabilizer (1 tsp.)
juice of 1 lemon
50 ml Chartreuse or verbena liqueur (1.5 fl. oz.)

Linden Tea Sorbet
1 L water (34 fl. oz.)
300 g sugar (10.5 oz.)
75 g glucose (3 oz.)
3 tea bags linden tea
5 g stabilizer (1 tsp.)
juice of 1 lemon

Tea Sorbet
1 L water (34 fl. oz.)
300 g sugar (10.5 oz.)
150 g glucose (5 oz.)
5 g stabilizer (1 tsp.)
tea leaves or bags
juice of 1 lemon

Special Sorbets

Avocado Sorbet
600 g avocado pulp (21 oz.)
400 ml water (13.5 fl. oz.)
200 g sugar (7 oz.)
150 g invert sugar or juice of 1 lemon (5 oz.)
10 g stabilizer (2 tsp.)

Tomato Sorbet
1 L tomato juice (34 fl. oz.)
400 ml water (14 fl. oz.)
400 g sugar (14 oz.)
150 g glucose (5 oz.)
10 g stabilizer (2 tsp.)

Carrot Sorbet
1 L carrot juice (34 fl. oz.)
400 ml water (13.5 fl. oz.)
500 g sugar (17.5 oz.)
150 g glucose (5 oz.)
juice of 1 lemon
10 g stabilizer (2 tsp.)

Les Sorbets
(Sorbets)

PREPARATION	**0** min	
Assemble the Equipment Prepare, Weigh, and Measure the Raw Ingredients		• Check to make sure all the equipment is clean. • Pasteurize the fruit pulp if fresh fruit is being used. • Prepare the sugar syrup at 1260 D.
PROCEDURE	**5** to **30** min	• Times given are for procedure after the pasteurization of the fruit pulp.
Stir the Fruit Pulp in a Mixing Bowl Whisk in the Sugar Syrup		• Combine the fruit pulp with the stabilizer. • Whisk the 1260-D sugar syrup into the fruit pulp.
Check the Density	**10** min	• The finished mixture should be at 1130 to 1135 D. • Adjust the syrup to the correct density by adding either water or sugar syrup at 1260 D.
Add Coloring		• This is optional.
Strain the Mixture Churn the Sorbet	**12** min	• Strain the mixture into a stainless steel bowl. • Put the sorbet mixture into the ice-cream machine as soon as possible.
STORAGE:		• The sorbet mixture should not be stored for over 24 hours. It should be kept in the refrigerator until needed.

Les appareils à bombes (Bombes)

Definition

Bombes are frozen desserts based primarily on egg yolks and sugar syrup. The cooked sugar is added to the yolks in much the same way as when poaching sugar syrup and yolks together for crème anglaise. The mixture is then flavored in a wide variety of ways, with liquor, liqueur, or other natural flavorings. Bombes can also be flavored with fruit pulp or juice in the same way as ice creams and sorbets.

Bombes are often filled with other frozen mixtures that are in themselves variations on the standard bombe mixture.

Usually a bombe is filled with a softer, lighter frozen filling while the outside mixture is firmer like a regular ice cream. Both the outside layer and inner filling of bombes are flavored in a wide variety of ways.

Uses

Bombe mixtures are the basis for other frozen desserts such as frozen parfaits and frozen soufflés. There are three methods used to prepare bombe mixtures:

- adding sugar cooked to the soft ball stage, 120°C (248°F), to the yolks
- cooking the yolks with sugar syrup in a bain-marie (double boiler) on a low flame
- cooking the yolks in sweetened milk on the stove (crème anglaise method)

One of the most important factors in successfully making a bombe mixture is correct cooking of the egg yolks. If the egg yolks are insufficiently cooked, the bombe mixture will not have the necessary light, rich texture. Nor will the frozen bombe be as appealing in appearance. Moreover, they will not combine properly with the whipped cream, and the mixture will separate once frozen. Grains of frozen egg yolk will then appear at the bottom of the mold.

It is also important to avoid overcooking the yolks. Egg yolks coagulate at 80° to 85°C (175° to 185°F). If they come to a boil, they will coagulate and become granular. It is of course possible to then strain the mixture, but it will not have as good a consistency and the taste may be adversely affected.

Preparation

Make sure that all the necessary equipment is perfectly clean.

Make sure that all the ingredients are fresh. This is especially important with egg yolks, which should be freshly separated. The egg yolks hold the bombe together and give it its rich consistency.

The sugar syrup used for the bombes must come to a boil. Carefully check its density. If the density is too low, it will not sufficiently cook the yolks, and the bombe will have a granular texture when it freezes.

Be careful to sift the sugar before measuring it and to skim off any froth that floats to the top as the sugar is brought to a boil.

A. Cooked-Sugar Method

Equipment

Equipment for cooking sugar
Fine-mesh sieve or cheesecloth
Plastic pastry scraper
Mixing bowl and hand whisk or mixing bowl and whisk attachment for electric mixer
Stainless steel or plastic bowl for storing mixture

Basic Recipe

20 egg yolks
300 g sugar (10.5 oz.)
100 ml water (3.5 fl. oz.)
Cook the sugar and water to a syrup of 125°C (257°F).

Procedure

Cooking the Sugar

Follow the instructions for cooking sugar given in volume 2, pages 14 to 17.

Preparing the Egg Yolks

Beat the egg yolks with a whisk in a clean mixing bowl. This helps to prevent overcooking them when the hot syrup is added.

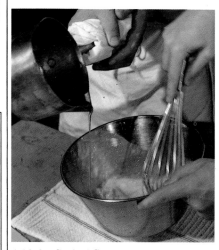

Add the Cooked Sugar

Pour the cooked sugar into the beaten egg yolks in a thin, steady stream. Quickly beat the yolks until all the sugar has been added.

Preparation of bombe mixtures requires experience with cooked sugar and egg yolks. Each step must be carefully executed in order to have successful results. Correctly adding the cooked sugar to the egg yolks is especially important. Carefully set up the work area before beginning to work so that all materials and equipment are at hand throughout the procedure. Only traditional pastry equipment is required.

Straining the Mixture

Quickly strain the mixture through a fine-mesh sieve to remove any particles of sugar or coagulated egg yolk. The mixture should be strained directly into a mixing bowl or the mixing bowl.

Beating the Mixture

Beat the mixture at medium to high speed in the electric mixer or rapidly by hand until it has completely cooled.

Checking the Beaten Mixture

The mixture should be smooth and completely cool and should form a ribbon when lifted out of the bowl with the whisk.

Flavoring the Bombe Mixture

The bombe mixture can be flavored with liqueur, liquor, fruit, or natural flavoring.

Either Italian meringue or whipped cream is then added to the bombe mixture, depending on the final mixture being prepared.

Bombe Mixtures
(Cooked-Sugar Method)

PREPARATION	0 min	
Assemble the Equipment Prepare, Weigh, and Measure the Raw Ingredients		• Make sure that all the equipment is perfectly clean. • Make sure that all the raw ingredients are fresh. • Separate the eggs just before preparing the mixture.
PROCEDURE	5 min	
Cook the Sugar Prepare the Egg Yolks		• Cook to 125°C (257°F). Follow the precautions given in volume 2. • Beat the egg yolks to prevent them from coagulating when the cooked sugar is added.
Add the Cooked Sugar	18 min	• Pour the sugar into the egg yolks in a steady stream. Do not stop beating.
Strain the Mixture Beat the Mixture	20 min	• Strain directly into the bowl for mixing. • Beat the mixture until completely cool.
Check the Mixture	28 min	• The mixture should be completely cool and form a ribbon when lifted above the bowl with a whisk.
Add Flavoring Add Whipped Cream Add Italian Meringue	30 min	• Use natural flavoring, fruit, liquor, or liqueur. • Use whipped cream for frozen parfaits. • Use Italian meringue for frozen soufflés.

STORAGE: • Cooked-sugar bombe mixtures can be frozen for several weeks if protected from frost.

B. Sugar-Syrup Method

Equipment

Equipment for making sugar syrup
Fine-mesh sieve or cheesecloth
Plastic pastry scraper
Mixing bowl and hand whisk or mixing bowl and whisk attachment for mixer
Stainless steel bowl for holding the finished mixture

Basic Recipe

300 g sugar (10.5 oz.)
250 ml water (8.5 fl. oz.)
16 egg yolks
Prepare a 1260-D sugar syrup with the sugar and water.

Procedure

Preparing the Sugar Syrup

Bring the syrup to the simmer for 1 minute (see volume 2, pages 14 to 17).

Preparing the Egg Yolks

Lightly beat the egg yolks to stabilize them before adding the hot syrup.

Adding the Syrup

Pour the hot syrup in a steady stream over the beaten egg yolks. Continue beating until all the syrup has been added.

Straining the Mixture

Strain the egg yolk/sugar syrup mixture through a fine-mesh sieve or through cheesecloth. This straining is optional and only necessary if lumps or particles appear in the mixture.

Cooking the Mixture

Place the bowl with the egg yolk/sugar syrup mixture either in a bowl of simmering water (bain-marie) or directly over a low flame. When heating the mixture in simmering water, stir it from time to time to make sure that it heats evenly. If heating the mixture directly over a flame, stir or whisk constantly. In either case, never let the mixture exceed 85°C (185°F), or the yolks will curdle.

Checking the Mixture

The egg yolk/sugar syrup mixture is completely cooked when it starts to thicken and lose volume.

Straining the Mixture

The mixture should be strained through a fine-mesh sieve when the cooking is complete to eliminate particles of egg yolk.

Final Beating

Beat the mixture either in the electric mixer at medium to high speed or by hand until it has completely cooled.

Checking the Mixture after Beating

The bombe mixture should be cool, creamy, and form a ribbon when lifted above the mixing bowl with the whisk.

Flavoring the Bombe Mixture

Flavor the bombe mixture with liqueur, liquor, fruit, or other natural flavors.

Once the bombe mixture has been flavored, it should be combined with either whipped cream for parfaits or Italian meringue for frozen soufflés.

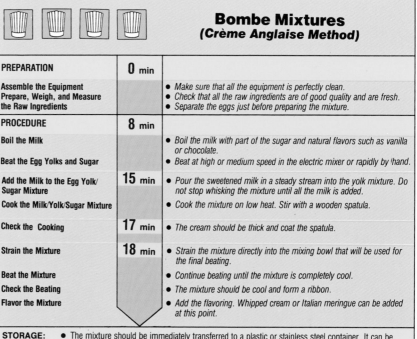 Bombe Mixtures (Sugar-Syrup Method)		
PREPARATION	**0** min	
Assemble the Equipment Prepare, Weigh, and Measure the Raw Ingredients		• Make sure that all the equipment is scrupulously clean. • Check the raw ingredients for quality and freshness. • Separate the eggs just before preparing the mixture.
PROCEDURE	**5** min	
Prepare the Sugar Syrup Prepare the Egg Yolks		• Simmer the water and sugar for 1 minute. • Lightly beat the egg yolks to prevent them from coagulating when the syrup is added.
Add the Hot Syrup Strain the Mixture Cook the Mixture	**15** min	• Pour the syrup into the egg yolks in a steady stream. Continue whisking until all the syrup has been added. • The mixture can be strained directly into the mixing bowl (optional) • Beat the mixture over a bowl of hot water or directly over a low flame. When beating over a flame, do not stop beating.
Check the Mixture Strain the Mixture Beat the Mixture Check the Consistency Flavor the Mixture	**45** to **60** min	• When the mixture has cooked, it will have lost volume and thickened. • Strain to remove particles of cooked yolk. • Beat the mixture until it has completely cooled. • When it has cooled, it should be thick and form a ribbon. • Continue in the same way as when preparing a bombe mixture using the cooked-sugar method.
STORAGE:		• The sugar-syrup bombe mixture can be frozen for several weeks if protected from frost.

C. Crème Anglaise Method

Equipment

Saucepan
Wooden spatula
Whisk
Measuring cup
Plastic pastry scraper
Mixing bowl and whisk attachment for electric mixer
Stainless steel or plastic bowl for finished mixture

Basic Recipe

500 ml milk (17 fl. oz.), boiled with 120 g sugar and flavoring (4.5 oz.)
16 egg yolks, worked with 300 g sugar (10.5 oz.)

Procedure

Preparing the Milk/Sugar Mixture

Boil the milk with the 120 g (4.5 oz.) of sugar. If a natural flavoring is being used, it should be added at this time. Boiling the milk also sterilizes it and prevents the mixture from souring.

Working the Egg Yolks with Sugar

Beat the 300 g (10.5 oz.) of sugar and egg yolks together until the mixture becomes thick and smooth.

Adding the Hot Milk to the Egg Yolks

Remove the milk from the stove and add it in a steady stream to the beaten egg yolks and sugar. Beat continuously with a whisk while adding the milk.

Cooking the Yolk/Milk/Sugar Mixture

Pour the mixture back into the saucepan and return it to the stove. Stir the mixture with a wooden spatula over the heat in the same way as when preparing a crème anglaise (see volume 2, pages 24 to 26). In no case should the temperature of the mixture exceed 85°C (185°F).

Checking the Cooking

Check the cooking with a wooden spatula in the same way as when preparing crème anglaise. This mixture should be much thicker and should thickly coat the spatula.

Straining the Mixture

Strain the mixture through a fine-mesh sieve to remove any coagulated egg yolk.

Beating the Mixture

Beat the strained mixture at medium to high speed until it has completely cooled. When the mixture is cool, light, and quite thick, it can be flavored with fruit or liqueurs. Whipped cream or Italian meringue is then added.

Bombe Mixtures (Crème Anglaise Method)		
PREPARATION	**0** min	
Assemble the Equipment Prepare, Weigh, and Measure the Raw Ingredients		• Make sure that all the equipment is perfectly clean. • Check that all the raw ingredients are of good quality and are fresh. • Separate the eggs just before preparing the mixture.
PROCEDURE	**8** min	
Boil the Milk Beat the Egg Yolks and Sugar		• Boil the milk with part of the sugar and natural flavors such as vanilla or chocolate. • Beat at high or medium speed in the electric mixer or rapidly by hand.
Add the Milk to the Egg Yolk/Sugar Mixture Cook the Milk/Yolk/Sugar Mixture	**15** min	• Pour the sweetened milk in a steady stream into the yolk mixture. Do not stop whisking the mixture until all the milk is added. • Cook the mixture on low heat. Stir with a wooden spatula.
Check the Cooking	**17** min	• The cream should be thick and coat the spatula.
Strain the Mixture	**18** min	• Strain the mixture directly into the mixing bowl that will be used for the final beating.
Beat the Mixture Check the Beating Flavor the Mixture		• Continue beating until the mixture is completely cool. • The mixture should be cool and form a ribbon. • Add the flavoring. Whipped cream or Italian meringue can be added at this point.
STORAGE:		• The mixture should be immediately transferred to a plastic or stainless steel container. It can be frozen for several weeks if well protected from frost.

Sugar-syrup- or milk-based ices

Definition

These ices are based either on pasteurized milk or sugar syrup that is then flavored with fruit or other natural flavoring. In some cases heavy cream or butter is added.

Uses

Sugar-syrup- and milk-based ices are extremely versatile and can be flavored in a wide variety of ways. They can, of course, be molded in the same way as other ice creams.

Equipment

Saucepan
Whisk
Fine mesh strainer or cheesecloth
Plastic pastry scraper
Stainless steel or plastic container
Water bath (bain-marie)

Basic Recipe Using Milk

Vanilla Ice

1 L milk (34 fl. oz.)
200 g sugar (7 oz.)
30 g trimoline (1 oz.)
5 g stabilizer (1 tsp.)
2 ml vanilla extract (½ tsp.)
50 g butter (1.5 oz.)

These ices are simple and straightforward to prepare but require careful attention to cleanliness and hygiene. The mixture must be thoroughly pasteurized before being churned. Allow 15 minutes for the preparation of the mixture before churning. An ice-cream machine is necessary.

Basic Recipe Using Sugar Syrup

Strawberry Ice

1 L boiled water (34 fl. oz.)
300 g sugar (10 fl. oz.)
80 g trimoline (3 oz.)
5 g stabilizer (1 tsp.)
500 g fruit pulp (17.5 oz.)

Lemon Ice

1 L boiled water (34 fl. oz.)
400 g sugar (14 oz.)
100 g trimoline (3.5 oz.)
5 g stabilizer (1 tsp.)
250 ml lemon juice (8.5 fl. oz.)

Preparation

The same precautions used with ice creams and sorbets should be followed in the preparation of ices. Make sure that all the equipment is scrupulously clean and that all the ingredients are of excellent quality and perfectly fresh.

Procedure

Milk-based Ices (with natural flavorings)

Combine the ingredients and bring them to a simmer. Let them simmer gently for 1 minute to pasteurize the mixture.

Strain the mixture through a fine-mesh sieve or through cheesecloth directly into

a stainless steel mixing bowl. Place the bowl immediately into another bowl of ice so that it cools quickly to 15°C (60°F). This rapid cooling helps kill bacteria. If the mixture is to be stored for more than 6 hours before being churned into ice cream, it should be chilled to 6°C (43°F). In any case, the mixture should never be held for more than 24 hours before being churned.

Sugar-Syrup-based Ices (strawberry and lemon)

Combine the ingredients and bring them to a simmer. Let them simmer gently for 1 minute to pasteurize the mixture.

Strain the mixture through a fine-mesh sieve or through cheesecloth directly into a stainless steel mixing bowl.

Add food coloring if necessary and reinforce the flavor with additional fruit or liqueur if desired.

Churn the mixture in the ice-cream machine as soon as possible.

Ices can be stored in the same way as other ice creams and sorbets.

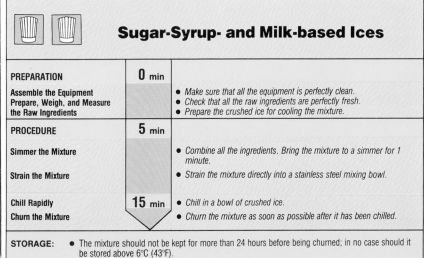

Sugar-Syrup- and Milk-based Ices

PREPARATION	**0** min	
Assemble the Equipment Prepare, Weigh, and Measure the Raw Ingredients		• Make sure that all the equipment is perfectly clean. • Check that all the raw ingredients are perfectly fresh. • Prepare the crushed ice for cooling the mixture.
PROCEDURE	**5** min	
Simmer the Mixture		• Combine all the ingredients. Bring the mixture to a simmer for 1 minute.
Strain the Mixture		• Strain the mixture directly into a stainless steel mixing bowl.
Chill Rapidly	**15** min	• Chill in a bowl of crushed ice.
Churn the Mixture		• Churn the mixture as soon as possible after it has been chilled.
STORAGE:		• The mixture should not be kept for more than 24 hours before being churned; in no case should it be stored above 6°C (43°F).

115

Les parfaits (Parfaits)

History

The word *parfait* has a different meaning in French than in English. In English a parfait is usually thought of as an assortment of different-flavored ice creams that are served together in a glass, sometimes with various toppings. In French, a parfait is a bombe mixture that is folded with whipped cream and then frozen.

The parfait became popular in France during the latter half of the nineteenth century. It is a lovely dessert because it is usually lighter and less sweet than ice cream. It also has a delightful, creamy texture.

Definition

Parfaits are frozen desserts based on bombe mixtures that can be prepared using cooked sugar, sugar syrup, or crème anglaise. The bombe mixture is then folded with whipped cream and flavored in a wide variety of ways.

In France, the ingredients used in a parfait are not as strictly controlled as those used in ice cream. In no case, however, may a parfait be called an ice cream.

Parfaits are never churned in an ice-cream machine but are simply placed in the freezer to set.

Uses

Parfaits can be molded in cylindrical or cone-shaped molds. They can also be used as fillings for molded ice creams or bombes. They are sometimes used as fillings for frozen cakes or as the bases for frozen soufflés.

Parfaits are usually based on bombe mixtures. Any of the three methods for making the bombe mixture can be used. A fourth technique is also sometimes used for preparing parfaits and frozen soufflés. This technique involves cooking down fruit pulp, letting it cool, and then folding it with whipped cream. All four methods produce excellent results.

A. Cooked-Sugar Method

Equipment

Equipment for cooking sugar syrup
Mixing bowl and whisk attachment for electric mixer or hand whisks and mixing bowls
Measuring cups
Plastic pastry scraper

Professional Recipes

Liquor-flavored Parfait

20 egg yolks
300 g sugar (10.5 oz.) plus 100 ml water (3.5 fl. oz.), cooked to 125°C (257°F)
150 to 200 ml liquor (5 to 7 fl. oz.)
1 L heavy cream (34 fl. oz.), whipped

Liqueur-flavored Parfait

20 egg yolks
300 g sugar (10.5 oz.) plus 100 ml water

(3.5 fl. oz.), cooked to 125°C (257°F)
100 to 150 ml liqueur (3.5 to 5 fl. oz.)
1 L heavy cream (34 fl. oz.), whipped

Fruit-flavored Parfait

20 egg yolks

300 g sugar (10.5 oz.) plus 100 ml water (3.5 fl. oz.), cooked to 125°C (257°F)
500 g fruit pulp or puree (17.5 oz.)
1 L heavy cream (34 fl. oz.), whipped

Preparation

Make sure that all the equipment is perfectly clean.

Check the freshness and quality of all the raw ingredients. Use egg yolks that have just been separated. Take the necessary precautions when preparing the sugar syrup (see volume 2, pages 14 to 17). Use only pasteurized heavy cream or crème fraîche. Make sure that the cream and the equipment are well chilled before beating.

Procedure

Cook the sugar: Take the usual precautions for preparing cooked sugar. Cook the syrup to the correct stage and temperature, 125°C (257°F).

Prepare the egg yolks: Beat the yolks lightly in a stainless steel bowl to help stabilize them and prevent coagulation during the addition of the cooked sugar.

Add the cooked sugar: Pour the cooked sugar in a steady stream over the beaten egg yolks. Continue beating until all the sugar has been added.

Strain the mixture: The mixture should be strained immediately after the addition of the sugar through a fine-mesh sieve or through cheesecloth.

Beat the bombe mixture: The egg yolk/cooked sugar mixture should be beaten at medium to high speed until it has thickened and completely cooled.

Check the beating: The bombe mixture should be cold and form a ribbon in the same way as génoise batter (see génoise, volume 1).

Flavor the bombe mixture: Immediately transfer the beaten bombe mixture to a clean mixing bowl and flavor it with the liquor, liqueur, or other natural flavoring. Fold the flavoring carefully into the bombe mixture with a whisk. Put the mixture in the refrigerator, 5°C (40°F).

Beat the cream: Chill the cream before beating it. Beat it to soft peaks (see

whipped cream, volume 2, pages 56 to 57).

Fold together the whipped cream and bombe mixture: Pour the flavored bombe mixture into the whipped cream and fold them together with a skimmer. Finish combining them with a few rapid strokes with a whisk. The finished mixture should be smooth and completely homogeneous.

Mold the parfait mixture: A variety of different-shaped molds can be filled with

the parfait mixture. It is best to freeze the empty molds ahead of time or to line them with ice cream. The parfait mixture can also be used to fill cakes and vacherins.

Freeze the parfait: Place the molds of parfait in the freezer as soon as they have been filled. Make sure they are frozen all the way through.

Unmold the parfait: Parfaits should be removed from the molds in the same way as ice creams.

Decorate the parfait: Parfaits are usually decorated with whipped cream applied with a pastry bag.

Equipment

Heavy-bottomed saucepan
Whisk
Plastic pastry scrapers
Fine-mesh sieve or cheesecloth
Measuring cups
Mixing bowls
Bowl for beating egg whites
Flexible whisk or electric mixer bowl and
    whisk attachments
Bowl for holding finished mixture

Professional Recipe

500 ml milk (17 fl. oz.) plus 120 g sugar (4.5 oz.) plus 2 vanilla beans split lengthwise, simmered together
16 egg yolks plus 300 g sugar (10.5 oz.), beaten together
850 ml heavy cream (28.5 fl. oz.), whipped

Alternative Recipes

Coffee: 80 g ground coffee (3 oz.), infused in hot milk

Chocolate: 100 g cocoa powder (3.5 oz.) or 300 g couverture chocolate (10.5 oz.)

B. Crème Anglaise Method

Chestnut: 500 g chestnut puree (17.5 oz.)

Pistachio: 150 g pistachio paste (5 oz.)

Praline: 160 to 200 g praline paste (5 to 7 oz.)

Caramel and hazelnut are also flavoring possibilities.

Preparation

Make sure that all the equipment is at hand and perfectly clean. Prepare, weigh, and measure all the raw ingredients. Carefully separate the eggs. Chill the bowl and whisk for whipping the cream in the freezer or refrigerator.

Procedure

Prepare the Crème Anglaise

See volume 2, pages 24 to 26, or crème anglaise method for bombe mixtures, this volume, page 113.

Reminder

Bring the milk, sugar, and vanilla beans to a simmer on top of the stove.

Cut the vanilla beans in half lengthwise and scrape the inside to loosen the tiny grains of vanilla. Stir these along with the beans into the milk. If vanilla is not being used, add the chosen flavoring to the simmering milk.

Lightly whisk the egg yolks with some of the sugar. Add the hot sweetened milk to the egg yolk/sugar mixture while beating.

Return the mixture to the stove and cook it in the same way as crème anglaise.

Strain the mixture through a fine-mesh sieve or cheesecloth.

Beat the mixture with the electric mixer at medium to high speed or rapidly by hand until it has completely cooled. This usually takes about 10 minutes. The mixture should have a thick texture and make a ribbon when lifted over the bowl with the whisk. The final steps for preparing the mixture are the same as the cooked-sugar method.

C. Sugar-Syrup Method

Equipment

Equipment for preparing sugar syrup
Mixing bowl attachment and whisk attachment for electric mixer or hand whisk and mixing bowls
Measuring cups
Plastic pastry scraper
Bowl for the finished mixture

Recipe

300 g sugar (10.5 oz.) plus 250 ml water (8.5 fl. oz.), cooked to make a syrup 1260 D
16 egg yolks
1 L heavy cream or crème fraîche (34 fl. oz.), whipped
flavoring

Alternative Recipes

Coffee: 25 ml coffee extract (1 fl. oz.) plus 20 g instant coffee granules (⅔ oz.)

Chocolate: 80 g bitter baking chocolate (3 oz.), melted, or 250 g couverture chocolate (9 oz.)

Chestnut: 400 g chestnut puree (14 oz.) thinned with 100 ml rum (3.5 fl. oz.)

Assorted liquors or liqueurs: 150 to 200 ml liquor or liqueur of choice (5 to 7 fl. oz.)

Preparation

Assemble all the equipment and make sure that it is perfectly clean.

Prepare, weigh, measure, and check the quality and freshness of all the raw ingredients.

Carefully separate the eggs. Save the whites for another use.

Chill the bowl and whisk to be used for whipping the cream.

Procedure

Reminder

Prepare the sugar syrup by boiling together the sugar and water. Be sure that they are allowed to boil for at least a minute.

Prepare the egg yolks by beating them lightly with a whisk.

Pour the hot sugar syrup on the beaten yolks while beating rapidly.

Strain the mixture through a fine-mesh sieve or cheesecloth directly into a stainless steel mixing bowl.

Cook the mixture by heating it in a water bath or directly over a low flame. If using a direct flame, the mixture must be stirred continuously. When using a water bath, this process requires 30 to 45 minutes but does not require such constant attention.

Once the mixture has been cooked, beat it by hand or in the electric mixer.

Finish the preparation in the same way as when using the cooked-sugar method.

D. Fruit-based Parfaits

Recipe

1 L unsweetened fruit pulp or puree (34 fl. oz.)
700 g sugar (24.5 oz.)
1 L heavy cream or crème fraîche (34 fl. oz.), lightly whipped
several drops fruit flavoring (optional)

Procedure

Certain fruit pulps are extremely liquid and need to be reduced by three-quarters. This should be done in a clean stainless steel bowl in a bain-marie. For example, 1 kg (35 oz.) of fruit puree should be cooked down until it weighs 750 ml (26.5 oz.).

Strain the fruit puree if necessary. Stir in the sugar until it dissolves.

Chill the mixture in the refrigerator.

Beat the heavy cream or crème fraîche until it has the texture of Chantilly cream. Do not overbeat it.

Pour the chilled fruit pulp over the beaten cream and gently stir the two to-

gether with a whisk. The mixture should be completely smooth and homogeneous without streaks of unincorporated cream.

The finished mixture is then used to fill molds, which are often already lined with a layer of ice cream.

Alternative Recipe

This mixture can easily be converted into a bavarian cream by adding gelatin leaves. This bavarian mixture can then be used to fill cakes and other desserts.

Fruit Bavarian

See recipe above

Before the whipped cream is combined with the fruit/sugar mixture, soften 12 leaves (24 g) gelatin (1 oz.) and dissolve them into the mixture. (Be sure to weigh the gelatin leaves, as they come in different sizes.)

Les soufflés glacés (Frozen soufflés)

Definition

Frozen soufflés are smooth and light-textured creams based on a variety of different fruits, liquors, and natural flavorings. They are prepared in much the same way as parfaits. The only difference is that the basic bombe mixture is combined with Italian meringue and sometimes whipped cream instead of whipped cream alone.

Here we have divided frozen soufflés into two categories:

Frozen soufflés flavored with natural flavorings, liqueurs, and liquor: These mixtures are based on a basic bombe mixture that is then folded with Italian meringue and whipped cream.

Frozen soufflés flavored with fruit: These soufflés are based on reduced fruit pulp or puree that is then combined with whipped cream and Italian meringue. Italian meringue lightens the mixture and gives it a stiffer texture, which makes it easier to freeze by itself without the support of an ice-cream lining.

Uses

Usually these mixtures are frozen in soufflé molds and presented as frozen soufflés. They can also be used, however, to fill other dessert molds in the same way as parfait mixture.

Equipment

Equipment for cooking sugar or preparing sugar syrup

Equipment for preparing Italian meringue
Equipment for preparing Chantilly cream
Mixing bowl
Plastic pastry scraper
Hand whisk

Basic recipe

Starting with bombe mixture

Liqueur-flavored Frozen Soufflé
(using Cointreau, Grand Marnier, Curaçao, for example)
20 egg yolks
300 g sugar (10.5 oz.) plus 100 ml water (3.5 fl. oz.), cooked to 125°C (257°F)
100 to 150 ml liqueur (3.5 to 5 fl. oz.)
400 g Italian meringue (14 oz.)
500 ml heavy cream (17 fl. oz.), whipped

Liquor-flavored Frozen Soufflé
(rum, Kirsch, whiskey, for example)
16 egg yolks
300 g sugar (10.5 oz.) plus 100 ml water (3.5 fl. oz.), cooked to 125°C (257°F)
100 to 150 ml liquor (3.5 to 5 fl. oz.)
400 g Italian meringue (14 oz.)
1.5 L heavy cream (50.5 fl. oz.), whipped

Natural-flavored Frozen Soufflé
(coffee, chocolate, hazelnut, for example)
20 egg yolks
300 g sugar (10.5 oz.) plus 100 ml water (3.5 fl. oz.), cooked to 125°C (257°F)
100 g bitter baking chocolate (3.5 oz.)
400 g Italian meringue (14 oz.)
1.5 L heavy cream (50.5 fl. oz.), whipped

Preparation

Make sure that all the necessary equipment is assembled and perfectly clean.

Separate the eggs just before the yolks are needed.

Carefully follow directions for preparing Italian meringue (see volume 1, pages 82 to 83) and for whipped cream (see volume 2, pages 56 to 57).

Preparing the Molds

Frozen soufflés are usually molded in traditional soufflé molds, which can be made of porcelain, earthenware, or stainless steel. A strip of paper is wrapped around the upper rim of the soufflé mold to hold the mixture in place while it is freezing. The paper should be wrapped three or four times around the sides of the soufflé mold so that it is somewhat rigid and will support the weight of the

mixture. The paper should reach 3 to 4 cm (1.5 to 2 in.) above the top edge of the mold. The paper should then be at-

tached with a rubber band or tape. When the soufflé is frozen in this way, it looks like a real soufflé that has risen up out of the mold.

It is also possible to attach a metal cake ring to the top of the soufflé mold instead of using paper. When using this method, be sure that the cake ring is attached to the mold in several places with tape.

A third method sometimes used is to mold the top half of the soufflé (the part that will eventually rise above the mold) separately in cake rings placed on sheets of aluminum foil. The top halves are then allowed to set in the freezer and are flipped out onto the bottom halves of the soufflés as they are needed.

This last method of preparing the top halves of the soufflé separately offers several advantages:

- the frozen soufflés are easier to store because they can be stacked until needed
- the tops and bottoms can be stored separately and put together as they are needed
- the surfaces of the soufflés can be decorated more easily because the decoration can be placed on the base of the frozen lid and then turned over

Procedure

Prepare the bombe mixture: Prepare the mixture using the methods described for preparing bombe mixtures and parfaits (pages 111 to 112, 116 to 117).

Flavor the mixture as desired: The mixture can be flavored with liquor, liqueur, or other natural flavorings.

Prepare the Italian meringue: see volume 1, pages 82 to 83.

Whip the cream: see volume 2, pages 56 to 57.

Combine the ingredients: Gently fold the Italian meringue into the beaten and flavored bombe mixture using a whisk.

Fold in the whipped cream after the Italian meringue and bombe mixture have been combined.

Molding the Soufflé Mixture

Attach a strip of paper (or aluminum foil) to the top of the mold with tape or a rubber band. Carefully fill the mold almost to the top of the strip.

Pieces of sponge cake soaked in liquor or liqueur can be placed in the soufflé mixture when the molds are half full to accent and reinforce the flavor.

Freezing the Soufflés

Place the soufflés in a cold freezer, −20° to −25°C (−5° to −15°F), for at least 4 hours.

Storage

The soufflés can be kept frozen for several weeks provided they are protected from frost.

Decoration

The decoration of the soufflé should correspond to its style and flavor. Possi-

bilities include Chantilly cream, ladyfingers around the sides, marzipan flowers and leaves, cake crumbs, cocoa powder, chocolate shavings, and toasted nuts (craquelins). It is also possible to spray the soufflé with liquid chocolate.

Presentation

Remove the strip of paper or cake ring from the top of the soufflé. Wipe the sides of the soufflé mold and place it on a paper doily.

Serving

The soufflé should be served after the center has softened slightly.

Frozen Soufflés Based on Fruit Pulp or Purée

Basic recipe

Fruit Soufflé

1 L fruit pulp or purée (34 fl. oz.), reduced 25 to 30 percent
few drops of food coloring
500 g Italian meringue (17.5 oz.)
1 L heavy cream (34 fl. oz.) whipped

Preparation

Make sure that all the equipment is scrupulously clean. Separate the eggs just before they are needed.

Follow the directions for preparing Italian meringue given in volume 1 (pages 82 to 83) and for preparing whipped cream given in volume 2 (pages 56 to 57). The preparation of the soufflé molds is the same as described above.

Procedure

Reduce the Fruit Pulp or Puree

Reduction of the fruit pulp or puree takes about 40 minutes in a bain-marie. The fruit pulp or puree is reduced to reinforce the flavor without relying on extract or flavoring. It also contributes to a thicker, creamier soufflé base. The reduced fruit puree can be strained through a fine-mesh sieve if necessary. Reduction is optional.

Prepare the Italian Meringue

See volume 1, pages 82 to 83.

Prepare the Whipped Cream

See volume 2, pages 56 to 57.

Make sure the whipped cream is light and smooth. Be careful not to overbeat it.

Combining the Ingredients

Chill the reduced fruit pulp or puree and fold it with the chilled Italian meringue. Gently combine the two with a whisk.

Once the Italian meringue and fruit puree have been combined, gently fold in the whipped cream. Finish combining the three components with a rapid circular movement of the whisk. Do not overbeat, or the mixture will lose volume and lightness. If the soufflé mixture is overworked, the acidity from the fruit puree may cause the cream to become grainy.

Les biscuits glacés

Definition

Biscuit glacé is based on a mixture that is prepared like génoise batter except that it contains no flour and is served frozen. The mixture is light and airy and is based on egg yolks that are beaten over a heat source and then flavored with liquor, liqueurs, or natural flavorings. This mixture is then combined with Italian meringue and whipped cream in much the same way as for frozen soufflés.

Equipment

Mixing bowl and whisk attachment for
  electric mixer
Mixing bowls
Plastic pastry scrapers

Measuring cups
Hand whisk
Saucepan
Skimmer
Pastry brush

Uses

Biscuit glacé is traditionally frozen in square or rectangular ice-cream molds. This mixture can also be used as a filling or center for other frozen desserts.

Professional Recipes

Chocolate Biscuit Glacé

16 egg yolks
400 g sugar (14 oz.)
600 g chocolate (21 oz.), melted
400 g Italian meringue (14 oz.)
1 L heavy cream or crème fraîche (34 fl.
  oz.), whipped

Fruit-flavored Biscuit Glacé

16 egg yolks
350 g sugar (12.5 oz.)
100 g glucose (3.5 oz.)
500 g fruit pulp or puree (17.5 oz.)

400 g Italian meringue (14 oz.)
1 L heavy cream or crème fraîche (34 fl.
  oz.), whipped

Recipe for a Small Quantity

4 egg yolks
100 g sugar (3.5 oz.)
150 g chocolate (5 oz.), melted
100 g Italian meringue (3.5 oz.)
300 ml heavy cream or crème fraîche (10
  fl. oz.), whipped

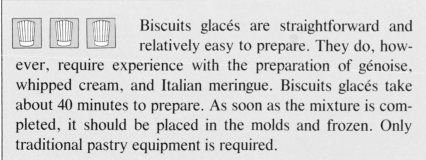

Biscuits glacés are straightforward and relatively easy to prepare. They do, however, require experience with the preparation of génoise, whipped cream, and Italian meringue. Biscuits glacés take about 40 minutes to prepare. As soon as the mixture is completed, it should be placed in the molds and frozen. Only traditional pastry equipment is required.

Preparation

Make sure that all the equipment is scrupulously clean.

Carefully separate the eggs.

Chill the mixing bowl and whisk for whipping the cream in the refrigerator or freezer.

Procedure

Combining the Egg Yolks and Sugar

Whisk together the yolks and sugar with the whisk attachment in an electric mixer or in a stainless steel bowl with a hand whisk.

Heating the Egg Yolk/Sugar Mixture

Heat this mixture in the same way as when preparing génoise (see volume 1,

pages 72 to 75). Beat the egg yolks with the sugar over a gentle heat source (low flame or bain-marie) until the mixture reaches 45°C (115°F).

Beating the Mixture

Beat the mixture off the heat either by hand or with an electric mixer until it has completely cooled.

Checking the Consistency

The mixture should be beaten until it has completely cooled, is light and

frothy, and forms a ribbon when lifted above the bowl with the whisk.

Flavoring the Mixture

Add the desired flavoring to the egg yolk/sugar mixture.

Preparing the Italian Meringue

See volume 1, pages 82 to 83.

Whipping the Cream

See volume 2, pages 56 to 57. It is best to beat the cream at the same time as the egg yolk/sugar mixture is being prepared.

Folding the Italian Meringue and Whipped Cream Together

Fold the meringue and whipped cream together until the mixture is smooth and homogeneous. Do not overwork the mixture.

Folding the Egg Yolk/Sugar Mixture into the Italian Meringue/Whipped Cream Mixture

Pour the beaten egg yolk/sugar mixture into the Italian meringue/whipped cream mixture. Fold the mixtures together gently with a whisk.

Molding the Finished Mixture

Put the finished biscuit glacé into the appropriate molds immediately.

Storage

The finished ice-cream cake can be stored for several weeks in a cold freezer, −25° to −30°C (−10° to −20°F).

Les Biscuits Glacés

PREPARATION Assemble the Equipment Prepare, Weigh, and Measure the Raw Ingredients	**0** min	• Make sure that all the equipment is perfectly clean. • Separate the eggs. • Chill the heavy cream or crème fraîche along with the whisk and bowl used for beating. • Melt the chocolate if it is being used.
PROCEDURE Combine the Egg Yolks with the Sugar	**5** min	• Use the whisk and mixing bowl.
Heat the Egg Yolk/Sugar Mixture Beat the Egg Yolk/Sugar Mixture	**15** min	• Heat the mixture over a heat source. Beat continuously until the mixture reaches 45°C (115°F). • Beat the mixture off the heat until it has completely cooled.
Check the Consistency Prepare the Italian Meringue Whip the Cream	**20** min	• Make sure that the mixture forms a ribbon when cooled. • Prepare the meringue while beating the egg yolk/sugar mixture. • The cream should be whipped until light and frothy.
Fold Together the Italian Meringue and the Whipped Cream Add the Egg Yolk/Sugar Mixture to the Whipped Cream/Italian Meringue Mixture	**35** min	• Carefully fold together the whipped cream and Italian meringue. Make sure that the meringue is completely cool before combining it with the cream. • Carefully fold the egg yolk/sugar mixture into the whipped cream/Italian meringue mixture by hand with a whisk.
MOLDING THE MIXTURE	**40** min	• Put the finished mixture immediately into ice-cream molds.
STORAGE:		• The ice-cream cake can be frozen for several weeks if well protected from frost, −25°C to −30°C (−10° to −20°F).

Les sabayons glacés (Frozen sabayon)

History

Frozen sabayon is based on sabayon sauce (see volume 2, page 82). Sabayon sauce is a derivative of the Italian zabaglione, which is based on egg yolks, sugar, and wine. Zabaglione is always prepared with Marsala wine, which has a distinctive, full flavor. The French version, sauce sabayon, is usually prepared with a dry white wine.

Definition

Frozen sabayons are extremely light and frothy and should have a creamy consistency. Although they are most often derived from the classic French sabayon sauce, which is based on dry white wine, frozen sabayons can be prepared with almost any type of wine. They are particularly successful when prepared with wines that have a pronounced character, such as Muscat, Tokay, Riesling, Gewurztraminer, or with fortified wines such as sherry, Madeira, port, or Malaga. They can also be prepared with Champagne and flavored with liqueurs such as Grand Marnier, Cointreau, or Curaçao. The finished sabayon sauce is combined with whipped cream before it is frozen.

Here we describe two methods for the preparation of frozen sabayons:

A. **génoise method**

B. **crème anglaise method**

Uses

Sabayon is usually frozen in ice-cream molds to serve as the filling for other ice-cream preparations. It is also used for frozen ice-cream coupes, for which it is used along with other frozen dessert preparations.

Génoise Method

Equipment

Mixing bowl and whisk attachment for electric mixer
Mixing bowls
Plastic pastry scrapers
Measuring cups
Hand whisk

Professional Recipe

20 egg yolks
500 g sugar (17.5 oz.)
500 ml Champagne or wine (17 fl. oz.)
1 L heavy cream or crème fraîche (34 fl. oz.), whipped

Alternative Recipe

16 to 20 egg yolks
400 to 600 g sugar (14 to 21 oz.)
400 to 600 ml Champagne or wine (13.5 to 21 fl. oz.)
1 L heavy cream or crème fraîche (34 fl. oz.), whipped

Recipe for a Small Quantity

8 egg yolks

200 g sugar (7 oz.)
200 ml Champagne or wine (6.5 fl. oz.)
500 ml heavy cream or crème fraîche (34 fl. oz.), whipped

Preparation

Assemble all the necessary equipment and make sure that it is clean.

Prepare, weigh, and measure the raw ingredients. Carefully separate the eggs. Save the egg whites for another purpose.

Place the mixing bowl containing the heavy cream in the refrigerator.

Procedure

See sabayon sauce, volume 2, pages 82 to 83).

Combining the Egg Yolks and Sugar

Whisk together the egg yolks and sugar in a stainless steel bowl or with the electric mixer.

Heating the Egg Yolk/Sugar Mixture

The egg yolk/sugar mixture should be heated in the same way as when warming the eggs for a génoise (see volume 1, pages 72 to 75). Beat the mixture continuously while it is being heated until it reaches 45°C (115°F).

Beating the Egg Yolk/Sugar Mixture

Remove the egg yolk/sugar mixture from the heat source and beat it vigorously by hand or with an electric mixer while adding the hot wine or Champagne.

Checking the Consistency

The mixture is ready when it has completely cooled, is light and airy, and forms a ribbon on the surface of the bowl when lifted with a whisk.

Whipping the Cream

The whipped cream should be light and airy. Do not overbeat it.

The preparation of the sabayon mixture requires constant attention. It is helpful if the techniques used for the preparation of génoise, whipped cream, and crème anglaise have already been mastered. The preparation of the sabayon mixture usually takes about 30 minutes and requires traditional pastry equipment.

Folding the Egg Yolk/Sugar Mixture with the Whipped Cream

Slowly add the egg yolks/sugar mixture to the whipped cream. Combine the

two mixtures carefully by hand with a whisk.

Anglaise Method

Equipment

Saucepan
Wooden spatula
Mixing bowls
Whisk
Plastic pastry scrapers
Measuring cups
Cheesecloth or fine-mesh sieve
Bowl for finished mixture

Professional Recipe

500 ml Champagne or wine (17 fl. oz.)
400 g sugar (14 oz.)
150 g glucose (5 oz.)
20 egg yolks
1 L heavy cream or crème fraîche (34 fl. oz.), whipped

Alternative Recipe

500 ml Champagne or wine (17 fl. oz.)
350 g sugar (12.5 oz.)
20 egg yolks
1 L heavy cream or crème fraîche (34 fl. oz.), whipped
300 g Italian meringue (10.5 oz.)

Recipe for a Small Quantity

250 ml Champagne or wine (8.5 fl. oz.)
250 g sugar (9 oz.)
10 egg yolks
500 ml heavy cream or crème fraîche (17 fl. oz.), whipped

Preparation

Same as génoise method.

Procedure

Heating the Wine or Champagne

Heat the wine or Champagne in the saucepan to about 90°C (195°F).

Beating the Egg Yolks with the Sugar

While the wine or Champagne is heating, vigorously beat together the egg yolks and sugar with a whisk until the mixture turns pale yellow or white.

Molding and Decorating the Sabayon Mixture

The sabayon mixture should be molded immediately in ice-cream molds or decorative glasses. It can be decorated with whipped cream when it is removed from the molds or served in the glasses.

Storage

Frozen sabayon can be kept for several weeks in a cold freezer, −25° to −30°C (−10° to −20°F), if well protected from frost.

Adding the Hot Wine or Champagne

Pour the hot wine or Champagne in a steady stream into the egg yolk/sugar mixture. Beat the mixture until all the liquid has been added. Put the mixture back in the saucepan and on the stove over a low flame.

Cooking the Mixture

See crème anglaise, volume 2, pages 24 to 26.
Heat the mixture over a low flame while stirring with a wooden spatula. Continue to heat the mixture to 85° to 90°C (185° to 195°F) or until it coats the back of the spatula.

Checking the Consistency

The sabayon is ready when it coats the back of the spoon. The best way to verify that it has reached the correct stage is to lift the spatula out of the hot mixture and hold it sideways at a 45-degree angle over the mixture. Draw a line in the sabayon clinging to the spatula with a finger. The top border of sabayon should stay where it is and not flow into the streak formed by the finger. As soon as this stage is reached, remove the saucepan from the stove.

Straining the Sabayon

Immediately strain the mixture through a fine-mesh sieve or cheesecloth into a clean mixing bowl.

Cooling the Sabayon

Stir the sabayon from time to time while it is cooling to prevent the formation of a crust on its surface.

Whipping the Cream

Whip the cream while the sabayon is cooling

Folding the Sabayon Mixture into the Whipped Cream

Add the sabayon mixture to the whipped cream. Stir it in carefully but thoroughly with a whisk.

If Italian meringue is being used, combine it with the whipped cream first and then add the sabayon mixture.

Alternative

The cooked sabayon can also be beaten in the electric mixer.

Molding and Storing

The same as for the génoise method discussed above.

			Les Sabayons Glacés (Frozen Sabayon)
PREPARATION	**0** min		
Assemble the Equipment Prepare, Weigh, and Measure the Raw Ingredients			• Make sure that all the equipment is perfectly clean. • Check that all the raw ingredients are fresh and of good quality. • Separate the eggs.
PROCEDURE	**5** min		
Combine the Egg Yolks with the Sugar			• Use a whisk and mixing bowl.
Heat the Egg Yolk/Sugar Mixture	**15** min		• Stir the mixture continuously over a low flame.
Beat the Egg Yolk/Sugar Mixture			• Beat the mixture off the heat. • Add the hot wine or Champagne to the egg yolk/sugar mixture while beating.
Check the Consistency	**20** min		• The mixture is ready when it has completely cooled and forms a ribbon.
Whip the Cream			• The cream can be whipped while the egg yolk/sugar mixture is being beaten with the wine.
Fold the Sabayon into the Whipped Cream			• Carefully fold the sabayon into the whipped cream by hand with a whisk.
MOLDING	**25** min		• The sabayon should be placed immediately into ice-cream molds or glasses as soon as it is ready.
STORAGE:			• Put the molded sabayon mixture immediately into the freezer. Make sure that it is well protected from frost.

Les mousses glacées (Frozen mousses)

Definition

Frozen mousses are extremely light and creamy. They are prepared using one of two methods:

using eggs: these mousse mixtures are composed of egg yolks, milk, sugar, gelatin, whipped cream, and flavoring. A wide variety of flavorings can be used, including natural flavorings such as coffee, chocolate, and vanilla. Fruit pulp, liquor, or liqueur can also be used.

using fruit: these mixtures are based on sugar syrup, fruit pulp or puree, and whipped cream. They can be flavored with various fruit extracts. They can also be colored if necessary.

Uses

Frozen mousses are usually used as fillings for other frozen desserts, such as bombes, vacherins, frozen soufflés, and frozen cakes.

Egg Method (Anglaise)

Equipment

Saucepan, wooden spatula, plastic pastry scrapers, fine-mesh sieve or china cap, measuring cup, mixing bowls, copper mixing bowl for egg whites, whisks, stainless steel bowl for holding finished mixture

Professional Recipes

Frozen Coffee Mousse

500 ml milk (17 fl. oz.)
30 ml coffee extract (1 fl. oz.)
450 g sugar (16 oz.)
16 egg yolks
6 sheets (12 g) gelatin (½ oz.)
60 ml rum (2 fl. oz.)
500 ml heavy cream or crème fraîche (17 fl. oz.)

Frozen Mousses with Liquors or Liqueurs

500 ml milk (17 fl. oz.)
450 g sugar (16 oz.)
16 egg yolks
200 ml liquor or liqueur (6.5 fl. oz.)
6 sheets (12 g) gelatin (½ oz.)
500 ml heavy cream or crème fraîche (17 fl. oz.)

Frozen Fruit Mousses

500 ml milk (17 fl. oz.)
500 g sugar (17.5 oz.)
16 egg yolks
6 sheets (12 g) gelatin (½ oz.)
500 ml fruit pulp or puree (17 fl. oz.)
juice of one lemon
500 ml heavy cream or crème fraîche (17 fl. oz.)

Preparation

Assemble all the necessary equipment for the preparation of the mousse. Make sure that the equipment is perfectly clean.

Prepare, weigh, and measure all the raw ingredients. Be careful when separating the eggs.

Soak the sheets of gelatin in cold water.

Chill the bowl to be used for whipping the heavy cream or crème fraîche.

   Frozen mousses are relatively easy to prepare, provided that the directions are closely followed. Some of the stages in their preparation, such as making the crème anglaise! Italian meringue, and whipped cream, are quite delicate and require constant attention.

Several methods can be used for their preparation.

Frozen mousses should be placed in the final molds as soon as the mixture is ready.

Some mousse recipes require an ice-cream machine.

Mousses keep well in a cold freezer if protected from frost.

Procedure

Method A
(without an ice-cream machine)

Preparing the Crème Anglaise: See volume 2, pages 24 to 26, for more detailed instructions on making crème anglaise. Bring the sweetened milk containing the flavoring to a simmer. Beat together the egg yolks and sugar. Add the hot, flavored milk to the egg yolk/sugar mixture, stirring constantly. Stir the mixture over low to medium heat with a wooden spatula until it thickens.

Adding the Gelatin: Add the sheets of gelatin, which have been soaked in cold water and squeezed to remove excess water, to the crème anglaise. Stir the mixture with a whisk until the gelatin has completely dissolved.

Straining and Cooling the Cream: Immediately strain the cream through a fine-mesh sieve or china cap into a clean stainless steel bowl placed on ice.
Stir the cream while it is cooling to prevent the formation of a skin.

Whipping the Heavy Cream or Crème Fraîche: Whip the cream while the crème anglaise is chilling.

Flavoring the Crème Anglaise: Liquor or liqueur flavoring should be added after the crème anglaise has been chilled.

Combining the Whipped Cream and Crème Anglaise: Slowly add the flavored and chilled crème anglaise to the whipped cream. Gently combine the two creams with a whisk. Stop as soon as they are thoroughly combined.

Freezing the Mousse: The mousse should be placed in a mold and frozen as soon as the mixture is complete. Leave it in the freezer until it has frozen all the way through.

Storage

The mousse can be kept frozen for several weeks, provided it is well protected from frost.

Method B
(with an ice-cream machine)

Do not use any gelatin when preparing frozen mousses with this method.

Preparing the Crème Anglaise: Follow the procedure in method A.

Straining the Crème Anglaise: Strain through a fine-mesh sieve or china cap.

Churning the Crème Anglaise: Use the same method as when preparing other types of ice cream. Frozen mousses should be somewhat soft when they come out of the ice-cream machine.

Beating the Heavy Cream or Crème Fraîche: Beat the cream while the crème anglaise is in the ice-cream machine.

Flavoring the Crème Anglaise after Churning: Liquor or liqueur flavorings should be added to the mousse when it comes out of the ice-cream machine.

Combining the Crème Anglaise with the Whipped Cream: Fold the whipped cream into the soft, frozen crème anglaise mixture, using a wooden or rubber spatula.

Optional: 400 g (14 oz.) Italian meringue can be added to the mixture to provide a smooth texture. When using this method, it is best to combine the Italian meringue with the whipped cream before folding it with the frozen crème anglaise.
The final freezing of the mousse is the same as for method A.

Les Mousses Glacées
(Frozen Mousses, egg method)

PREPARATION Assemble the Equipment Prepare, Weigh, and Measure the Raw Ingredients	**0** min	• Make sure that all the equipment is perfectly clean. • Check that all the raw ingredients are fresh. • Soak the sheets of gelatin in cold water if they are being used.
PROCEDURE Without Ice-Cream Machine Prepare the Crème Anglaise Bring the Milk to a Simmer	**7** min	• The milk can be sweetened or flavored. • Beat until the yolks become pale yellow or white.
Work the Egg Yolks with the Sugar		• Add the hot milk in a steady stream to the yolk/sugar mixture.
Add the Milk to the Yolk/Sugar Mixture		• Cook the crème anglaise over a low flame.
Cook the Crème Anglaise		• Check the thickness of the cream with a wooden spatula.
Check the Consistency		• This is optional, depending on the method chosen.
Add Gelatin		• Strain immediately into a clean bowl. • Chill the crème anglaise over a bowl of crushed ice.
Strain the Mixture Chill the Crème Anglaise	**25** min	• Whip the heavy cream while the crème anglaise is chilling. • Flavor the cold crème anglaise with liquor or liqueurs.
Add the Crème Anglaise to the Whipped Cream	**40** min	• Add the crème anglaise to the whipped cream, using a small hand whisk.
PROCEDURE With Ice-Cream Machine Prepare the Crème Anglaise	**7** min	
Churn the Cream		• Same as above, but do not use gelatin.
Whip the Heavy Cream		• The cream should be somewhat soft when it comes out of the ice-cream machine.
Flavor the Crème Anglaise		• Whip the cream while the crème anglaise is chilling.
Whip the Cream		
Flavor the Cold Crème Anglaise	**35** min	• Flavor the frozen crème anglaise with liqueurs or liquor when it comes out of the ice-cream machine.
Add the Whipped Cream to the Frozen Crème Anglaise	**40** min	• Add the whipped cream to the frozen crème anglaise using a small spatula.
MOLDING		• Place the mousse immediately into the appropriate molds and freeze.
STORAGE:		• Frozen mousses will keep for several weeks in a cold freezer if well protected from frost.

Fruit Method

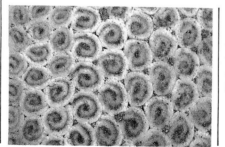

Equipment

Saucepan, measuring cup, skimmer, pastry brush, fine-mesh strainer, hydrometer, mixing bowl, whisk, plastic pastry scraper, stainless steel bowl for holding finished mousse

Professional Recipe

700 g sugar (24.5 oz.) plus 350 ml water (12 fl. oz.), cooked to a syrup of 1350 D

1 L fruit pulp or puree (34 fl. oz.)

2 L heavy cream or crème fraîche (67.5 fl. oz.)

Method A
(hand mixing)

Preparing and Cooling the Syrup: See the instructions regarding preparation of simple syrups in volume 2, pages 14 to 17. Bring the sugar and water to a simmer. Simmer for 1 minute to sterilize it. Transfer the syrup to a clean bowl and let it cool. Stir it from time to time.

Preparing the Italian Meringue: If it is to be used, prepare the Italian meringue while the syrup is cooling (see volume 1, pages 82 to 83).

Whipping the Heavy Cream or Crème Fraîche: Whip the cream while the sugar syrup is cooling.

Combining the Fruit Pulp or Puree with the Syrup: When the syrup is lukewarm, add the fruit pulp or puree all at once. Combine the mixture with a whisk.

Combining the Whipped Cream with the Cold Italian Meringue: If Italian meringue is being used, thoroughly combine it with the whipped cream.

Combining the Syrup/Fruit Mixture with the Whipped Cream: Pour the syrup/fruit mixture in a steady steam into the whipped cream or the whipped cream/ Italian meringue mixture. Fold the two mixtures together carefully with a whisk. When all the syrup mixture has been added, finish combining the mixtures with a rapid circular movement of the whisk. If the color seems too pale, a few drops of food coloring can be added at this point.

Freezing and Storage

Freezing and storing are the same as for egg-based frozen mousses, discussed on the preceding page.

Method B
(with an ice-cream machine)

When using this method, it is advisable to use the recipe containing Italian meringue.

Preparing the Sugar Syrup: Bring the sugar and water to a simmer for one minute to sterilize them (see volume 2, pages 14 to 17).

Adding the Fruit Pulp or Purée to the Hot Syrup: Thoroughly combine the fruit pulp or puree with the syrup, using a whisk.

Churning the Fruit/Syrup Mixture: Churn the mixture in an ice-cream machine. It should be somewhat soft so that it can be easily combined with the whipped cream

Whipping the Heavy Cream or Crème Fraîche: Whip the cream while the fruit mixture is being churned.

Combining the Whipped Cream with the Italian Meringue: Fold the whipped cream and Italian meringue together with a spatula.

Combining the Whipped Cream/Italian Meringue Mixture with the Frozen Fruit Mixture: Fold the whipped cream/Italian meringue mixture in stages into the frozen fruit mixture, using a spatula or a skimmer.

Molding and Storage

Follow the same recommendations given for egg-based frozen mousses, discussed on the preceding page.

Les Mousses Glacées
(Frozen Mousses, fruit method)

PREPARATION	0 min	
Assemble the Equipment Prepare, Weigh, and Measure the Raw Ingredients		• Make sure that all the equipment is perfectly clean. • Check all the raw ingredients to make sure they are fresh. • Chill the mixing bowl for the cream in the refrigerator.
PROCEDURE Without Machine	5 min	
Prepare the Sugar Syrup		• Simmer the syrup for 1 minute to sterilize it.
Chill the Syrup		• Stir the syrup from time to time while it is chilling.
Prepare the Italian Meringue		• Italian meringue is optional.
Whip the Heavy Cream or Crème Fraîche	10 min	• Whip the cream while the syrup is cooling.
Add the Fruit Pulp or Puree to the Syrup		• Combine the pulp or puree and syrup with a whisk.
Combine the Whipped Cream with the Italian Meringue		• Fold the two together gently but thoroughly.
Combine the Fruit Mixture with the Whipped Cream	20 min	• Add the fruit/sugar syrup mixture to the whipped cream. Combine using a small whisk.
Freeze the Mixture		• Put the mousse mixture into molds and freeze immediately.
PROCEDURE With Ice-Cream Machine	5 min	
		• See volume 1, pages 82 to 83.
Prepare the Italian Meringue		• Simmer the syrup for 1 minute.
Prepare the Sugar Syrup		• Combine the fruit pulp with the syrup, using a whisk.
Add the Fruit Pulp to the Hot Syrup		
Churn the Fruit/Syrup Mixture in the Ice-Cream Machine		• Churn the fruit/syrup mixture in the ice-cream machine. The mixture should be somewhat soft after churning.
Whip the Cream	20 min	• Whip the heavy cream or crème fraîche while the fruit/syrup mixture is in the ice-cream machine.
Combine the Italian Meringue with the Whipped Cream	25 min	• Use a whisk to combine the Italian meingue with the whipped cream.
Combine the Italian Meringue/ Whipped Cream Mixture with the Frozen Fruit Mixture		• Add the Italian meringue/whipped cream mixture to the soft, frozen fruit mixture, using a spatula or a skimmer.
STORAGE:		• Frozen fruit mousses can be kept in the freezer for several weeks if well protected from frost.

Les granités (Granités)

Definition

Granités are similar to sorbets, but they contain less sugar and have a characteristic grainy texture, which gives them their name. Less sugar is used in their preparation, so that their density is lower—usually it ranges from 1090 to 1110 D. They are based on a simple mixture of sugar syrup and fruit juice, which makes them particularly light and refreshing.

Uses

Granités are best served quite soft, even semiliquid. They can be served in sundae glasses or in various-shaped wine glasses.

Equipment

Mixing bowl
Whisk
Plastic pastry scraper
Measuring cup
Fine-mesh strainer or cheesecloth
Hydrometer
Equipment for preparing sugar syrup

Recipe

1 L fruit juice or pulp (34 fl. oz.)
500 ml sugar syrup (17 fl. oz.), at 1260 D

Preparation

Assemble all the necessary equipment and make sure it is perfectly clean.

Prepare, weigh, and measure all the raw ingredients. The basic preparation and precautions are the same as for sorbets (see pages 108 to 110).

Procedure

Add the fruit pulp to the cold syrup. Combine thoroughly with a whisk.

Add enough plain water or fruit juice so the final density is between 1090 and 1110 D.

Churning

Strain the mixture through a fine-mesh strainer or cheesecloth and churn it in the ice-cream machine. Follow the same precautions as when preparing sorbets and ice creams. The finished granité should have a loose, frothy texture and be somewhat grainy.

129

Les boissons glacées (Frozen milkshakes)

Definition

These desserts are similar to American milkshakes except that they are prepared directly in an ice-cream machine and are served before the ice cream freezes into a solid mass. American milkshakes are made like frappés, in a blender or milkshake machine. Frozen milkshakes are served in coupe-shaped or sundae glasses. They are similar to ice cream but are usually not quite as firm. These desserts are served topped with Chantilly cream.

Types of Frozen Milkshakes

Frozen coffee dessert
Coffee liégeois (Belgian style)
Café viennois (Viennese style)
Frozen chocolate milkshake
Frozen chestnut milkshake
Frozen vanilla, strawberry, coconut, black currant or raspberry milkshake
Frozen wine or Champagne
Frozen Irish coffee

Equipment

Saucepan
Whisk
Plastic pastry scraper
Stainless steel mixing bowl
Measuring cup
Fine-mesh strainer

Preparation

Assemble all the equipment and make sure it is perfectly clean.

Prepare, weigh, and measure the raw ingredients. Make sure that they are fresh.

Chill the glasses, coupes, or cups.

Frozen Coffee Milkshake (café liégeois)

Recipe

225 g ground coffee (8 oz.)
450 ml water (16 fl. oz.)
400 g sugar (14 oz.)
500 ml milk (17 fl. oz.)
half a vanilla bean
750 ml heavy cream or crème fraîche (25.5 fl. oz.)
500 ml Chantilly cream (17 fl. oz.)

Alternative Recipe

20 ml coffee extract (⅔ fl. oz.)
450 ml water (16 fl. oz.)
400 g sugar (14 oz.)
400 ml milk (13.5 fl. oz.)
1 L crème fraîche or heavy cream (34 fl. oz.)
a few drops of vanilla extract
500 ml Chantilly cream (17 fl. oz.)

Procedure

Preparing the Coffee

Bring the water to a simmer and add the ground coffee or the coffee extract and the split vanilla bean or vanilla extract.

Sweetening the Coffee

Add the sugar to the hot coffee and combine well with a whisk. Let the coffee cool.

Filtering the Coffee

When the coffee has cooled, strain it to remove any coffee grounds.

Adding the Milk and the Crème Fraîche

Stir the milk and then the cream into the strong coffee. Combine all the components thoroughly with a whisk.

Churning the Mixture

Churn the mixture until it is semiliquid. Do not wait until it is firm like ice cream or sorbet.

Serving

Serve immediately in coupes that have been previously chilled. Top each serving with a rosette of Chantilly cream.

Café Viennois (Viennese-style Frozen Coffee Milkshake)

Prepare this dessert in the same way as café liégeois or use the following method.

Coat the bottom of each coupe or sundae glass with 25 ml (1 fl. oz.) strong coffee (prepared in the same way as for coffee liégeois). Place a scoop of vanilla and a scoop of coffee ice cream over the coffee and spoon coffee liqueur over both scoops.

Decorate the dessert with a rosette of Chantilly cream.

Other Frozen Milkshake Desserts

Frozen Chestnut Milkshake

500 ml milk (17 fl. oz.)
250 g chestnut puree (9 oz.)
200 g sugar (7 oz.)
650 ml crème fraîche (22 fl. oz.)
500 ml Chantilly cream (17 fl. oz.)

Prepare using the procedure for frozen chocolate cream.

Frozen Vanilla Milkshake

500 ml milk (17 fl. oz.)
1 vanilla bean
250 g sugar (9 oz.)
800 ml crème fraîche (27 fl. oz.)
several drops vanilla extract if needed
500 ml Chantilly cream (17 fl. oz.)

Prepare using the procedure for frozen chocolate milkshake.

Frozen Fruit Milkshake

500 ml milk (17 fl. oz.)
350 g fruit pulp or puree (12.5 oz.)
juice of one lemon
700 ml heavy cream or crème fraîche (23.5 fl. oz.)
500 ml Chantilly cream (17 fl. oz.)

Combine the ingredients and bring the mixture to a simmer. Churn in an ice-cream machine, as for the frozen coffee milkshake.

Frozen Wine or Champagne

500 ml sugar syrup (17 fl. oz.), at 1260 D
300 ml Champagne or white wine (10 fl. oz.)
juice of two lemons
juice of two oranges
500 ml heavy cream or crème fraîche (17 fl. oz.)
500 ml Chantilly cream (17 fl. oz.)

Combine all of the ingredients and strain the mixture through a fine-mesh strainer.

Churn the mixture in an ice-cream machine, as for the frozen coffee milkshake.

Classic Irish Coffee

75 ml hot, sweet, strong coffee (3 fl. oz.)
25 ml good-quality whiskey (1 fl. oz.)
heavy cream

Frozen Irish Coffee

75 ml hot, sweet, strong coffee (3 fl. oz.)
25 ml good-quality whiskey (1 fl. oz.)
1 or 2 scoops vanilla ice cream
whipped cream

Frozen Chocolate Milkshake

Recipe

500 ml milk (17 fl. oz.)
150 g couverture chocolate (5 oz.)
200 g sugar (7 oz.)
750 ml heavy cream or crème fraîche (25.5 fl. oz.)
500 ml Chantilly cream (17 fl. oz.)
vanilla extract, optional

Procedure

Simmering the Flavored, Sweetened Milk

Add the sugar to the milk. Stir it well with a whisk to dissolve it. Chop the chocolate into cubes and add it to the milk. Bring these ingredients to a simmer. Stir the mixture from time to time while it is heating to dissolve the chocolate.

Adding the Heavy Cream or Crème Fraîche

When the milk, chocolate, and sugar have come to a simmer, add the heavy cream or crème fraîche. Combine well with a whisk.

Cook this mixture over a low flame, so that it is at 85° to 90°C (185° to 195°F) for 2 to 3 minutes.
Strain the mixture

Churning and Serving

Churn the mixture and serve it in the same way as the frozen coffee milkshake (café liégeois).

Variation

Pour a tablespoon of chocolate sauce into the bottom of each coupe or sundae glass. Add a scoop of chocolate ice cream to each. Sprinkle the ice cream with chocolate sprinkles and coat with chocolate sauce.

Decorate each with a rosette of Chantilly cream.

Ice-cream sodas

Definition

French ice-cream sodas differ only slightly from the American version, in that they always contain fresh fruit pulp or syrup. They always contain ice cream and sometimes sorbet. They are usually topped with whipped cream.

Recipes

Black Currant Ice-Cream Soda

50 ml black currant pulp (1.5 fl. oz.)
50 ml heavy cream (1.5 fl. oz.), whipped
250 ml carbonated water (8.5 fl. oz.)
2 scoops vanilla ice cream
Chantilly cream to garnish

Strawberry Ice-Cream Soda

50 ml strawberry pulp or syrup (1.5 fl. oz.)
50 g vanilla ice cream (1.5 oz.)
250 ml carbonated water (8.5 fl. oz.)
juice of half a lemon
vanilla extract
1 scoop vanilla ice cream
1 scoop strawberry sorbet
Chantilly cream to garnish

Variations

Other fruits, such as raspberries, blackberries, blueberries, red currants, peaches, pears, cherries, bananas, pineapples, lemons, and oranges can also be used.

Preparation

Gather all the necessary components. Make sure that the ingredients are either fresh or have been properly stored.

Chill the coupes in the refrigerator or freezer.

Procedure

Pour the fruit pulp or syrup into the bottom of the glass.

Add either the ice cream or the whipped cream. Gently mix with the fruit in the glass.

Gently pour the carbonated water along the inside walls of the glass. Rotate the glass so the soda is well distributed. Fill the glass three-quarters full and then add the scoops of ice cream.

Finish filling the glass with carbonated water.

Decorate the ice-cream sodas with Chantilly cream and pieces of fresh fruit.

Serve immediately.

Les frappés glacés (Frappés)

Definition

Frappés are blended frozen drinks containing a combination of ice cream, cold milk, fruit or other flavoring, and sometimes sorbet and heavy cream. They can be served in glasses or coupes.

Uses

Any type of sorbet or ice cream can be used for these refreshing drinks. Below are some examples:

- natural extracts and flavorings: vanilla, coffee, chocolate, hazelnut, almond, caramel
- fruit flavors: black currant, blueberry, strawberry, raspberry, blackberry, lemon, orange
- aromatic plants, wines, or liqueurs can also be used

Equipment

Blender
Ice-cream scoop
Measuring cup

Preparation

Make sure that the ice cream and sorbet is already prepared. Chill the coupes or glasses.

Recipes

Natural Flavorings and Extracts

Vanilla Frappé

1 scoop vanilla ice cream
100 ml very cold milk (3.5 fl. oz.)
20 ml heavy cream or crème fraîche (⅔ fl. oz.)

Coffee Frappé

1 scoop coffee ice cream
100 ml very cold milk (3.5 fl. oz.)
20 ml heavy cream or crème fraîche (⅔ fl. oz.)

Chocolate Frappé

2 scoops chocolate ice cream
100 ml very cold milk (3.5 fl. oz.)

Hazelnut Frappé

1.5 scoops praline ice cream
100 ml very cold milk (3.5 fl. oz.)

Caramel Frappé

2 scoops caramel ice cream
100 ml very cold milk (3.5 fl. oz.)

Fruit

Black Currant Frappé

1 scoop black currant sorbet
100 ml very cold milk (3.5 fl. oz.)
30 ml cold water (1 fl. oz.)
several drops lemon juice

Blueberry Frappé

1 scoop blueberry sorbet
100 ml very cold milk (3.5 fl. oz.)
30 ml cold water (1 fl. oz.)
15 ml blueberry puree (½ fl. oz.)

Strawberry or Raspberry Frappé

1 scoop strawberry or raspberry sorbet
100 ml very cold milk (3.5 fl. oz.)
15 ml cold water (½ fl. oz.)
several drops lemon juice

Aromatic Plants

Mint, Tea, Verbena, Lavender, or Linden Frappé

1 scoop appropriately flavored sorbet
100 ml very cold milk (3.5 fl. oz.)
15 ml cold water (½ fl. oz.)

Liqueurs, Wines, and Liquors

Muscat or Port Wine Frappé

1 scoop of Muscat or port sorbet
100 ml very cold milk (3.5 fl. oz.)
8 ml cold water (½ fl. oz.)
several drops lemon juice

Champagne Frappé

1 scoop Champagne sorbet
100 ml very cold milk (3.5 fl. oz.)
8 ml cold water (½ fl. oz.)
several drops vanilla extract

Kirsch or Vodka Frappé

1 scoop Kirsch or vodka sorbet
100 ml very cold milk (3.5 fl. oz.)
8 ml cold water (½ fl. oz.)
several drops orange or lemon juice

Procedure

Put the ice cream or sorbet in the bottom of the blender. Add the cold milk, the juice or extract, and the crème fraîche or heavy cream if they are being used. Add the cold water. Secure the lid.

Blend the mixture until it is completely smooth.

Serve the frappé immediately in the chilled coupes or glasses with a spoon or

a straw. Cookies (petits fours secs) can be served on the side.

Variation

For fruit frappés, pieces of fresh or canned fruit can be placed in the bottom of the blender and pureed before the addition of the other elements. Once the fruit is pureed, proceed as described above.

Les fruits givrés (Frosted fruits)

Definition

Frosted fruits are fruits from which the pulp has been removed. They are then frozen and filled with a sorbet or ice cream flavored with the fruit being used.

Fruits used for this style of presentation include oranges, lemons, mandarins, grapefruits, pineapples, melons, apples, pears, mangoes, and bananas.

Preparation

Carefully select the fruit. Make sure each is evenly shaped and has no imperfections.

Procedure

Hollowing Out the Fruit

Remove the top of the fruit. The top, which will be used in the presentation, should be approximately 4 cm (1.5 in.) in diameter. An additional round slice can also be cut from the fruit and used as a base to hold the fruit while it is being prepared and for its presentation. This step, however, is optional.

The fruit can be hollowed out with a special machine designed for this purpose or by hand with a small spoon. When hollowing out citrus fruit, the inside of the fruit should be pulled out carefully so that none of the white pulp is removed. Remove the pulp gently, being careful not to damage the skin of the fruit.

Freezing the Fruit

Put the hollowed-out fruit and their covers in the freezer. They should be completely frozen and hard before filling.

Preparing the Sorbet or Ice Cream

Prepare the sorbet or ice cream with the fruit juice or pulp.

Filling the Frozen Fruits

First Method

Fill the frozen fruit with ice cream or sorbet using a pastry bag with a fluted tip. Form a decorative rosette pattern on the top of each one.

Second Method

Fill the frozen fruit with sorbet or ice cream using an ice-cream scoop.

Finish the tops of the frozen fruit by adding a decorative rosette pattern, applied with a pastry bag.

Put the frozen covers on the fruit.

Serving

Each fruit can be decorated with pulled-sugar leaves or candied fruits.

Storing

As soon as they are assembled, place the fruit in a cold freezer, −25°C (−15°F). They will keep for several weeks at this temperature.

Les entremets glacés (Frozen specialties)

Definition

Frozen specialties encompass a wide range of constructed frozen desserts. The variety of frozen desserts available to the pastry chef is almost infinite. Not only is the entire repertoire of classic frozen desserts at his or her disposal, but the wide variety of techniques used for these desserts allows for the improvisation of personal specialties.

These desserts are divided into two main categories:

- *French classic desserts: These include the omelettes norvégienne (similar to baked Alaska), omelettes surprises, frozen vacherins, frozen charlottes, and frozen profiteroles. In this category, traditional techniques and styles of presentation are used.*

- *Frozen cakes: These are cakes prepared in metal cake rings that are 3.5 to 6 cm (1.5 to 2.5 in.) high or, occasionally, in standard génoise molds. The use of these rings allows the pastry chef considerable freedom in choosing the elements of a finished dessert. Here, the pastry chef can create imaginative, innovative preparations.*

Frozen Specialties Discussed

Several types of frozen cakes are presented in the following pages:

A. Omelettes norvégiennes (baked Alaska)
B. Frozen vacherins
C. Frozen charlottes
D. Frozen profiteroles
E. Frozen cakes

L'omelette norvégienne (Baked Alaska)

Definition

A baked Alaska, also called omelette surprise, is a well-known frozen dessert. It consists of one or more sorbets or ice creams encased in génoise and Italian meringue. It is sometimes called omelette surprise because there is no set recipe for what it should contain. The ice creams or sorbets in the middle are usually a surprise. Candied fruits can also be used in the center filling.

Ingredients

For 8 to 10 servings

2 rectangular sheets of génoise
1 sheet of sponge cake
1.5 L sugar syrup (50.5 fl. oz.), at 1260 D
150 ml liquor or liqueur (5 fl. oz.)
750 to 1000 ml sorbet or ice cream (25.5 to 34 fl. oz.)
250 to 300 g Italian meringue or special meringue (see below) (9 to 10.5 oz.)
confectioners' sugar

Recipe for Special Meringue

Italian Meringue Method

4 to 6 egg whites, beaten to almost stiff peaks and stiffened further with 100 g confectioners' sugar (3.5 oz.)
100 g sugar (3.5 oz.), cooked with 30 ml water (1 fl. oz.) to the soft ball stage
vanilla extract
3 egg yolks

The method of preparation is the same as for Italian meringue (see volume 1, pages 82 to 83) except that the additional yolks are quickly folded in at the end.

French Meringue Method

6 egg whites, beaten to almost stiff peaks and stiffened further with 200 g granulated sugar (7 oz.)
3 egg yolks, added quickly to the stiffened egg whites
vanilla extract

Preparation

Use an oval stainless steel or silver serving platter for presenting the finished baked Alaska.

Cut two even rectangles of génoise from a sheet. The two rectangles should measure 10 to 12 cm by 20 to 25 cm (4 to 5 in. by 8 to 10 in.). Trim the corners and edges of the two rectangles so they fit evenly and snugly into the bottom of the oval platter. The easiest way to do this is to place the pieces of cake directly over the platter and trim them following the platter's inner rim.

It is of course possible to trim the cake sections into any shape, but rectangles result in less waste.

Shape a sheet of sponge cake in the same way as the génoise. A third section of génoise can be used instead of the sponge cake.

Before the construction of the baked Alaska begins, it is a good idea to cover the bottom of the platter with a sheet of aluminum foil, but be sure it will not show.

Procedure

Constructing the Baked Alaska

Place the first section of génoise over the sheet of aluminum foil. The génoise should fit evenly over the bottom of the platter. Brush it liberally with the liquor- or liqueur-flavored sugar syrup and coat it with a thick layer of ice cream or sorbet.

If candied fruit is being used, sprinkle it over the ice cream or sorbet at this point.

Cover this layer with the sheet of sponge cake. A third layer of génoise can be used instead of the sponge cake. Brush this layer liberally with the flavored syrup. Cover this second layer with another thick layer of sorbet or ice cream. More candied fruit can also be added at this point if it is being used.

Cover the baked Alaska with the last sheet of génoise and brush it with the liquor- or liqueur-flavored syrup.

Press gently on the top of the baked Alaska to even out its shape.

Put the baked Alaska in a freezer at −20° to −30°C (−5° to −20°F).

Prepare the Italian or special meringue.

After the baked Alaska has been in the freezer for at least an hour, coat both the top and sides with the meringue, using a metal spatula. Decorate the baked Alaska using a pastry bag with a fluted tip. Just before the baked Alaska is to be glazed, sprinkle it with confectioners' sugar. Be sure to wipe off any sugar that has landed on the rim of the platter before glazing.

Glazing the Baked Alaska

Method A

Place the platter holding the baked Alaska on a sheet pan. Place one or more empty cardboard egg cartons on a second sheet pan and place the sheet pan with the baked Alaska on top of this. The egg cartons protect the bottom of the baked Alaska from coming in direct contact with the hot racks or floor of the oven.

Place the two racks with the baked Alaska in a very hot oven, 260° to 270°C (500° to 525°F) to color the surface of the baked Alaska lightly. The coloring should take no longer than 2 minutes. If the baked Alaska stays in the oven too long, the ice cream or sorbet will melt.

Method B

The top of the baked Alaska can also be glazed with a propane torch. Some chefs find this method more convenient and versatile because it allows for more

careful control of the areas to be colored —specifically the pastry bag decoration.

Serving

The baked Alaska can be served as soon as it is ready by pouring hot flaming rum over it in front of the customer. If the baked Alaska has been kept in the freezer, it should be quickly heated in the oven before serving so the rum will flame properly.

Storage

Baked Alaska can be stored for several weeks in a freezer, −20° to −30°C (−5° to −20°F). In commercial establishments, it is usually made ahead of time and kept frozen until needed. Only the coloring in the oven or with the torch is done at the last minute.

Note

Baked Alaska can be filled with any type of ice cream or sorbet. As many layers as desired can be made. To make more layers, just cut the sheets of génoise and the center sheet of sponge cake thinner and use additional layers. Between each layer of cake, spread a layer of ice cream or sorbet.

Les vacherins glacés (Frozen meringues)

Definition

Vacherins are constructed with shells or rings of meringue that are then filled with assorted sorbets and ice creams. They are usually quite high, 10 to 12 cm (4 to 5 in.), and are decorated with ice cream or Chantilly cream using a pastry bag with a no. 17 tip.

Preparation

Vacherins can be prepared in a variety of shapes and styles. See volume 2, pages 170 to 171, Individual Meringues and Meringue Cake Bases.

Meringue Shells

These shells, usually prepared in advance, can vary in height and style. They are generally prepared using one of two methods.

1. A meringue base is prepared by piping out meringue into a spiral round. The round is baked until dry. At the same time, four or five single rings of meringue of the same diameter as the base are also baked until dry. The shell is then constructed by placing these rings on the meringue base and attaching them with raw meringue. The whole construction is then slowly dried in the oven. It is finished with a thin coating of Swiss meringue. Additional decoration can be added at this point with a pastry bag. The shell is then dried once again in very slow oven.

2. Prepare a meringue base as described above. At the same time, prepare strips of meringue about the size of fat ladyfingers, using a pastry bag with a no. 12 tip. Dry these in the oven in the same way as the base. When both the base and the meringue strips have dried, the strips can be attached to the sides of the base with raw meringue and then decorated and baked to firm the seal.

Meringue Bases and Strips

It is best when preparing vacherins on a regular basis to prepare a number of

spiral meringue bases in advance. The meringue strips can also be prepared in advance. They should be piped out with a pastry bag using a no. 12 tip as discussed above or piped into decorative shapes using a fluted tip. They should be baked until completely dry.

If a prepared meringue shell is not being used, the ice cream or sorbet can be placed directly onto the meringue base, with the meringue strips simply pressed directly onto the sorbet or ice cream to form the sides of the cake. The finished cake should then be decorated with Chantilly cream using a pastry bag with a medium-size fluted tip.

Fillings

Regardless of the method used to prepare the base and sides of the vacherin, there are no rules for the types of ice creams or sorbets used as the filling. Any of the varieties discussed in this chapter, as well as candied fruits, chopped toasted nuts, macerated fruits, and fresh fruits, can be used.

Filling the Vacherin

Make sure that all the necessary ice creams or sorbets are at hand.

The meringue shell can be filled by simply scooping in ice cream or sorbet. It is also possible to fill the shell in a more elaborate way, using a metal cake ring. Select a metal cake ring 6 to 8 cm (2.5 to 4 in.) high. Place the ring into the meringue shell or simply on a meringue base. The ice creams or sorbets can then be layered into the cake ring. If several layers of ice cream or sorbet are being used, it is preferable to separate each of them with a thin layer of génoise brushed with liqueur- or liquor-flavored syrup. Make sure that the rings of génoise are prepared in advance so the layers can be constructed quickly; otherwise, the sorbet or ice cream might melt. If either the

ice cream or sorbet begins to melt, place the meringue shell containing the cake ring back in the freezer.

When all the layers are in the cake ring, place the shell and ring in the freezer to ensure that all the layers are frozen solid. Then remove the cake ring. If the cake has been constructed with only a meringue base, place meringue strips on the side of the cake.

The vacherin can then be decorated with Chantilly cream using a pastry bag with a medium-size fluted tip.

The top of the cake can be decorated with candied fruits, marzipan flowers, candied violets, or pulled-sugar decorations.

Variation

Vacherins can also be filled with scoops of ice cream or sorbet. When using this method, fill the meringue shell halfway up with one flavor of ice cream or sorbet.

Place scoops of different-flavored ice creams and sorbets on this base layer. Decorate the entire meringue cake with Chantilly cream using a pastry bag with a fluted tip. Decorate as described above.

Les charlottes glacées (Frozen charlottes)

Definition

Frozen charlottes are frozen desserts that are molded and presented in classic charlotte molds lined with ladyfingers. Usually they are filled with frozen mousse, parfait, a frozen soufflé mixture, or a frozen bavarian cream. Although the filling for frozen charlottes can be flavored according to taste, charlottes are traditionally based on fruit flavors.

Frozen charlottes have recently become extremely popular in France, where they are often available in a wide assortment of flavors and styles. Charlottes keep relatively well, provided the usual precautions for hygiene are followed.

Originally charlottes were constructed in charlotte molds. Today it is more typical to prepare them in metal cake rings.

Constructing the Charlottes

Place a cardboard disk in the freezer to chill. Place a metal cake ring over the frozen cardboard. Make sure the cake ring is at least 6 cm (2.5 in.) high.

Cut a strip of ladyfingers (see volume 2, Using Sponge Cake, pages 146 to 147) into two 6-cm-wide (2.5-in.) strips.

Line the metal cake ring with the ladyfinger strips. Make sure the strips fit tightly.

Place a layer of génoise or sponge cake on the cardboard at the bottom of the ring. Brush it liberally with appropriately flavored sugar syrup.

Fill the cake ring all the way to the top with the chosen frozen filling.

Put the charlotte in the freezer for 3 to 4 hours.

Decoration

Frozen charlottes can be decorated in many ways. Chantilly cream or frozen mousse can be piped out, and chocolate sauce, fruit purees, candied fruits, marzipan flowers, and pulled-sugar decorations can be used as well.

Presentation

Place the frozen charlotte on a doily and remove the cake ring. Frozen charlottes can be served with fruit or chocolate sauce served on the side.

Les profiteroles glacées au chocolat (Frozen profiteroles with chocolate sauce)

Definition

Frozen profiteroles are constructed in much the same way as regular profiteroles except that they are filled with ice cream and kept frozen until served. They should be served with hot chocolate sauce. Usually three to five profiteroles make up one serving, depending on their size.

Procedure

See volume 1, pâte à choux, pages 50 to 53, and volume 2, profiteroles, page 134, and sauce profiteroles, page 85.

Pipe out the pâte à choux into profiteroles using a pastry bag with a no. 7 to no. 9 tip. They can be sprinkled with slivered almonds before baking. After the profiteroles have baked and cooled, they can be filled in one of two ways.

- by poking a hole in the bottom of each with a pastry bag tip and then filling using a pastry bag
- by cutting off the top of each with a serrated knife and then filling the base, using a pastry bag with a fluted tip. When this method is used, the base should be finished with a decorative rosette pattern of ice cream. Replace the lids and place the profiteroles on stainless steel sheet pans in the freezer to firm up the ice cream before serving.

Prepare the chocolate sauce.

Presentation

Stack the profiteroles in a neat pile on a serving platter.

Pour the hot chocolate sauce over the profiteroles at the last minute, just before serving.

Roasted slivered almonds can be sprinkled over the profiteroles after they are covered with chocolate sauce.

Assembling frozen cakes in rings

These frozen cakes are prepared in metal cake rings. The cake rings should be from 3.5 to 6 cm (1.5 to 2.5 in.) high and should be well chilled in the freezer before use. Génoise molds can also be used.

Cake Bases

Frozen cakes are constructed using layers of génoise, sponge cake, meringue, or succès/progrès (see these headings in volume 1).

Fillings

Frozen cakes can be filled with any type of ice cream or sorbet. They can also be filled with frozen mixtures such as bombe mixture, parfait, frozen soufflé mixture, frozen mousse, or frozen sabayon, which do not require an ice-cream machine.

Different types of ice cream or other mixtures can, of course, also be used to form the different layers of the cake.

These cakes should be constructed layer by layer in metal cake rings.

Decoration

The decoration should correspond to the type of filling and flavoring used for the cake. There are no strict rules as to the type or style of decoration that should be used. The pastry chef is free to improvise and express his or her personal style. The table below lists some possible decorative preparations.

Chantilly cream, which should be applied carefully and discreetly	*Italian meringue or the special meringue for baked Alaska*
Sculpted chocolate or marzipan	*Pulled-sugar flowers*
Nougatine, craquelin, toasted almonds, roasted chopped or slivered almonds	*Candied fruits*
Poached or canned fruits	*Coulis and jellies*

Examples of frozen-cake decorations

 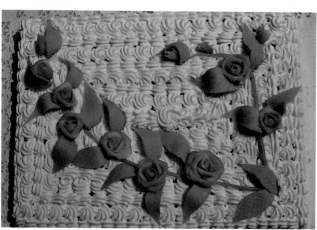

Constructing the Cakes

There are two basic techniques used for constructing frozen cakes in metal cake rings:

Upside-down construction
Upright construction

Upside-down Construction

This method allows the pastry chef to build the cake upside down over its decoration to obtain an inlaid effect (see volume 2, page 149).

Freeze a 4-cm-high (1.5-in.) metal cake ring and place it on a frozen sheet pan covered with a sheet of plastic or parchment paper.

Place candied or macerated fruit inside the ring in a decorative pattern and add a layer of ice cream or other frozen filling. If more than one type of flavor or filling is being used, separate each with a round of génoise or sponge cake. Brush the cake layers with liquor-flavored sugar syrup.

Finish the cake with a layer of meringue, succès/progrès, sponge cake, or génoise, which should come exactly to the top of the cake ring.

Place the cake in the freezer to harden the filling. Depending on the type of filling used, allow 4 to 6 hours in the freezer.

When the cake is thoroughly frozen, flip it over onto a cardboard disk or other support. The surface of the cake can then be given a final glazing with fruit coulis, jelly, or apricot preserves. Let the final glazing set by placing the cake back in the freezer for 10 minutes.

To unmold the cake, wave a propane torch around the sides to detach the metal cake ring, and carefully remove it.

The sides of the cake can now be decorated.

Variation

Ice cream or sorbet can be spread around the inside walls of the frozen cake ring. Trim the cake layers so they will not be seen when the dessert is finished. The final construction is then completed as described above.

Upright Construction

This is the classic method used for constructing cakes in metal cake rings (see volume 2, page 146).

Place a frozen metal cake ring that is about 4 cm (1.5 in.) high on a cardboard disk that is slightly larger than the cake ring.

Place a round layer of sponge cake, meringue, génoise, nougatine, or succès/progrès inside the cake ring, fitting it snugly in the ring and over the cardboard base.

Variation

These cakes can be constructed without interior layers of cake. Only a bottom layer of cake is required. Simply layer the ice creams or other fillings in a decorative way within the cake ring.

Note

Pastry chefs usually prefer to construct cakes using the upside-down method because it has certain advantages:

- Because the presentation surface of the cake is turned down against the surface of the sheet pan or cardboard, it has less chance of being altered or damaged in some way during storage.
- These cakes can be stacked without damaging the presentation surface. This enables the pastry chef to make a large quantity in advance, removing the metal cake rings as the cakes are needed. The final decoration can be done according to the whim of the chef or the specific requests of the customer.

Brush the layer of cake liberally with liquor-flavored sugar syrup (unless using meringue, succès/progrès, or nougatine).

Place the cake in the freezer for 4 to 6 hours, so that the frozen filling hardens. Finish the cake as described above for upside-down construction.

Add the ice cream or other frozen filling. If more than one filling is being used, separate each layer with a layer of some type of cake or meringue.

Finish constructing the cake with a layer of frozen filling. Smooth the cake's surface with a metal spatula. At this point, the surface can be decorated by streaking it with the edge of a serrated knife.

143

Examples of cakes

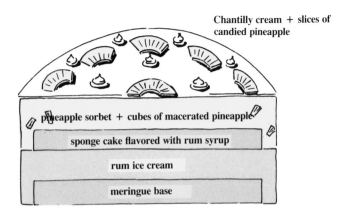

Chantilly cream + slices of candied pineapple

pineapple sorbet + cubes of macerated pineapple

sponge cake flavored with rum syrup

rum ice cream

meringue base

Le Délice des Iles (Island Delight)

Composition
meringue base
rum ice cream
sponge cake flavored with rum syrup
pineapple sorbet + cubes of macerated pineapple

Decoration
slices of candied pineapple
Chantilly cream

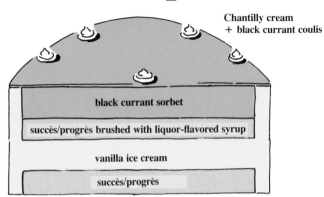

Chantilly cream + black currant coulis

black currant sorbet

succès/progrès brushed with liquor-flavored syrup

vanilla ice cream

succès/progrès

Délice de Dijon (Dijon Delight)

Composition
two layers of succès/progrès
vanilla ice cream (for one layer and sides)
black currant sorbet

Decoration
black currant coulis
Chantilly cream

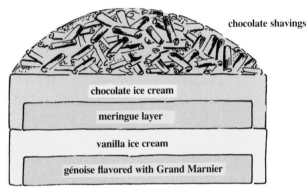

chocolate shavings

chocolate ice cream

meringue layer

vanilla ice cream

génoise flavored with Grand Marnier

Le Jour et Nuit Glacé (Frozen Day and Night Cake)

Composition
génoise base flavored with Grand Marnier syrup
vanilla ice cream
meringue layer
chocolate ice cream

Decoration
chocolate shavings on top

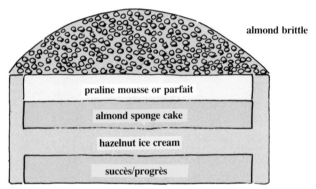

almond brittle

praline mousse or parfait

almond sponge cake

hazelnut ice cream

succès/progrès

Le Noisetier Glacé (Frozen Hazelnut Cake)

Composition
succès/progrès brushed with liquor-flavored syrup
hazelnut ice cream (for one layer and sides)
almond sponge cake soaked with liquor-flavored syrup
praline mousse or parfait

Decoration
almond brittle sprinkled on top

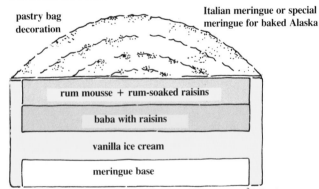

pastry bag decoration

Italian meringue or special meringue for baked Alaska

rum mousse + rum-soaked raisins

baba with raisins

vanilla ice cream

meringue base

Le Stanislas Glacé (Frozen Stanislas Cake)

Composition
meringue base
vanilla ice cream (for one layer and sides)
baba flavored with rum syrup containing raisins
rum mousse + rum-soaked raisins

Decoration
Italian meringue or special meringue for baked Alaska

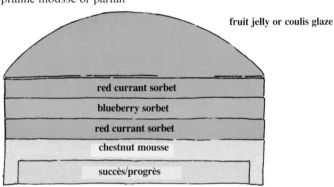

fruit jelly or coulis glaze

red currant sorbet

blueberry sorbet

red currant sorbet

chestnut mousse

succès/progrès

Le Privas (Chestnut-Mousse and Sorbet Cake)

Composition
succès/progrès
chestnut mousse
two layers of red currant sorbet
blueberry sorbet

Decoration
fruit jelly or coulis glaze

144

constructed in rings

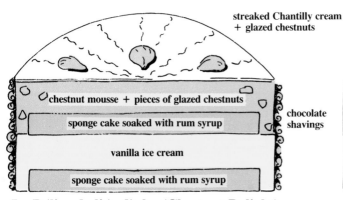

streaked Chantilly cream
+ glazed chestnuts

chocolate
shavings

Le Délice de l'Ardèche (Chestnut Delight)

Composition
two layers of sponge cake soaked
  with rum syrup
vanilla ice cream
chestnut mousse + pieces of glazed
  chestnuts

Decoration
chocolate shav-
  ings on the sides
streaked Chantilly
  cream + glazed
  chestnuts on the top

Chantilly cream and
coffee liqueur candies

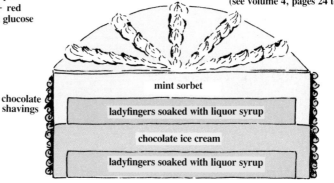

Le Délice Glacé au Moka (Mocha Delight)

Composition
two layers of génoise soaked with
  rum syrup
coffee ice cream
coffee mousse
rum-soaked raisins

Decoration
Chantilly cream
  and coffee li-
  queur candies

Chantilly cream piped
with a fluted tip + red
currant glaze with glucose

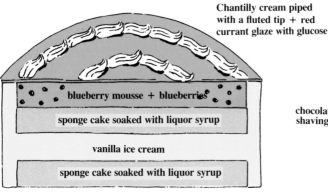

chocolate
shavings

Le Délice du Vivarais (Blueberry Delight)

Composition
two layers of sponge cake soaked
  with liquor syrup
vanilla ice cream (for sides and one
  layer)
fresh, canned, or frozen blueberries
blueberry mousse

Decoration
Chantilly cream
  + red currant
  containing glaze
  glucose (see volume
  4, pages 24 to 25)

Chantilly cream + green
fruit glaze containing glucose
(see volume 4, pages 24 to 25)

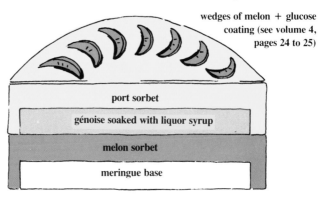

chocolate
shavings

Le Rafraîchissant (Chocolate Mint Cake)

Composition
two layers of ladyfingers (sponge
  cake) soaked with liquor syrup
chocolate ice cream
mint sorbet

Decoration
chocolate shav-
  ings on the sides
Chantilly cream
  and green fruit
  glaze containing
  glucose

toasted slivered almonds
+ couverture chocolate icing

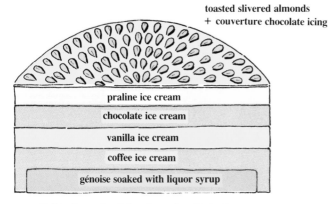

wedges of melon + glucose
coating (see volume 4,
pages 24 to 25)

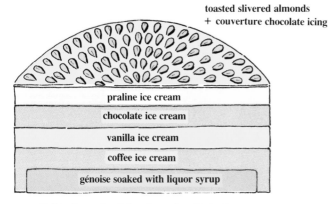

L'Arlequin (Harlequin Cake)

Composition
génoise soaked with liquor syrup
coffee ice cream
vanilla ice cream
chocolate ice cream
praline ice cream

Decoration
toasted slivered
  almonds + cou-
  verture choco-
  late icing (see
  volume 4, page 25)

Le Cavaillon (Melon Cake)

Composition
meringue base
melon sorbet
génoise soaked with liquor syrup
port sorbet

Decoration
wedges of melon
  + glucose coat-
  ing

Examples of frozen cakes

Les bûches glacées (Frozen logs)

Definition

Frozen logs are prepared either in trough-shaped molds (gouttières) specifically for this use or are rolled in the classic way used for making bûches de Noël. Any type of frozen filling can be used for logs.

Frozen logs are usually prepared using génoise or sponge cake and are filled with the same wide variety of frozen fillings used for frozen cakes in general.

Usually frozen logs are decorated using a pastry bag with a flattened fluted tip. In France, these tips are sold under the name "chemin de fer." If a premade flattened tip is unavailable, it is possible to flatten a regular fluted tip. Frozen logs can be coated with ice cream, Chantilly cream, Italian meringue, or the special meringue used for baked Alaska. Frozen logs containing fruit can also be glazed using coulis or jelly glazes containing glucose (see volume 4, pages 24 to 25).

Methods for Preparing Frozen Logs in Cylindrical Molds

A. Direct method
B. Lining the mold with génoise or sponge cake
C. Lining the mold with layered sponge cake (see volume 2, pages 146 to 147)
D. Lining the mold with wrinkled aluminum foil

Method A. Direct Method

Line the inside of a frozen trough-shaped mold with an even layer of ice cream or sorbet. Put the mold back in the freezer for 1 hour to let the layer harden.

Fill the inside of the ice-cream- or sorbet-lined mold with another flavored ice cream or sorbet.

Place a strip of sponge cake, génoise, meringue, or succès/progrès over the top of the ice cream or sorbet.

The different flavors of ice cream can also be separated with thin strips of génoise or sponge cake that have been liberally brushed with flavored sugar syrups.

When all the components have been placed in the mold, place it in the freezer for at least 3 hours before removing the log.

Unmolding the Log

The technique for unmolding the log is similar to removing frozen cakes from cake rings. Dip the bottom of the mold in hot water for several seconds and turn the log out onto a cold strip of cardboard. Place the unmolded log back in the freezer for 10 minutes to firm up the surface before beginning the final decoration

Decorating the Log

Completely cover the surface of the log with ice cream using a pastry bag with a flattened, fluted tip (chemin de fer). The surface can then be worked with a fork dipped in hot water or with a pastry scraper with a serrated edge to imitate the bark of a tree.

Chantilly cream can be used instead of ice cream to cover the logs.

Finishing the Log

Additional decorations can be added to the log, such as marzipan leaves and branches or holly berries and leaves, swirls of Chantilly cream, Christmas decorations, or meringue mushrooms.

Method B. Lining the Mold with Génoise or Sponge Cake

Line the inside of a frozen trough-shaped mold with a thin layer of génoise or sponge cake.

Fill the cake-lined mold with softened ice cream, sorbet, or other frozen filling in successive layers. Each of these layers can in turn be separated with thin layers of génoise or sponge cake. When all the filling and cake layers have been added, place a strip of meringue or génoise on top. This strip will form the base of the cake.

Place the mold in the freezer for 2 hours to allow the fillings to harden.

Unmolding the Log

Turn the mold onto a strip of cardboard and carefully remove the log.

Decorating the Frozen Log

Decorate the log with Italian meringue or the special meringue used for baked Alaska. Use a pastry bag with a flattened, fluted tip.

The decoration can be finished with marzipan leaves and branches.

Finishing the Log

The technique for finishing and serving the log is the same as for baked Alaska.

Variation

Sometimes frozen logs are coated with Chantilly cream instead of Italian meringue.

Method C. Lining the Mold with Layered Sponge Cake

Line the trough-shaped mold with a sheet of parchment paper or plastic wrap.

Line the inside of the paper with round slices of jelly-filled sponge cake (see volume 2, pages 146 to 147). Once the mold is lined with the slices of sponge cake, fill the inside with fruit-flavored ice cream, frozen mousse, or sorbet. Macerated fruits can also be added at this time. When the mold is filled, place a strip of meringue or succès/progrès on top.

Place the mold in the freezer for at least 2 hours to allow the fillings to harden.

Unmolding the Log

Dip the mold in hot water for several seconds to loosen the log. Turn the log out onto a strip of cardboard.

Finishing the Log

Coat the log with a flavored jelly glaze containing 50 percent glucose (see volume 4, pages 24 to 25). Decorate the log with Chantilly cream using a pastry bag with a fluted tip.

Method D. Lining the Mold with Wrinkled Aluminum Foil

Line a trough-shaped mold with a sheet of aluminum foil that has been crumpled and wrinkled in such a way that the surface of the log will have the appearance of bark. Cover the inside of the aluminum foil with a sheet of plastic wrap so that it will be easier to remove from the surface of the ice cream. Freeze the lined mold.

Fill the lined mold with any type of frozen filling. Make sure that the filling used is somewhat soft so that it can be easily molded. The layers of ice cream or other fillings can be separated with thin layers of génoise or sponge cake that have been soaked in liquor-flavored sugar syrup.

When the mold is filled, cover it with a strip of meringue, génoise, sponge cake, or nougatine.

Place the mold in the freezer for at least 2 hours to allow the fillings to harden.

Unmolding the Log

Dip the mold in hot water for several seconds and flip it over onto a strip of cardboard. Remove the sheet of aluminum foil and the plastic wrap from the log.

Decoration

Additional decoration can be added to the log as described for the other three methods.

Preparing Frozen Logs without Molds

The method is the same as when preparing classic logs (see volume 2, page 157).

Preparing the Ice Cream

It is important that the ice cream have the correct soft consistency before it is used in a log. It should have the consistency of butter cream. If the ice cream is kept in an extremely cold deep-freeze, it is a good idea to transfer it to a less-cold freezer the night before it is to be used. The best method, however, is to use ice cream fresh from the ice-cream machine.

Preparing the Génoise

The method is the same as for regular logs and rolled cakes (see volume 2, pages 156 to 157).

Filling and Rolling the Log

It is best to fill frozen logs with ice creams, egg-based ice creams, or sorbets.

Spread the softened ice cream or sorbet over the surface of the génoise or sponge cake using a large metal spatula or a pastry bag with a flattened tip.

Sprinkle the surface of the ice cream with macerated, frozen fruit (optional).

Roll the log in the same way as when preparing regular logs or rolled cakes.

Put the log in the freezer to harden. Coat the log using a pastry bag with a flattened tip. The log is finished in the same way as a classic butter-cream-filled log or rolled cake.

Frozen logs can be decorated in the same way as classic logs.

Variations

Finish the decoration of the log using a pastry bag with a regular fluted or flattened fluted tip using one of the following methods:

- Chantilly cream: create a classic or improvised decoration
- Italian meringue or special baked Alaska meringue: these can be colored just before serving with a propane torch.

These last methods work very well for decorating frozen tree trunks (see photos above).

149

Les crêpes glacées surprises (Frozen filled crêpes)

Definition

These are freshly prepared, hot crêpes that are filled just before serving with frozen preparations such as ice cream, egg-based ice cream, or sorbet. They are often topped with fresh fruit or fruit sauces and syrups.

Composition

To make the crêpes, see the instructions in volume 1, pages 98 to 101. They can be filled with any frozen filling and served with any kind of sweet sauce or topping.

Decoration

Frozen filled crêpes can be decorated with Chantilly cream, fresh or candied fruits, roasted chopped or slivered almonds, almond craquelées, nut brittle, nougatine, sweet sauces, fruit coulis, fruit preserves, or other garniture.

Variation

Any of the possibilities suggested for sundaes (see following pages) can be used to fill crêpes.

Procedure

Using a Single Hot Crêpe

Place the hot crêpe on a dessert plate.

Place two scoops of the frozen ice cream in the center of the crêpe.

Cover the ice cream with fruit. The fruit can be macerated, but this is optional.

Fold the crêpe over itself and decorate with one of the suggestions above. Frozen filled crêpes can also be flambéed in front of the guests.

Using Two or More Hot Crêpes

Place a hot crêpe on a dessert plate.

Place scoops of the chosen flavor of ice cream or sorbet on top of the crêpe.

Sprinkle the ice cream with fresh fruit or other flavorings and cover with a second crêpe. The crêpes can be decorated at this point or another layer can be added.

Decoration

Layers of frozen filled crêpes can be coated with Italian meringue or the special meringue used for baked Alaska (see baked Alaska, page 137). The layer can then be colored at the last minute with a propane torch.

Frozen filled crêpes can be served with petits fours, individual meringues, fruit sauce, or coulis.

Les meringues glacées (Frozen meringues)

Definition

These are decorative meringue shells, similar to vacherins, that are filled with a wide variety of frozen preparations. They are most often filled with ice cream or sorbet and topped with Chantilly cream.

Composition

Meringue shells (see meringues, volume 1, pages 81 to 91), ice cream or sorbet, fresh or candied fruits (macerated fruit can also be used)

Decoration

Frozen filled meringues can be decorated with fresh or canned fruits and fruit sauces.

Procedure

Freeze the dessert plates. Place one or more scoops of ice cream in their centers.

Place decorative prebaked meringue shells around the ice cream. Decorate with Chantilly cream, using a pastry bag with a fluted tip.

The top of the frozen meringue can then be topped with fruit sauce or coulis (this is optional).

Les coupes glacées (Sundaes and parfaits)

Definition

Sundaes are different types of ice creams, sorbets, and/or fresh fruits served in large frozen glasses. They usually include additional ingredients, such fruit sauce, chocolate sauce, crème anglaise, or chopped nuts. The English term *parfait* should not be confused with the French term, which denotes a specific type of ice cream (see page 116). In English usage, a parfait is a layered sundae served in a tall, narrow glass.

Sundaes are popular both in America and France. They are extremely adaptable because they can be made with an almost unlimited variety of ice creams and sorbets and topped with different types of sauces and garnitures.

Preparation

In the following recipes, the quantities of ice cream or sorbet are given in scoops. In some cases, however, it is preferable to fill the coupes or sundae glasses using a pastry bag with a plain or fluted tip. When using a pastry bag, it is important to be extremely well organized, as it is imperative to work quickly so none of the components melts.

When working with ice cream, it is important to remove it from the freezer at least an hour in advance so it is not too hard. If the ice cream is kept in a deep-freeze, it should be transferred to a less cold freezer for several hours (or the night before) so that it can soften.

Place the ice-cream coupes or sundae or parfait glasses in the freezer for at least 10 minutes before filling them.

Check all the pastry equipment, including the ice-cream scoop, the pastry bag and tips, and the plastic pastry scraper, to make sure that it is perfectly clean. Check the cleanliness of the work surfaces.

Prepare all the necessary ingredients in advance, including those to be used for decoration.

Constructing the Sundaes or Parfaits

Direct Method
(most often used)

Place the scoops of ice cream directly in the bottom of the ice-cream coupe or sundae or parfait glass using an ice-cream scoop or a pastry bag.

Add the fruit, nuts, sauces, or other garnitures. Sprinkle the top of the sundae with liquor or liqueur if they are called for in the recipe and top with Chantilly cream.

The top of the sundae can then be decorated with fresh fruit, canned fruit, or other decorations.

On Syrup-Flavored Cakes
(ladyfingers or génoise)

Soak a thin sheet of génoise or pieces of ladyfingers with liquor- or liqueur-flavored sugar syrup. Place the syrup-soaked cake in the bottom of the frozen coupe.

Place the scoops or piped-out ice cream on top of the moistened cake. The final assembly and decoration is the same as when using the direct method.

On a Base of Fruit or Fruit Coulis

Line the walls of the coupe with the fruit garniture, fruit coulis, or other sauce. Sprinkle the fruit or other garniture with an appropriate liqueur or liquor if desired.

Finish adding the scoops of ice cream or sorbet in the same way as when using the direct method.

Sundae suggestions

Melbas

Although these desserts were originally prepared with peaches (peach Melba), other fruits such as pears, strawberries, and black currants can be substituted with equally satisfying results.

History

Peach Melba is one of the great classic French desserts.

It was invented by Auguste Escoffier for the coloratura soprano Nelly Melba, who was staying at the Savoy Hotel in London. One evening, after singing Wagner's *Lohengrin* at Covent Garden, she returned to the hotel to dine with the duc d'Orléans. When the time came for dessert, Escoffier, the most famous chef of the era, had the idea of presenting a peach with vanilla ice cream and raspberry coulis on a swan carved from ice, to pay homage to Nelly Melba and her singing of *Lohengrin*.

Coupe Pêche Melba (Peach Melba)

Composition

2 to 3 scoops vanilla ice cream
1 or 2 peach halves (canned or, preferably, freshly poached and peeled)
Kirsch (optional)
Raspberry or red currant coulis or preserves

Decoration

toasted slivered almonds
Chantilly cream

Coupe Poire Belle Hélène (Pears with vanilla ice cream and chocolate sauce)

Composition

2 to 3 scoops vanilla ice cream
1 to 2 poached or canned pear halves
several drops Kirsch or poire William (optional)

Decoration

hot chocolate sauce
roasted slivered almonds
Chantilly cream

Coupe Exotique (Tropical Sundae)

Composition

1 scoop passion-fruit ice cream
1 scoop lime sorbet
1 scoop coconut ice cream
pineapple cubes soaked in rum

Decoration

Chantilly cream

Coupe du Père Labat (Chocolate Rum Sundae)

Composition

1 or 2 scoops rum ice cream
1 scoop chocolate ice cream
rum-soaked raisins

Decoration

chocolate sauce
Chantilly cream

Banana Split

Composition

2 or 3 different-flavored ice creams
1 banana, sliced lengthwise down the middle
sprinkling of rum (optional)

Decoration

chocolate sauce or fruit sauce, such as raspberry, strawberry, or apricot sauce
Chantilly cream

Coupe Stanislas (Rum Vanilla Sundae)

Composition

1 thin base of savarin, well soaked with rum-flavored sugar syrup
1 to 2 scoops vanilla ice cream
1 scoop rum ice cream

Decoration

Chantilly cream
chocolate sauce (optional)

Coupe Salpicon (Raspberry, Strawberry, and Vanilla Sundae)

Composition

fresh or canned fruits, cut into cubes and macerated in liqueur or liquor
1 scoop vanilla ice cream
1 scoop strawberry sorbet
1 scoop raspberry sorbet

Decoration

Chantilly cream
fruit (optional)

Coupe Coeur Fidèle (Vanilla Chestnut Sundae)

Composition

2 scoops chestnut ice cream
1 scoop vanilla ice cream
pieces of glazed chestnuts

Decoration

Chantilly cream
chocolate sauce

Coupe Cévenole (Blueberry Chestnut Sundae)

Composition

1 scoop vanilla ice cream
1 scoop blueberry sorbet
1 scoop chestnut ice cream

Decoration

Chantilly cream containing chopped blueberries
blueberry coulis

Coupe Marylin (Pistachio Pear Sundae)

Composition

2 scoops pistachio ice cream
1 pear half
several drops Kirsch

Decoration

Chantilly cream
chocolate sauce

Coupe Pralinette (Chocolate Hazelnut Sundae)

Composition

2 to 3 scoops hazelnut ice cream
roasted hazelnuts
chocolate sauce

Decoration

Chantilly cream
hazelnut brittle

Coupe Pompadour (Strawberry Peach Sundae with Grand Marnier)

Composition

1 scoop peach sorbet
1 scoop strawberry sorbet
1 scoop Grand Marnier ice cream
several strawberries macerated in Grand Marnier

Decoration

Chantilly cream

Coupe Abricotine (Apricot Sundae)

Composition

2 to 3 scoops apricot sorbet
candied apricots macerated in orange Curaçao

Decoration

Chantilly cream
roasted slivered almonds

Coupe Arlésienne (Vanilla Ice Cream with Candied Fruits)

Composition

ladyfingers soaked in curaçao-flavored sugar syrup
macerated candied fruits
macerated raisins
2 to 3 scoops vanilla ice cream
vanilla crème anglaise

Decoration

Chantilly cream

Coupe Bébé (Caramel Peach Sundae)

Composition

½ poached or canned peach
2 scoops peach ice cream
1 scoop caramel ice cream
caramel sauce

Decoration

Chantilly cream
nut brittle

Coupe Arlequin (Rum, Vanilla, and Chocolate Sundae)

Composition

ladyfingers soaked in rum-flavored sugar syrup
1 scoop vanilla ice cream
1 scoop chocolate ice cream
macerated raisins

Decoration

Chantilly cream
chocolate sauce

Coupe Antillaise (Pistachio, Vanilla, and Banana Sundae)

Composition

ladyfingers soaked in Curaçao-flavored sugar syrup
1 to 2 scoops pistachio ice cream
1 scoop vanilla ice cream
banana slices sprinkled with Curaçao

Decoration

Chantilly cream

Coupe Antoinette (Anisette Sundae)

Composition

ladyfingers sprinkled with anisette
2 to 3 scoops vanilla ice cream
diced candied fruit macerated in liquor or liqueur

Decoration

Chantilly cream

Coupe Andalouse (Apricot Vanilla Sundae)

Composition

2 scoops apricot sorbet
1 scoop vanilla ice cream
apricots soaked in Curaçao
roasted slivered almonds

Decoration

Chantilly cream

154

Coupe Croquante (Chocolate Almond Sundae)

Composition

1 scoop chocolate ice cream
1 to 2 scoops praline ice cream
almond brittle

Decoration

Chantilly cream flavored with praline paste
roasted whole almonds

Coupe Fleur de Paris (Caramel, Chocolate, and Fruit Parfait)

Composition

1 scoop caramel ice cream
1 scoop chocolate ice cream
1 scoop lemon sorbet
1 scoop mint sorbet
caramel sauce

Decoration

Chantilly cream
chocolate shavings

Coupe Isabelle (Vanilla Rum Sundae)

Composition

2 scoops rum ice cream
1 scoop vanilla ice cream
raisins macerated in rum

Decoration

Chantilly cream
chocolate sauce

Coupe Brasilia (Banana Caramel Sundae)

Composition

banana slices macerated in Cointreau
1 scoop caramel ice cream
1 scoop banana ice cream
crème anglaise
nut brittle

Decoration

Chantilly cream

Coupe Amarena (Cherry Sundae)

Composition

1 scoop Kirsch ice cream
1 scoop cherry sorbet
1 scoop vanilla ice cream
cherry liqueur or Grand Marnier

Decoration

Chantilly cream
maraschino cherries

Coupe Délice (Peach, Pear, and Apple Sundae)

Composition

chunks of apples, pears, and peaches
1 scoop apple sorbet
1 scoop pear sorbet
1 scoop peach sorbet
chocolate sauce or Calvados

Decoration

Chantilly cream

155

Coupe Surprise du Chef (Assorted-Fruit Parfait)

½ scoop pineapple sorbet
½ scoop raspberry sorbet
½ scoop mandarin sorbet
½ scoop pear sorbet
½ scoop black currant sorbet
½ scoop peach sorbet
½ scoop vanilla ice cream
½ scoop pistachio ice cream
pieces of fresh or canned fruits (pears, peaches, pineapples, raspberries, black currants)

Decoration

Chantilly cream
nut brittle
roasted slivered almonds

Coupe des Alpes (Honey Vanilla Sundae)

Composition

2 scoops honey ice cream
1 scoop vanilla ice cream
roasted slivered almonds and hazelnuts

Decoration

Chantilly cream

Coupe Désirée (Strawberry, Grand Marnier, and Cherry Sundae)

Composition

2 scoops strawberry sorbet
1 scoop Grand Marnier ice cream
cherries macerated in Kirsch

Decoration

Chantilly cream

Coupe Légère (Herb Tea Sundae)

Composition

1 scoop verbena tea sorbet
1 scoop linden tea sorbet
1 scoop tea sorbet
juice of two lemons

Decoration
thinly sliced lemons

Coupe Caprice (Chestnut Berry Sundae)

Composition

chocolate ladyfingers soaked in rum-flavored sugar syrup
1 scoop chestnut ice cream
1 scoop blueberry sorbet
1 scoop blackberry sorbet
crème de cassis liqueur

Decoration

Chantilly cream
walnut halves

Coupe Canaries (Banana, Pineapple, and Vanilla Sundae)

Composition

ladyfingers soaked in liquor-flavored sugar syrup
diced or sliced bananas
1 scoop vanilla ice cream
1 scoop banana sorbet
1 scoop pineapple sorbet

Decoration

Chantilly cream
chocolate spaghetti or shavings

Coupe Béatrice (Blueberry Peach Sundae)

Composition

2 to 3 scoops blueberry sorbet
1 poached or canned peach half

Decoration

Chantilly cream
chocolate sprinkles or shavings

Coupe Belle Epoque (Cherry Vanilla Sundae)

Composition

macerated sour cherries
1 scoop vanilla ice cream
1 scoop cherry sorbet
cherry cream sauce
crème anglaise
nut brittle

Decoration

Chantilly cream
sour cherries

Coupe Délire (Delirious Parfait)

½ scoop blueberry sorbet
½ scoop hazelnut ice cream
½ scoop pear sorbet
½ scoop caramel ice cream
½ scoop mint sorbet
½ scoop chocolate ice cream
pieces of pears, peaches, and bananas

Decoration

Chantilly cream
blueberry or chocolate sauce
meringue shells

Coupe Arc-en-ciel (Rainbow Parfait)

Composition

assortment of sorbets: lemon, pineapple, orange, strawberry, raspberry, black-berry, black currant, melon, mango, and passion fruit are just a few of the possibilities

Decoration

fresh fruit coulis

Coupe Délice de Cavaillon (Melon Sundae)

Composition

2 to 3 scoops melon sorbet
melon balls or pieces macerated in Cointreau

Decoration

Chantilly cream

Coupe Tendresse (Passion-fruit Peach Sundae)

Composition

2 to 3 scoops passion-fruit sorbet
chunks of fresh or canned peaches

Decoration

Chantilly cream

Coupe Mercédès (Strawberry Vanilla Sundae)

Composition

candied or fresh strawberries
strawberry coulis flavored with Kirsch
2 scoops praline ice cream
1 scoop vanilla ice cream
nut brittle

Decoration

Chantilly cream
strawberries

Coupe Charmante (Black Currant Sundae)

2 to 3 scoops black currant sorbet
assorted diced fruits
crème de cassis liqueur

Decoration

Chantilly cream
black currants

Coupe Bamba (Rum Lemon Sundae)

Composition

diced fruit macerated in rum
2 to 3 scoops lemon sorbet
candied lemon zests

Decoration

Chantilly cream

157

Ice sculpture

Definition

Although ice sculpture requires considerable skill and practice, the raw ingredient is simply frozen water. In traditional buffet presentations, ice sculpture plays a role in showcasing frozen desserts, ice creams, and even certain drinks and aperitifs. Ice sculptures sometimes serve as pedestals or even as containers for cold foods and drinks, but usually they are purely decorative.

Occasionally, ice sculptures are also made by freezing water in special molds, but professionals tend to use this method only to make small sections of a larger sculpture. The traditional techniques of ice sculpture, hewing the ice with a series of sharp tools, is one of the most artistic areas of the pastry chef's work. Of all the different methods used by the pastry chef to enhance the presentation of fine foods, ice sculpture is one of the most fanciful and creative.

Despite the beauty and appeal of ice sculpture, it is only rarely executed. This is probably because of the considerable work and skill required to create something that will last only a few hours. Ice sculptures are also extremely heavy and cumbersome to carry and store.

Not only does ice sculpture require considerable skill, but a set of expensive tools and equipment is also needed.

Large freezers are necessary to store the finished sculptures and the large blocks of ice used as the raw material.

Preparation

The first stage in the preparation of an ice sculpture is the choice of the subject. In America, blocks of ice come in standard blocks of 300 pounds each. With the necessary equipment, the pastry chef can also prepare his or her own blocks of ice appropriate to the needs of a particular sculpture. This is particularly effective for small ice sculptures, for which standard pastry equipment can be used to freeze the blocks. Examples of small subjects, shown in the above photo, include little angels, miniature animals, candelabras, doves, and swans.

Preparing the Blocks of Ice

The blocks of ice must be frozen several days in advance. This is especially true for large blocks that require considerable time to freeze all the way through. In general, allow 24 to 72 hours for complete freezing. The length of time, of course, depends to some degree on the temperature of the freezer.

Several methods can be used to prepare blocks of ice. Whatever the method, however, be careful that the blocks are well formed and do not contain cracks or large air pockets. Inexperienced pastry chefs sometimes forget that water expands once it starts to freeze. Take this into consideration when choosing a container for the block.

As water freezes, it tends to freeze from the outside in. This can be a problem, because a sheet of ice is likely to form on the outside surface of the block before it has frozen all the way through to the center. When the center finally does freeze, it expands and causes the outer section of the block, which has already frozen, to crack. For this reason, it is necessary to break up the outer layer of frozen ice from time to time during the freezing of the block.

First Method

Fill a metal tray with very cold water. Make sure the water is as cold as possible. Place the container of water in the freezer, but avoid placing it directly on the floor. At this point, the water can be colored or filled with flowers and other ornaments if this style of decoration is desired.

Protect the container of water from the floor of the freezer by placing it on several cake racks or a refrigerator or freezer rack or on several layers of cardboard. This prevents the water on the outer surface of the container from freezing too quickly.

Regularly check the water to make sure that it is not freezing too quickly. If ice starts to form on the walls of the container or on the top surface, break it apart. An ice pick or sharp knife works best for this.

If a block of ice 60 × 30 × 20 cm (24 × 12 × 8 in.) is desired and if 15°C (60°F) water is placed in a freezer at −20°C (−5°F), it will probably be necessary to break up the ice after the first 8 hours and every 6 to 8 hours after that. Plan to break up the ice at least three times while it is freezing.

Approximately 48 hours will be necessary to freeze the above example under the given conditions.

Second Method

Place thin sheets of water on clean, flat sheet pans. Place these in the freezer until thin layers of ice form. Break the ice up and place it in a deep tray as explained above. Fill the tray with cold water to the desired level. From this stage on, the procedure is the same as for the first method.

This second method has the advantage of requiring that the ice be broken up only once while freezing. It is also quicker.

It is also possible to modify this method by simply using ice cubes for the first stage. A large number of ice cubes are, of course, required so it is best to use this method only if a large ice-making machine is available.

Additional time can also be saved if a water cooler is available. It provides very cold water, which hastens the freezing.

Third Method

Some pastry chefs like to add a small amount of salt or potassium nitrate (which functions in the same way) to the water before freezing. This provides a softer ice that is easier to sculpt. There are two main disadvantages to this method, however. Ice containing salt freezes at a lower temperature than plain ice, so more time and a colder freezer is required. Moreover, salted ice also melts more quickly, so the sculpture will not last as long once presented.

The technique for freezing salted ice is the same as discussed above. Add 5 g (1 tsp.) of salt or potassium nitrate per L (34 fl. oz.) of water. It is best to dissolve the salt or potassium nitrate in hot water to ensure it is thoroughly dissolved before adding it to the cold water.

Although ice is easiest to work with when it is at a temperature of −5°C (23°F), it is rarely at this temperature because freezers are usually considerably colder.

When ice is transferred to another freezer in order to bring it to a more workable temperature, allow at least 48 hours for the temperature change to reach the center of the block.

Equipment

It is difficult to give an exact list of the equipment needed to sculpt ice. Each chef has his or her personal preferences. Usually, however, several different-size chisels represent the absolute minimum.

Equipment for the Preliminary Shaping

Japanese ice sculptors use special long saws with thin pointed teeth, which work particularly well for ice sculpture. Because these are hard to obtain in both France and America, the second-best instrument is a small electric chain saw. A chain saw has the advantage of being fast even when the ice is hard.

Chain saws are extremely dangerous. It is important not only to take the standard precautions for working with chain saws but certain precautions particular to cutting ice as well.

Even though chain saws are usually well insulated, remember that, as the ice starts to melt, you will be standing on a wet floor. For this reason it is advisable to wear rubber boots as an added precaution against electric shock.

Remember also that working with a chain saw always causes chips of ice to spatter. Always wear a thick apron or even two thick canvas aprons separated by sheets of plastic. A long bibbed apron is advisable to protect the legs and torso from accidents. Goggles should be worn to protect the eyes. Always hold the chain saw steadily with two hands. Make sure that the cord is always behind you.

Equipment for Sculpting

Many different tools are used for sculpting ice, but in general they are the same kinds of tools as those used for wood sculpture. Long chisels, 40 to 60 cm (16 to 24 in.) are best. They should have good solid handles because considerable force is required to cut the ice. Make sure that all the tools are kept sharp. Chisels for ice sculpture are usually sharpened on only one side of the blade, like scissor blades.

Equipment for Smoothing

A hacksaw blade is useful for giving the final touches to small or fragile sections of a sculpture. A hard sponge or a wool rag can also be used to round off or smooth edges.

Preparation

The solid block of ice can be unmolded in several ways:

a. Dip the container holding the ice in warm water (water that is too hot can cause the ice to crack).

b. Turn containers with large blocks over onto a large rack (such as an oven rack). Wipe the back of the container with a towel soaked in hot water. Pull off the container.

c. Transfer the ice to a large or walk-in refrigerator set at 0°C (32°F) and leave it for 10 to 12 hours. If there is enough time, this is the best method. The block will not only be easier to remove from the mold, but will be softer and easier to carve.

Carving the Ice

Tips

When first learning how to carve ice, work on subjects with simple lines (for example, fish). This allows time to familiarize yourself with the texture and feel of the ice. It also will allow for the development of some of the basic techniques of ice sculpture.

Once these basic techniques are familiar, it is quite easy to progress to larger and more elaborate shapes, such as swans, deer, or angels. As the ice sculptures become larger, the general shape and contour will take on more importance.

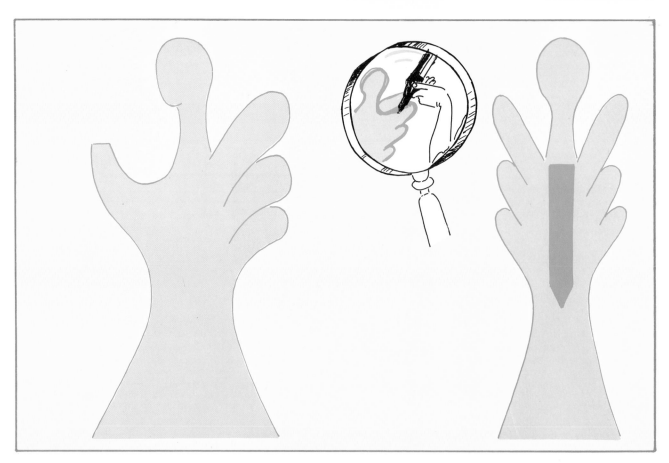

Know your subject! Before beginning the actual cutting of the ice, it is important to visualize clearly the basic shapes and surfaces of the sculpture. To do this, it is often helpful to draw the basic lines of the sculpture on a blackboard. Try to make a drawing that is the actual size of the projected sculpture. Sculpting a smaller version of the subject from another material, such as modeling clay, may also be helpful.

When working with a model, place the model directly in front of where you will be sculpting the ice. Make sure the angle of the model is the same as the positioning of the ice.

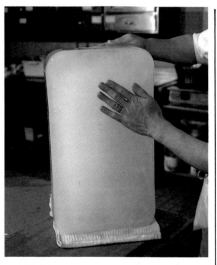

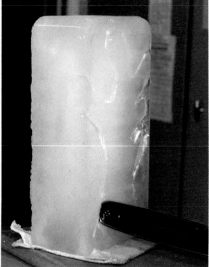

Preliminary Shaping

1. Examine the block of ice to see if it symmetrical. Note if there are any cracks or chips. If there are, try to position the block so they will end up on the least visible sides of the sculpture. Find the nicest-looking side of the block and designate it for the first outline of the sculpture.
2. Make sure that the base of the block is perfectly flat. If not, cut a slice off the end of the ice with the chain saw to make sure that it is flat.

3. Place the block of ice on a wet towel placed on a cutting board. The towel will help prevent the block from sliding. The cutting board elevates the block slightly so it is easier to cut all the way down to the base.

Check to make sure that the block of ice is seated firmly on the work surface. It is best to set the block on a solid work table. Ideally, the base of the block should be at waist level.

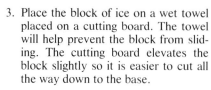

4. Cut a coarse outline of the sculpture into the side of the ice with the tip of the chain saw.

5. Remove sections of ice that will not be needed in the final sculpture. Be sure to keep the ice well balanced.

6. Cut the front of the sculpture and then the back.

7. Brush over the cut surfaces of the ice with the chain saw to make the profile as even as possible.

At this point it is advisable to stand back from the ice to see if the basic shape and proportions are correct. The finishing touches will be given to the sculpture with hand tools.

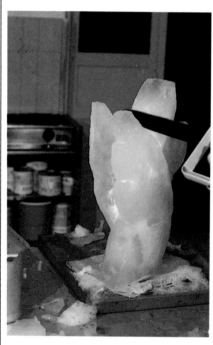

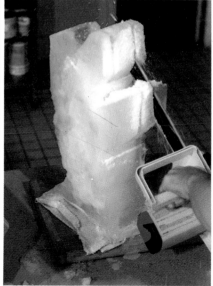

When carving the ice with the hand tools, treat the ice gently to prevent it from chipping.

Never strike the ice with the equipment. This can cause it to crack.

When using a chisel, always keep the flat side (the unsharpened side) against the ice (see drawing on page 160).

When carving with the chisel, the left hand should guide the blade and keep it

at a 30- to 45-degree angle in relation to the surface of the ice. The right hand directs the chisel and provides the force. Try to avoid a jerky or chipping movement when using the chisel, as this can cause the ice to crack.

Always be conscious of the size and shape of tool that should be used on a particular area of the sculpture.

Finishing the Sculpture

Finish the more fragile sections of the ice sculpture (such as angel wings) before moving on to the more solid parts. Otherwise, the fragile parts are liable to break.

Final Checking

At this stage, it is important to stand back from the sculpture and view it from several different angles. Remember that it will be seen from different positions once it is on display.

Polishing and Smoothing the Sculpture

Now the finishing touches can be added to the sculpture. A hacksaw blade is particularly well suited to this. When using a hacksaw blade, hold one end in each hand and keep the blade at a 30-degree angle in relation to the surface of the ice.

Feel the surface of the ice with the palms of the hands to determine if the surface is smooth and even.

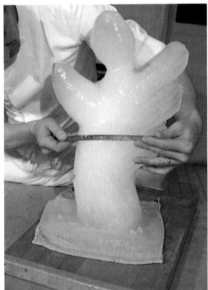

Finish polishing the surface of the ice with a scrub pad or woolen rag. Wool gloves are also useful for polishing and moving the sculpture.

At times, the pastry chef may wish to highlight certain elements (such as the eyes of an animal) of the ice sculpture by using colors. Traditionally, however, ar-

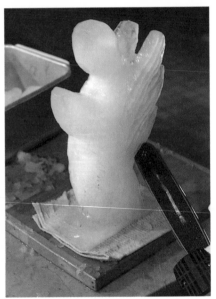

Enhancing the Presentation

It is sometimes advantageous to present the ice sculpture, which is usually white, with colored crushed ice to provide an attractive background. Crushed ice that has been lightly tinted blue works particularly well. Pulled-sugar decorations are also an attractive accompaniment to ice sculpture.

Fresh-cut flowers are often presented with ice sculpture. Their bright colors lend a dramatic effect to the stark white of the sculpture.

Note

In the examples and photos presented above, we have avoided giving specific examples of decoration, preferring to give free rein to the creativity of the reader.

tificial colors are never used. Instead, colored objects such as flowers were actually frozen in the ice before it was sculpted.

Ice sculptures should be presented just before guests arrive to prevent the sculptures from melting before the guests can appreciate them.

Presenting the Ice Sculpture

Ice sculptures should be presented on racks set inside deep metal trays, so they do not get the tables and the reception area wet. The tray and racks should be covered with a clean, presentable tablecloth.

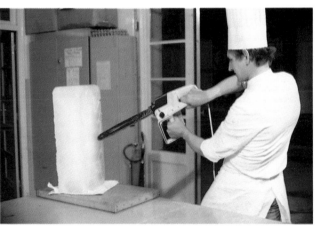

Chapter 4 Sugar work

〰〰〰〰〰〰〰

Introduction

Sugar work requires the mastery of various techniques; it is an important means of decoration and is perhaps the most artistic area of pastry making.

The eight types of sugar work	
1. Pastillage	5. Poured sugar
2. Molded sugar	6. Turned sugar
3. Rock sugar	7. Pulled sugar
4. Spun sugar	8. Blown sugar

This section is devoted to the eight categories of sugar work, specifically the various techniques and difficulties involved in each.

The categories listed here are arranged from the easiest to the most difficult. Learning in this order will help develop skills necessary for understanding the types that follow. Sometimes techniques or difficulties will overlap within two categories; for example, some pieces made out of pastillage, a fairly easy medium, may be more difficult to build than pieces made from blown sugar, a more difficult medium to prepare.

Definition

Except for pastillage, the categories for sugar work are based on cooked sugar, although each is prepared in a different way. The cooking of the sugar and recipes in each category are very much alike; how they are prepared after cooking varies.

The difficulty of this work will largely depend on the individual. Sugar work is considered an art form and requires the same creative abilities as any art form, including understanding the harmony of colors and being able to work with the hands in an inventive way.

This section will give the reader a good foundation for sugar work. Improving from this point requires hours of practice to develop manual dexterity and an understanding of the techniques.

Choosing the Proper Raw Materials

Sugar (Sucrose)

It is important to use as pure a granulated sugar as possible, meaning sugar free of impurities such as flour and dust that might fall into an open bin. It is best to use sugar cubes or sugar from small, closed packages, which are more likely to be clean.

Cooking Sugar

Before working with sugar, it is important to understand its structure. The sugar used in cooking—granulated, confectioners', and the like—is sucrose, a disaccharide made up of two simple sugars:

• glucose (also called dextrose)
• fructose (also called levulose)

Sucrose can be purchased in several forms, which will be discussed below under the heading of raw materials.

The temperature at which glucose molecules liquefy so that they are completely dissolved in water is considerably lower than that for fructose, and so also for sucrose, which contains fructose. Thus, the more glucose in a recipe (in the form of glucose syrup, for example), the lower the temperature at which the sugar will dissolve. A recipe high in glucose will have the same consistency at a low temperature as a recipe low in glucose at a higher temperature does. This is why different recipes require different temperatures to reach the same density.

When cooking sugar, it is really the consistency and density that are important, more so than the temperature. The temperatures given correspond to specific consistencies and densities. As the quality of the sugar can vary (companies usually maintain consistency, although seasonal changes can affect the sugar), it may be necessary to adjust the temperature through trial and error until the proper consistency is reached.

Although a recipe high in glucose is cooked to a lower temperature than one low in glucose, as more acid (cream of tartar or lemon juice) is used in a recipe, a higher temperature will be required.

Some form of acid is sometimes used when cooking sugar to help break down the sucrose into its two component sugars, glucose (dextrose) and fructose (levulose) when cooked in water (this process is called hydrolysis). The acid also prevents the sugar from crystallizing as it cooks.

Adding acid to sugar can cause the finished product to sweat or melt quickly. It therefore should not be used during periods of high humidity, when raining, or in coastal areas.

Glucose Syrup

Glucose syrup is often used in cooking sugar. Glucose syrup is a compound consisting of dextrose, maltose, and dextrine and should not be confused with the simple sugar glucose. When glucose is called for in recipes throughout the four volumes of this series, use glucose syrup. It should be clean and free of dust or other foreign matter. Glucose can also be found in a powder form (rarely used), which is highly concentrated and should be diluted in water or other liquid from the recipe before adding it to the sugar and cooking.

The recipes for the various types of sugar work differ only slightly. It is therefore important to follow the advice and corresponding temperatures given for each recipe (see the chart on cooking sugar, page 166).

Liquid (Water)

Almost all liquid used for cooking sugar is pure water. Avoid hard water (high in minerals), which could affect the finished product and cause small grains to appear in some types of sugar work, such as pulled and blown sugar, which should have a smooth, satiny look.

Acids

Used in small quantities, acids help hydrolyze (break down) the sucrose to prevent crystallization. It is important to be exact when measuring the amount needed.

An acid in powder form (cream of tartar) is usually diluted in some of the liquid taken from the recipe before adding it to the sugar.

Acid in liquid form (lemon juice or vinegar) is added to the cooking sugar just before the final temperature is reached.

Coloring

Food coloring exists in various forms and is used accordingly. When using a powder, dissolve it in a little boiling water and dilute with a strong, clear liquor so the color is not affected. Powdered or paste coloring are diluted in clear, strong liquors, rather than in water. The liquor will quickly evaporate when it comes in contact with the hot cooked sugar and so will not dilute the sugar as water would.

Cooked sugar is colored either

- halfway through the cooking
- at the end of cooking

When colorings are added after cooking, it is possible to separate the cooked sugar into batches before cooking so more than one color can be made from one batch of cooked sugar.

Note

Cooked sugar stirred to make it crystallize (fondant, molded sugar, and rock sugar) tends to sweat less, is less susceptible to humidity, and stores well. Once this type of sugar is recooked, it is difficult to make it recrystallize. When cooking with fondant, it is best to use the following recipe:

15 ml vinegar (1 Tbsp.)
1 to 2.5 ml cream of tartar (¼ to ½ tsp.)
1 kg white fondant (35 oz.)

Cook to 160° to 162°C (320° to 323°F).

Variations of this recipe can be used for thread, poured, turned, pulled, and blown sugar. The chart below can be used as a guide for variations on recipes for sugar work (other than pastillage). It is good to experiment with these recipes to see which works best for the type and quality of sugar available and the climate.

Recipes for Cooking Sugar

Sugar	Glucose	Acid	Cream of Tartar	Water	Temperature
1 kg granulated sugar (35 oz.)	250 g (9 oz.)	—	—	400 ml (13.5 fl. oz.)	148°C (298°F)
1 kg granulated sugar (35 oz.)	150 g (5 oz.)	—	—	350 ml (12 fl.oz.)	150°C (302°F)
1 kg sugar cubes (35 oz.)	100 g (3.5 oz.)	—	1 g (¼ tsp.)	350 ml (12 fl. oz.)	153°C (307°F)
1 kg sugar cubes (35 oz.)	100 g (3.5 oz.)	1 ml lemon juice (¼ tsp.)	1 g (¼ tsp.)	350 ml (12 fl. oz.)	155°C (311°F)
1 kg sugar cubes (35 oz.)	15 g (1 Tbsp.)	—	2 g (½ tsp.)	400 ml (13.5 fl. oz.)	160°C (320°F)
1 kg sugar cubes (35 oz.)	—	—	2 g (½ tsp.)	400 ml (13.5 fl. oz.)	160°C (320°F)
1 kg fondant (35 oz.)	—	15 ml vinegar (1 Tbsp.)	1 g (¼ tsp.)	—	162°C (323°F)

Raw Materials

Raw Materials	Effects	When to Add	Precautions, Advantages, Inconveniences
Glucose	Slows crystallization	After water comes to a boil	Lowers the final cooking temperature Must be weighed carefully
Cream of Tartar	Aids in hydrolyzing sugar Slows crystallization	Mix with sugar before adding water, or better, dilute in water used for cooking sugar and add before cooking	Dries out the sugar, raises final cooking temperature Final product is more sensitive to humidity Pours more easily
Acids (citric, lemon juice, vinegar)	Prevents grains in final product	At the end of cooking	Use in small amounts; for example, 1 g cream of tartar (¼ tsp.) to 200 g glucose (7 oz.) Final product will sweat more readily Changes final cooking temperature

Le pastillage
(Pastillage)

History

The word *pastillage* first appeared in the beginning of the nineteenth century in the *Universal Dictionary of the French Language* by Claude Boiste. Originally a variation of the batter was used to make lozenges called pastilles, the derivation of the word pastillage.

Pastillage was often used during the nineteenth century, when presentation pieces were more popular.

Antonin Carême was the most talented chef and pastry chef of his time. He created many presentation pieces out of pastillage, sculpting temples, fountains, and castles in remarkable detail.

In Mexico, a type of pastillage called *alfeñique* is still used for funeral ceremonies to make birds, mermaids, lambs, flowers, and pitchers.

In France, pastillage is usually used only for gala events or competitions to make large display pieces or small pieces such as animals, figurines, and flowers.

Definition and Use

The batter for pastillage is based on confectioners' sugar and is dried until firm after being shaped. While moist, it is pliable and can be colored. The batter is not particularly difficult to make, stores well, and is used to create a variety of shapes. Pastillage can be considered the modeling clay of the pastry chef.

Pastillage is used only for decorative purposes; it is not edible.

Depending on the size of the piece made, it takes approximately 48 hours for individual pieces to dry before they can be assembled. For each millimeter (¹⁄₁₆ in.) of thickness, allow 24 hours for a piece to dry thoroughly.

A few drops of citric acid or lemon juice added to the batter will act as a bleach for pieces that are to be left white. A small drop of blue coloring will also help brighten white, uncolored pastillage.

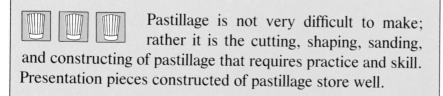 Pastillage is not very difficult to make; rather it is the cutting, shaping, sanding, and constructing of pastillage that requires practice and skill. Presentation pieces constructed of pastillage store well.

Equipment

Fine-mesh drum sieve, pastry cutter, small bowl, small saucepan, measuring cup, plastic wrap

Recipes

1.5 kg confectioners' sugar (53 oz.)
16 g gelatin (½ oz.), approximately 8 sheets
125 ml water (4 fl. oz.)
juice of half a lemon

Alternative Recipe A

1 kg confectioners' sugar (35 oz.)
10 g gelatin (⅓ oz.), approximately 5 sheets
50 ml water (1.5 fl. oz.)
50 ml white distilled vinegar (1.5 fl. oz.)

Alternative Recipe B

750 g confectioners' sugar (26.5 oz.)
150 g cornstarch (5 oz.)
50 g gum arabic (1.5 oz.)
150 to 200 g egg whites (5 to 7 oz.)

Alternative Recipe C

1 kg confectioners' sugar (35 oz.)
75 g gum arabic (2.5 oz.)
5 to 6 egg whites, strained

Alternative Recipe D

250 g confectioners' sugar (9 oz.)
250 g cornstarch (9 oz.)
150 g rice flour (5 oz.)
25 g gum arabic (1 oz.)
2 to 3 egg whites, strained
several drops lemon juice

Preparation

Before the pastillage is made, it is important to prepare the molds or templates to be used. Although pastillage can be covered to prevent it from drying out during use, if left out for long periods of time, it loses its malleability and will be difficult to work with, cracking or tearing easily and producing a weak structure.

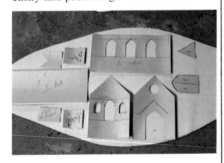

Procedure

Soak the sheets of gelatin in cold water to soften them.

Sift the confectioners' sugar through a fine-mesh drum sieve directly onto a clean marble, forming a mound.

Drain the sheets of gelatin and gently squeeze out the excess water. Dissolve the gelatin in 125 ml (4 fl. oz.) of water (if using the first recipe) over low heat, stirring constantly with a very clean wooden spatula. Only warm the mixture enough

to dissolve the gelatin. The water must never come to a boil, or the gelatin will be rendered useless.

Pour the water and gelatin in a well made in the mound of confectioners' sugar. Add the lemon juice or citric acid if used.

Incorporate the confectioners' sugar with the fingertips into the well of liquid

until all is added. Occasionally scrape the marble so the batter is brought into one pile.

Work the batter with two hands and fraise (scrape the batter against the marble) until homogeneous.

The batter should now be smooth, white, and have the consistency of sweetened tart dough. It should be malleable so that it can be easily rolled out without cracking.

Note

If the pastillage is to be colored, it is best to add the coloring along with the other liquids. Use only small amounts of coloring to tint the pastillage to obtain pastel colors—remember, a little coloring goes a long way.

Storage

Once the batter is made, cover the unused portion in plastic wrap or in an airtight container at room temperature. If placed in a cold area, the gelatin may break down and lose its bonding properties.

General Rules for Working with Pastillage

The modeling, cutting, shaping, molding, and coloring are all left to the imagination of the individual. However, a few precautionary measures should be followed to obtain the best possible results.

When rolling out the pastillage, always work on a very clean surface and lightly dust the surface with cornstarch or confectioners' sugar to prevent the pastillage from sticking. To obtain a very even thickness, it is best to use a variable-gauge rolling pin. This type of rolling pin is equipped with changeable rings that fit on each end. The batter is rolled out to the desired thickness, which occurs when the ring touches the marble.

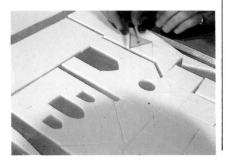

Work with only the amount of batter needed. This will prevent unneeded batter from drying out or forming a crust.

Generally, pastillage is rolled out into fairly thin pieces, about 2 to 3 mm (1/16 to 1/8 in.) thick. Pieces used as supports are left considerably thicker, depending on the weight to be supported.

Pastillage must be shaped or molded before it dries.

Any leftover trimmings should immediately be wrapped airtight. Do not wait until shaping a piece before putting away trimmings, which will quickly dry out. If they become a little dry, trimmings can

be worked a bit before being used or mixed in with fresh batter.

Pastillage can be molded in metal, plaster of paris, wood, or plastic molds.

Drying and Assembling Pieces

Individual pieces should be dried slowly at room temperature to prevent cracks from forming. Never place pastillage in a hot proof box to speed up the drying process.

Flat pieces should be turned over halfway through drying so they will dry evenly and not buckle.

Before attaching pieces together, the edges can be gently sanded to smooth them. Sanding can also be used to change the shape of a piece slightly as well as even a piece out.

Royal icing or pastillage heated and stirred in a saucepan until supple can be used to glue pieces together. Heated pastillage dries quickly and forms a strong bond. It is also possible to attach pieces together with tempered white chocolate.

Flat pieces, especially those used for paintings, can be smoothed out before drying by rubbing the surface with a sponge moistened (not dripping) with very hot water in a circular motion. The heat of the sponge will make the pastillage shiny as well as smooth. The gelatin in the pastillage softens to form a glaze which, when dry, makes the surface impermeable. This procedure is necessary for surfaces painted with diluted colors that would otherwise penetrate the pastillage, bleed, and run into other colors.

Volume 4 of this series explains how to paint on pastillage with food coloring

Le sucre massé (Molded sugar)

Definition

In French, the word *masser* indicates the sugar is stirred or worked until it begins to solidify and becomes opaque.

Uses

Molded sugar is poured into various molds and can be used for supports. This type of cooked sugar has a wide range of uses and was popular in the nineteenth century for elaborate presentation pieces for large buffets. It can also be used to make small, delicate pieces. Molded sugar can be displayed with other types of sugar work to augment a piece, such as swans made from molded sugar placed in front of a display piece made of pastillage.

Equipment

Saucepan, pastry brush, bowl, thermometer, wooden spatula, molds

Recipes

A. 1 kg sugar (35 oz.)
   300 ml water (10 fl. oz.)

B. Fondant

Preparation

Prepare the molds or forms. Molds should be very clean and lightly oiled with a pastry brush. It is best to use melted paraffin wax or warmed vegetable oil on porous molds.

Imprints can be made in plastic modeling clay. Cover the piece used to make the imprint with cornstarch so it can be easily removed from the clay. After the imprints are made, brush all cornstarch out of them before oiling.

Molds often come in two pieces and must be carefully assembled after oiling. They can be held tightly closed with rubber bands or string to secure them and prevent the sugar from dripping out.

Molded sugar is fairly simple to make. Once cooked, it is poured into various molds or forms. Molded sugar stores very well after being shaped.

Method A

Procedure

Cook the sugar and water in a heavy-bottomed saucepan to 117° to 120°C (242° to 248°F), soft ball to firm ball stage. When it reaches the proper temperature, remove the saucepan from the heat and set it aside for 3 to 5 minutes.

After 3 to 5 minutes, stir the sugar with a wooden spatula. The working and stirring of the sugar gives it its opaque quality. When the sugar begins to thicken and

whiten, quickly pour it into the prepared molds or forms. It is important to work quickly at this point, as the sugar will

continue to crystallize and may become difficult to pour.

Another technique for obtaining the quality needed for this type of cooked sugar is to add a few pinches of granulated sugar to the cooked sugar just before removing it from the heat. This will bring about the desired look without stirring.

Fill each mold to the rim without stopping so the piece will be solid, without cracks.

Cooling

Allow each piece to cool completely before unmolding. See more on cooling in method B.

Method B (preferred)

In a saucepan, heat the quantity of fondant needed just to the boiling point.

Careful! The fondant should not be overheated, that is, heated to the point that it becomes thin and clear. Remove the fondant from the heat when the first bubbles break the surface.

Allow the fondant to rest for 3 to 4 minutes. Do not stir it. Pour it into the prepared molds in one step as for method A. This method is preferred, as the resulting product is more opaque because of the finer crystallization of the sugar.

Cooling

Cool the molds and imprints at room temperature. Try to keep the molds and imprints stationary, as any sudden movement can deform the sugar as it sets and cause it to crack.

The cooling time needed depends on the size and thickness of the piece. Allow approximately 10 to 15 minutes for pieces sized and shaped like the columns shown in the photos on this page.

Once the pieces are cool, remove them carefully from their molds. They will still be fragile at this point and should be handled gently.

It takes several days for each piece to harden and become solid.

After unmolding, each piece should be examined carefully and gently scraped to remove any slight imperfections. Often joints need to be scraped. This should be done with a sharp knife, frequently wiped on a damp towel to prevent scrapings from sticking to the finished pieces.

Assembly

Pieces to be attached should be thoroughly dry, firm, and strong. Royal icing or heated pastillage can be used to glue the pieces together.

Storage

Molded sugar is not very sensitive to humidity, as compared to some other types of cooked sugar. Molded and assembled pieces can be stored at room temperature for up to several months.

Le sucre rocher (Rock sugar)

Definition

Rock sugar is seldom used for decoration. Its name is derived from its porous, rough, rocklike appearance. Royal icing is added to the cooked sugar to achieve its characteristic look.

Utilisations
Uses

Rock sugar can be easily shaped and cut to create presentation pieces. It can also be passed through a drum sieve or food processor and used to decorate various cakes.

Equipment

Saucepan and cover, pastry brush, bowl, whisk or wooden spatula, sheet pan, metal spatula, molds lined with oiled parchment paper or aluminum foil

Recipes

1 kg sugar (35 oz.) plus 300 ml water (10 fl. oz.), cooked to the hard crack stage, 145°C (293°F)

100 g firm royal icing (3.5 oz.)

Procedure

Cook the sugar and water in a saucepan large enough to hold 8 liters (8 quarts) of liquid, as the sugar will expand when the royal icing is added.

Once the sugar has reached the proper temperature, take it off the heat, add the royal icing, and mix rapidly with a whisk

Rock sugar, not often used, is fairly easy to make when the given key points are followed. It stores well.

or wooden spatula. This procedure must be done quickly, but be careful to avoid being burned by the popping bubbles of sugar.

Immediately remove the whisk or wooden spatula after the mixture has been well blended.

The mixture will rise, resembling milk brought to a boil. Do not stir or touch the mixture as it rises.

When the sugar stops rising, run a metal spatula around the inside of the

saucepan to loosen the sugar from the sides. Pour the contents of the saucepan out onto an oiled sheet pan. The cooked sugar will now resemble a sponge or pumice stone.

Allow the cooked sugar to cool before shaping or grinding it.

Once cool, rock sugar stores well in a dry area for up to several months.

Note

Rock sugar can be colored for various decorative purposes. The coloring can be added either at the end of cooking the sugar or to the royal icing, which creates shadows and shading.

Le sucre filé (Spun sugar)

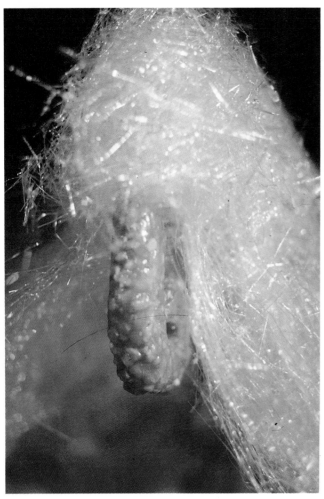

Uses

Spun sugar is used to decorate presentation pieces (croquembouches, bases for baskets, snow, centers of flowers, and birds' nests). It can also be shaped into swans, trees, and other figures.

Although spun sugar can be used in various ways, its application is limited to dry pieces. Spun sugar requires a dry environment, or it will quickly melt.

 Spun sugar is fairly easy to make, depending on how it is shaped. It should be stored in a very dry environment.

Preparation

It is important to have all equipment in place before the spun sugar is finished cooking.

During cooking, prepare either a section of marble by lightly oiling it or the bottom of several sheet pans by cleaning and lightly oiling them. It is best to have a surface area of approximately 2 meters (6.5 feet) long.

If available, cut the attached ends of a whisk so the ends extend straight out (like a feather duster). It is also possible to place several brochettes in a base (such as an apple), making sure they will fit into the saucepan in which the sugar is cooked.

Procedure

Follow the recipe and cooking procedure for poured sugar (page 177).

Cook the following to 152°C (305°F) in a copper sugar pan or heavy-bottomed saucepan:

1 kg sugar (35 oz.)
400 ml water (13.5 fl. oz.)
125 g glucose (4.5 oz.)
10 g baking soda (2 tsp.), only for opaque spun sugar

Spun sugar is rarely made opaque, only when used for special decorations, to create snow, mist, or fog.

After the cooked sugar has reached the proper temperature, remove it from the heat and allow it to cool for a few minutes until it thickens somewhat.

Place the pan of cooked sugar on top of a kitchen towel near the work area.

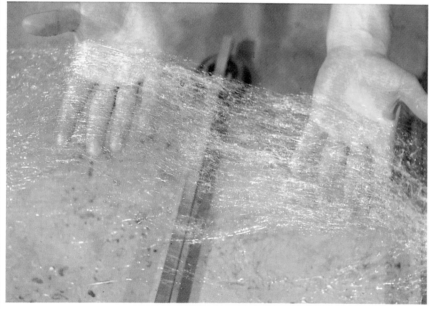

Spinning the Sugar

Dip the cut-off whisk or brochettes in the cooked, cooled sugar, lift it for a second over the saucepan to let the first large drops of cooked sugar fall off, and then shake the cooked sugar off the utensil in quick movements back and forth over the oiled surface.

Dip the utensil into the cooked sugar and repeat the procedure until a veil of threads is obtained.

Gently lift up the mass of spun sugar when the desired volume has been obtained and shape it immediately.

Spun sugar should be stored in airtight containers with dehydrating packets. Storage time will depend on the amount of humidity the spun sugar absorbs.

Le sucre coulé (Poured sugar)

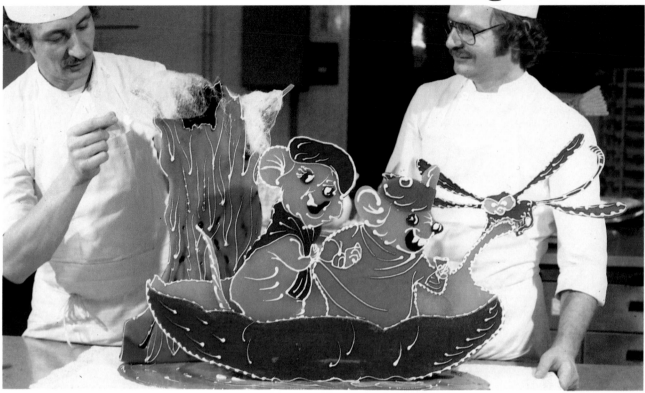

Definition

Poured sugar is cooked sugar that is poured into various free-form shapes or into templates on a flat surface, such as an oiled pastry marble or sheet pan.

Various colors and shapes can be made, including presentation pieces assembled from several sections.

There are two types of poured sugar:

A. **Opaque poured sugar**

B. **Royal poured sugar**

A. Opaque Poured Sugar

Uses

Poured sugar can be used to create various shapes, such as hearts, and figures, including well-known figures such as Mickey Mouse, which can be decorated with a paper cone filled with royal icing. Elaborate presentation pieces can be made for exhibitions, pastry shop displays, wedding cakes, or as a way to present petits fours.

Preparation

Before the sugar can be cooked, it is very important that all equipment and forms be prepared.

Trace the design or figure on parchment paper or very firm marzipan (a sheet of marzipan that has been rolled out and dried).

For large pieces, the borders are made with 1-cm-thick (⅜-in.) strips of plastic modeling clay or marzipan.

It is important that the strips are carefully applied, as they will determine the shape of the piece.

Attach the strips firmly to the surface by pressing on the outside edge. Trim or shape the inside of the strips so the lines are well defined.

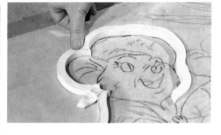

    Poured sugar can be used in various ways.

It is important to study and prepare the design to be made. Several precautions should be followed when pouring cooked sugar. Poured-sugar objects store well, especially those made from opaque poured sugar.

Oiling the Surface

Using a paintbrush, evenly and lightly

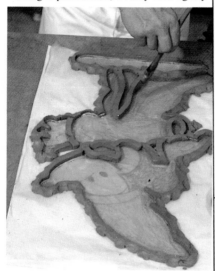

oil all surfaces and borders that will come in contact with the poured sugar.

Thickness of the Poured Sugar

The thickness of the poured sugar depends on how the piece is to be used. For example: 3 to 5 mm (⅛ to ¼ in.) is sufficient for the center of a piece that will be displayed lying prone. For pieces to be used as supports or parts of an exhibition

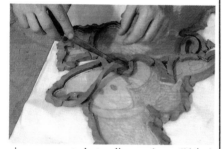

piece presented standing, a 1-cm (⅜-in.) thickness is necessary.

Cooking the Sugar

Recipe

1 kg sugar (35 oz.)
400 ml water (13.5 fl. oz.)
125 g glucose (4.5 oz.)
10 g baking soda (2 tsp.), dissolved in a little water

Preparation

It is best to start cooking the sugar the day before it is to be used. Mix the sugar with the water in a heavy-bottomed saucepan. Wash down any sugar on the sides of the saucepan with a wet pastry brush, skim, and bring the mixture to a boil. Add the glucose and bring to a boil again, this time for 1 minute.

Remove the saucepan from the heat. Check that the sides of the saucepan are clean; brush them with a wet pastry brush if necessary. Cover the saucepan with a clean, damp towel and a saucepan cover. Allow the sugar mixture to cool.

When cooking the sugar a day ahead, use 500 ml (17 fl. oz.) of water per 1 kg (35 oz.) of sugar.

Cooking the Sugar

The following day, pour the sugar mixture in a clean copper sugar pan. Use only as much of the mixture as needed.

Cook the sugar, and approximately 10 g (2 tsp.) of baking soda dissolved in water. When the sugar reaches 125°C (257°F), coloring can be added. The coloring should be either a very concentrated liquid or a powder diluted in a little water and a clear, strong liquor.

Slow down the cooking as the sugar approaches the correct temperature. Stir the sugar with the thermometer to assure an even cooking and control the temperature more accurately.

When the sugar reaches the proper temperature, stop the cooking by placing the bottom of the pan in cold water for a few seconds.

Cooking Temperatures

- transparent sugar for bases: 152°C (305°F)
- for second layer: 150°C (302°F)
- opaque white and blue: 145°C (293°F),
- any other color: 150°C (302°F)

Pouring the Sugar

The cooked sugar should be poured immediately. Pour the cooked sugar in a circular motion, in a fine stream to ensure an even layer. Pour the sugar first over any rough or bumpy areas in the border. Avoid repouring over a section (unless covering it entirely with a second layer).

To prevent sugar from dribbling off the spout or edge, pass a piece of chalk over the spout to cut the sugar cleanly after it is poured.

Pieces that will have several different colors require two steps:

1. Pour clear cooked sugar (half the final thickness) over the entire surface of the form (the sections do not need to be separated);
2. Separate the sections with plastic modeling clay or marzipan. Pour each color of cooked sugar, one at a time, waiting for the first to cool before pouring the next. Remove the separating strips after the poured sugar has cooled, and check to be certain no traces of the strips or oil remain.

More delicate sections, such as tall trees, can be strengthened by placing a fine wire between the two layers of poured sugar.

Cooling

Allow the poured sugar to cool to approximately 40°C (104°F), which can be tested by touching the surface. At this temperature the sugar will be firm yet slightly malleable. This is the best time to transfer the piece directly onto a marble or sheet pan to prevent it from sticking to the work surface.

To lift a piece that was poured directly onto a marble, delicately release the entire border of the piece with the tip of a thin knife. Air will pass under the piece, releasing it completely so it can be lifted in one piece. Slide it over to a cold section of marble, or slip a sheet pan or presentation base underneath it.

Supports

Support pieces can be made with any remaining cooked sugar. Their size is determined by the size of the piece supported. They should be attached in such a way that they cannot be seen from the front, to reinforce the piece, especially weaker sections, so it will be well balanced.

Attach the support pieces with sugar cooked to the hard crack stage, 150°C (302°F). Make certain all the pieces are completely cold before assembling.

The base of the piece is usually made out of marbled poured sugar (see page 181).

Uses

Royal poured sugar is used mostly for presentation pieces or to augment a presentation piece.

Definition

Royal poured sugar is made from two types of cooked sugar made in two steps. The first step involves making a base of clear poured sugar (without baking soda). The second step consists of covering the poured sugar with a layer of fondant molded sugar (see page 171) mixed with royal icing. The royal icing helps the fondant molded sugar to dry quickly and provides a finer appearance.

Procedure

Place the chosen design on a flat surface such as a marble and cover it with a sheet of plastic wrap to protect the design. Place a sheet of parchment paper over the piece.

With a paper cone or pastry bag and no. 5 or no. 7 tip (depending on the size of the lines to be drawn) filled with royal icing, trace over the outlines of the design.

Allow the royal icing to develop a crust, which takes approximately 1 hour.

When it has hardened slightly, lightly oil the parchment paper inside the border of royal icing.

The base is made by pouring a layer of clear poured sugar cooked to 155°C (311°F) in one piece inside the border of

B. Royal Poured Sugar

royal icing. This is the same step as for making a base for opaque poured sugar, described on the previous page.

Allow the layer of poured sugar to cool and become firm.

Trace over the design inside the border with a paper cone filled with royal icing, making lines approximately 2 mm (¹⁄₁₆ in.) thick.

Trace over the design to separate the different colors in the design as well.

Prepare the royal fondant sugar by placing two parts white fondant to one part royal icing in a saucepan.

Mix the two sugars and heat them slowly to no more than 50°C (122°F). The mixture can be thinned with a little sugar syrup at 1260 D if necessary so it can be easily piped out of a pastry bag.

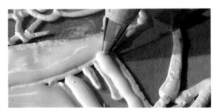

Fill a pastry bag with a no. 5 tip with the royal fondant sugar and cover the entire surface of the design by filling in between the traced lines. Allow the sugar to dry and form a crust, which takes approximately 24 hours. After this time the piece can be colored with an airbrush or sponge and paintbrush.

Storage and Assembly

Follow the procedure for opaque poured sugar.

Presentation bases of poured sugar

Presentation bases made from poured sugar are fairly simple to construct and can be used to present dishes for a buffet or to present cakes in a restaurant or in the window of a pastry shop.

Numerous shapes can be made with poured sugar, such as hearts for a wedding or engagement party or a horseshoe for a New Year's celebration.

Decorations used to complement the poured-sugar supports can be made from pulled or blown sugar or marzipan, which holds up well uncovered on presentation pieces.

Opaque poured-sugar presentation supports should last for approximately 6 to 8 weeks if kept in a dry, dust-free area.

Preparation

It is best to make a model of the piece to be constructed, taking into consideration the theme, size, number of cakes or dishes to be presented, and additional decoration to be added.

Prepare a frame for the supports with plastic modeling clay, marzipan, or royal icing piped from a pastry bag with a no. 6 or no. 7 tip onto parchment paper.

After allowing the frame to dry, lightly oil the interior.

Prepare and cook the quantity of opaque poured sugar needed. The cooked sugar can be colored with one shade or marbled (see marbled sugar, page 181).

Pour an even layer of cooked sugar into the frames, leaving enough to make the base.

After the sugar has cooled completely, the piece is assembled by attaching each section with cooked sugar using the recipe for the poured sugar:

1 kg sugar (35 oz.)
400 ml water (13.5 fl. oz.)
125 g glucose (4.5 oz.)
10 g baking soda (2 tsp.), dissolved in a small amount of water (for opaque poured sugar)

Tips on Assembling Presentation Supports

Place the base on a strong, steady support.

Prepare and attach all the sections possible before attaching them to the base.

Construct the piece before attaching the sections to the base to verify the final piece is balanced, sturdy, and attractive.

To ensure stability, make sure each piece is level when attached.

Check that each section is properly secured. Secure the joints if necessary by melting them together with a hot knife.

Decorations can be used to hide joints and slight imperfections.

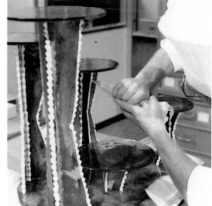

Poured sugar piped from a paper cone

Poured sugar can be piped out of a paper cone to create various designs for decorative purposes.

Procedure

Fill a large parchment-paper cone no more than half full with poured sugar, following the recipe given on page 177, leaving out the baking soda so the sugar will be clear and shiny.

Close the paper cone carefully to prevent burns.

Hold the paper cone in a towel folded over several times. Cut the tip of the paper cone to pipe out a line approximately 2 mm (1/16 in.) thick.

While piping, occasionally heat the cone under a heat lamp or in an oven to prevent the sugar from becoming firm and difficult to pipe out.

Pipe out the sugar using the thread technique (see volume 4, page 56) on a lightly oiled sheet pan.

When the pieces have completely cooled, gently lift them. Several pieces can be attached with the poured sugar piped out of the cone to form various shapes or objects.

Examples

Butterflies on a dessert containing fruit
Fountains on a frozen dessert

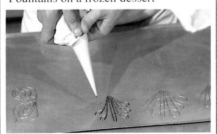

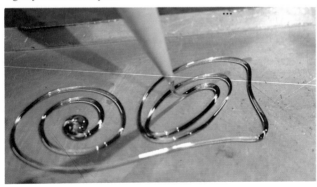

Marbled poured sugar

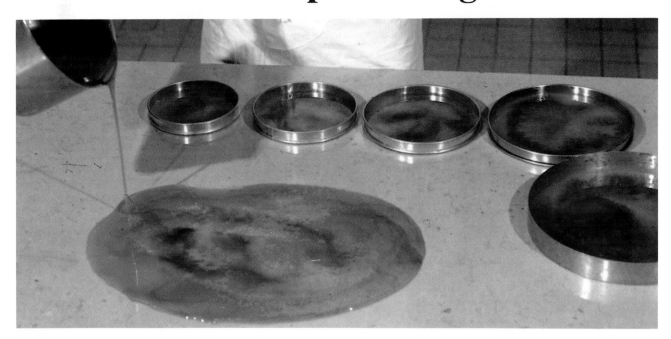

Poured sugar can be given a marbled appearance using either of two methods, each of which offers a slightly different result.

1. Coloring after Pouring

This first method is best for small pieces.

Cook the sugar to 150°C (302°F), using the same recipe for opaque poured sugar given on page 177. Pour the cooked sugar onto a lightly oiled surface into the desired shape or form; an oiled tart ring or cake ring can be used, or the sugar can be poured free-form onto an oiled marble as in the above photograph.

Sprinkle a few drops of coloring over the poured cooked sugar. One color or several different colors can be used, such as yellow, red, green, blue, or brown. It is best to use concentrated or powdered food coloring diluted in a strong liquor. Draw the tip of a paring knife or brochette through the drops of coloring to create free-form lines until the desired effect is achieved.

2. Coloring the Sugar before Pouring

When coloring is added to the cooked sugar before pouring, a more realistic marble effect can be created.

Cook the sugar to 152°C (305°F), using the recipe for opaque cooked sugar on page 177.

When the proper temperature has been reached, remove the cooked sugar from the heat and allow it to rest for 2 to 3

minutes in the saucepan until it thickens somewhat. Sprinkle the chosen colors directly into the saucepan of cooked sugar. Use two or three drops of each color.

Return the colored cooked sugar to the stove and reheat it until the first bubbles break the surface. Depending on the amount of sugar cooked, it may be necessary to stir the sugar gently with a ther-

mometer or wooden spatula to help disperse the colors throughout the mixture.

From this point on, the cooked sugar is treated in the same way as opaque poured sugar.

Storage

Marbled opaque poured sugar stores fairly well in a cool, dry area.

The baking soda helps prevent the pieces from absorbing humidity and sweating.

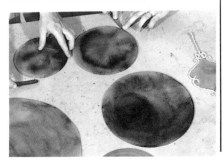

Le sucre tourné (Turned sugar)

Turned sugar is somewhat similar to the more popular pulled sugar (page 184). Although turned sugar is easier to work with and stores better than pulled sugar, it does not offer as fine a result as pulled sugar and is not as versatile.

The cooled cooked sugar is turned and worked as it is shaped. Once the desired shapes are formed, it is best to let the pieces rest for several days before presenting them. Their appearance will change and improve during this time.

Equipment

The equipment required for turned sugar is the same as for pulled sugar (page 184), plus metal rulers and containers with airtight covers to store the pieces of cooked sugar that are not immediately presented.

Recipe

1 kg sugar (35 oz.)
400 ml water (13.5 fl. oz.)
100 g glucose (3.5 oz.)

Cook the above ingredients to 145°C (293°F).

Note that acid is not used in this recipe, as it would prevent the sugar from having the proper texture and appearance.

Testing the recipe may indicate that certain weather conditions or the quality of the sugar makes it necessary to cook the sugar to a slightly lower temperature to prevent it from absorbing humidity which would make it difficult to work with.

Turned sugar is not very difficult to prepare; however, the shaping requires skill and experience. Some special equipment is needed for this work.

Although not as popular as pulled sugar, turned sugar stores well.

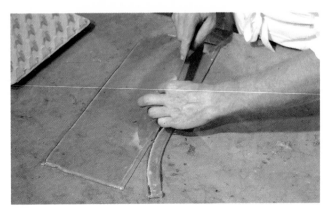

Procedure

Turned sugar is made in two stages.

Stage 1: Cooking and Pouring the Sugar

The sugar is cooked following the usual precautions. The glucose is added after the sugar/water mixture has been skimmed and the sides of the saucepan or copper sugar pan have been brushed down.

Stop the cooking at 145°C (293°F). Allow the sugar to rest for several minutes. During this time make a frame with the metal rulers and lightly oil the surface inside the rulers.

Pour the sugar inside the frame. Allow the sugar to set.

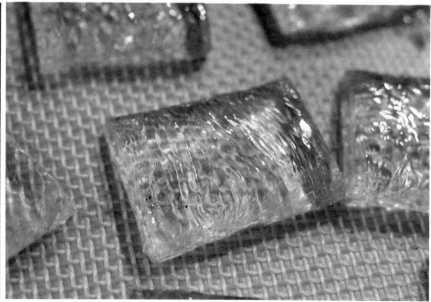

Once set, remove the rulers and cut the rectangle of cooked sugar into strips and the strips into squares. Place them on a sheet of silicone or parchment paper.

At this point the cooked-sugar squares can be placed in airtight containers and stored in a cool, dry area for up to 1 week.

Stage 2: Working and Shaping the Sugar

Place three to five cooked sugar squares under a heat source such as a heat lamp with an infrared bulb used for pulled sugar. The number of squares heated at a time will depend on how quickly they are worked and the piece made. The squares should be heated and softened evenly.

Coloring

Turned sugar can be colored after it is worked and shaped with a brush or airbrush, or the pieces can be colored as they are being worked. For the latter, use powdered coloring mixed with a small amount of cornstarch. Dip the fingertips

in the color/cornstarch mixture while working the sugar to obtain the desired color.

As the square of cooked sugar becomes soft and malleable under the heat of the lamp, massage, stretch, and turn the piece in the hands so it is worked evenly.

After working the sugar until it is malleable and has a matted look, stretch and form the piece to the desired shape, making a petal or leaf out of each square as for pulled sugar, described on pages 187 and 198.

Note

If the turned sugar is not being colored as it is worked, occasionally rub the fingertips in white fondant while working with each piece. The film of fondant on the fingertips will enter the sugar and bring about the matted look and desired texture more quickly.

Storage

Shaped turned-sugar pieces can be stored in airtight containers for several weeks in a cool, dry area.

Le sucre tiré (Pulled sugar)

Definition

Both pulled sugar and blown sugar are worked while the sugar is still hot after cooking until a shiny satinlike appearance is achieved.

Slight variations can be made in recipes for pulled and blown sugar depending on the subject made, although the technique for cooking and pulling the sugar is always the same.

Working with pulled and blown sugar is considered the most artistic area of pastry making and requires many hours of serious practice.

The unlimited possibilities for self-expression and artistic creation with pulled and blown sugar merit the many hours of required practice.

Beginners should carefully follow all key points and advice to obtain a good foundation for sugar work.

Uses

Pulled sugar offers the greatest artistic creativity of all the types of sugar work. Each individual can display his or her own style when making flowers and leaves, ribbons, and other objects.

Equipment

Equipment for Cooking the Sugar

Copper sugar pan or stainless steel saucepan, thermometer, pastry brush, metal spatula, bowl, tablespoon, teaspoon

Equipment for Working the Sugar

Lightly oiled work surface (marble), triangle or knife

Equipment for Pulling the Sugar

Heat lamp with a 800- to 1,200-watt infrared bulb. It is best to have an adjustable lamp. Although a lamp is preferable, it is possible to use an oven as a heat source. To protect the eyes from long exposure to infrared light, wear infrared-blocking sunglasses when using the heat lamp for extended periods of time.

 Pulled sugar requires some special equipment.

Certain precautions should be followed throughout the procedure. Dexterity and many hours of practice are required for this work. Pulled sugar offers unlimited artistic possibilities.

Finished pieces should be stored in a dry area.

Marble or clean drum sieve to place the pulled sugar on or a sheet of silicone paper on a cutting board or sheet pan. Scissors, molds, as needed.

Recipe (fondant)

1 g cream of tartar (¼ tsp.)
15 ml white distilled vinegar (1 Tbsp.)
1 kg white fondant (35 oz.)

Cook the above ingredients to 160°C (320°F).

Note: Depending on the fondant used, it may be necessary to:

- cook the mixture to 158°C (316°F) if the fondant is too firm and hot while pulling the sugar
- add 100 to 150 g (3.5 to 5 oz.) of glucose to the recipe if the fondant is too soft and not hot enough when pulling the sugar

Add a liquid or powdered coloring to the sugar when it reaches 130° to 140°C (266° to 284°F).

It is also possible to color the sugar with concentrated colors diluted in a strong, clear liquor after the sugar has been cooked and poured onto the marble.

This recipe cannot be used for white or blue colored sugar. To make these two colors, use the recipe given for blown sugar (page 214).

Preparation

Before proceeding with this recipe, read the entire section on pulled sugar and review all the recipes given in this chapter on cooking sugar, the various products used, and why and when they are used.

To obtain the best results, it is best to follow the same recipe carefully once it has been perfected. A few drops of acid, a fraction more or less of cream of tartar, a few degrees higher or lower in the cooking of the sugar—each can entirely change the final results.

For beginners the recipe with fondant is given here, as it is one of the least difficult, although not the most commonly used.

Procedure

Clean a copper sugar pan or stainless steel saucepan with vinegar and coarse salt. Rinse it well with water. Place 1 g (¼ tsp.) cream of tartar dissolved in 15 ml (1 Tbsp.) white distilled vinegar into the clean pan. Add 1 kg (35 oz.) fondant.

Heat the mixture on the stove and stir with a wooden spatula until it is well blended. Remove the spatula and heat the mixture.

After the mixture comes to a boil, wash down the insides of pan with a pastry brush and water.

Place the thermometer in the pan and watch the temperature. Be careful not to let the thermometer touch the bottom of the pan (most candy thermometers come with an adjustable clip so they can be attached to the side of the pan), or over a hot spot on the stove, which would falsify the temperature reading.

Cook the mixture over the highest flame that still stays beneath the bottom of the pan and does not lap up around the sides.

Coloring

The mixture can either be colored toward the end of cooking, around 130° to 140°C (266° to 284°F), or after it has been poured onto the marble. The latter makes it possible to obtain several different colors from the same batch of sugar and is recommended when making ribbons. It is best to use highly concentrated colors dissolved in very little water and diluted with a very strong clear liquor.

Cook the sugar to the proper temperature and slow down the cooking for the last five degrees C (ten degrees F).

Gently stir the mixture to ensure an even cooking toward the end of cooking. Stop the cooking when the correct temperature, 160°C (320°F), has been reached by dipping the bottom of the pan in cold water for a few seconds.

Pulling the Sugar

Allow the sugar to cool for 1 to 2 minutes in the pan and turn on the heat lamp or other heat source to be used.

Pour the cooked sugar onto a lightly oiled work surface. As the border of the cooked sugar becomes firm, fold it over

itself toward the center of the mass with a knife or metal spatula, as shown in the photograph.

Continue this procedure until the cooked sugar becomes somewhat firm. Treating the sugar in this way allows it to cool sugar evenly.

The sugar should be firmer now and is ready to be pulled. This is done by stretching it and folding it over itself. Repeat this procedure twenty to thirty times, working the entire mass of sugar evenly. Remember, the sugar is still very hot at this point and should be handled

carefully with the fingertips to prevent burns and to prevent the hands from sweating, which would cause the sugar to crystallize, rendering it useless. For this step, it is advisable to wear surgical gloves to prevent burns.

Once the sugar is shiny and has a sat-

inlike sheen throughout, the stretching and folding can be stopped.

Place the pulled sugar under a heat lamp or another heat source hot enough to keep it malleable.

The pulled sugar is now ready to be used.

In all cases, regardless of what is to be done with the pulled sugar, it should be kept malleable under a heat source without becoming too hot or cold. Occasionally fold the pulled sugar over itself so it will continue to maintain an even temperature and satiny appearance.

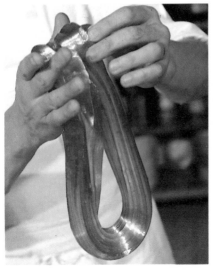

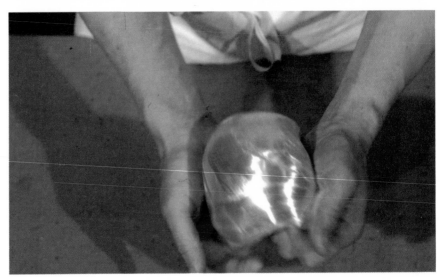

Making a rose

The Basic Flower: A Rose

Regardless of the type of flower or leaf made in pulled sugar, the basic technique for preparing the sugar is always the same.

It is important to understand how to make a rose, which is considered the most basic flower in pulled-sugar work. After mastering the technique for making a rose, it will seem relatively easy to make other types of flowers. Each individual brings his or her own personality into this work, so that different results will be apparent when making the same type of flower.

It takes approximately 12 to 15 hours of practice for someone at an intermediate level in pastry making to make an attractive rose.

Shaping the Pulled Sugar

Rose Petals

The pulled sugar is left under the heat source throughout the procedure so that it remains malleable yet somewhat firm. The pulled sugar should have the consistency of firm marzipan.

Pinch a nut-size piece of pulled sugar between the thumb and index finger. Stretch it using the thumb and index fingers of both hands to spread and flatten it crosswise; it should still be attached to the ball of pulled sugar.

Taper and thin out the edge to the thickness of a thin knife blade. Pull the petal at the base with one quick movement to detach it from the ball of pulled sugar.

This is the basic procedure for making all types of petals out of pulled sugar.

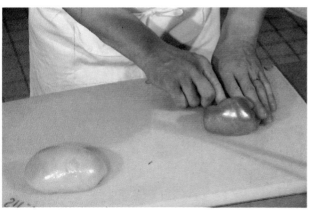

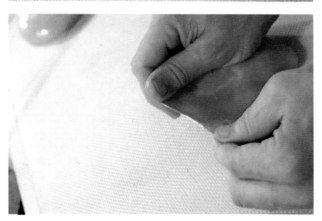

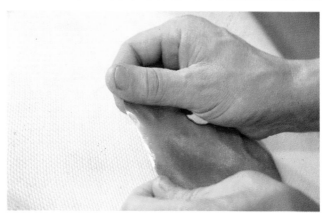

187

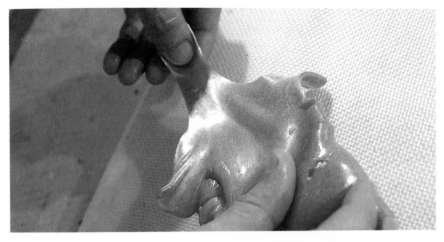

Making a Rose with Thirteen Petals

There are several possible styles for making roses, and the number of petals needed depends on the shape and size of the rose to be made.

To start the rose, the bud is always the first piece shaped. Pinch a piece of pulled sugar between the thumb and index finger so it is cupped halfway around the thumb; hold the pulled sugar at the base of the thumbnail between the thumb and index finger of the other hand and pull in one quick stroke to detach the pulled piece from the ball of pulled sugar.

While the piece of pulled sugar is still on the thumb, fold the base up around the thumbnail. Remove the piece from the thumb and lay it on the index and middle fingers. Fold the base inside and roll the sides around the folded base to form a cone shape that is wider at the bottom and tapered at top to form a point.

Place the bud on a sheet of plastic or aluminum foil away from the heat source. The bud will remain a little soft for a short time. Be careful not to distort the shape.

To make a petal, pull off a piece of sugar to be the same height as the bud, fold the base, but leave the petal open and attach it to the base of the bud. The bud should fit inside the petal and be of the same height.

Pull a second petal and attach it to the bud at the base so that it overlaps the first petal. Repeat this step with a third petal. The three petals should encircle the bud, overlapping.

The next petal should be slightly larger and wider than the first three petals. Lightly pinch the top of the petal between the index finger and thumb to form a point, giving it a realistic look. Make four such petals. Attach these petals to the base. They should be of the same height as the flower.

The exterior petals are pulled slightly longer and wider. After making the point at the top of the petal, gently bend the edges back around the point, as shown in the first three photos on the opposite page. These petals are attached to the base slightly lower than the others were. For this last row, make five identical petals overlapping around the flower.

The base of the rose should be flat so it will sit upright.

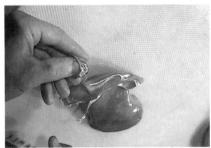

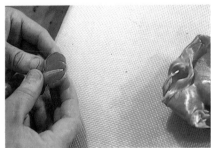

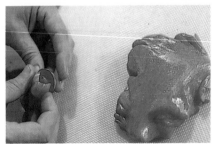

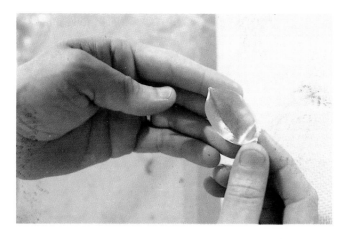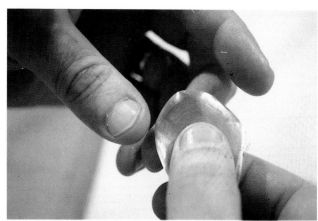

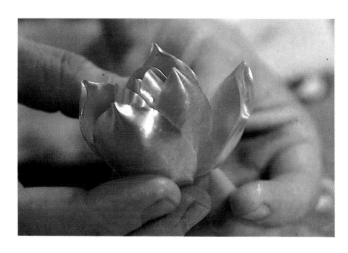

Pulled-sugar flowers

Introduction

The rose is not only the most popular and often-made pulled-sugar flower, but learning how it is made provides an understanding of basic techniques for working with pulled sugar. It is important to master making a rose before going on to other flowers, which will then come more easily.

Preparation

Before deciding on which flower to make, it is important to know how the flower will be presented. If the flower is used to decorate a dessert, the size and color of the dessert should be taken into consideration. If the flower is set in a bouquet of pulled-sugar flowers, the bouquet should consist of assorted flowers varying in color, size, and shape.

Sometimes flowers are attached to stems and/or leaves, which are made before the flowers.

Composition of Flowers

Most flowers are assembled in two steps.

1. Constructing the Different Components

Depending on how the flower is to be presented determines if stems, leaves, pistils, and stamens will be made and their size and shape. These elements are made separately. Flowers can be lifelike or imaginary.

2. Assembling the Flower

The petals, stem, leaves, pistils, and stamens are usually attached by heating the base of the flower or leaves with a low flame such as that from a small alcohol burner.

Daffodils

Daffodils are made in two steps, as are narcissus and lilies. The daffodil is always attached to a stem whose length is determined by how it will be presented.

Procedure

Use yellow-colored pulled sugar to form six long slender petals cut with a scissors at an angle (to form the pointed tips) from the ball of pulled sugar. Curve the petals slightly so they arch upward in the middle.

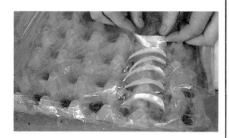

The trumpet of the daffodil is more difficult to make than the outer petals. Pull a strip of pulled sugar from the mass ap-

proximately 10 cm (4 in.) long and 3 cm (1 in.) wide. Keeping the strip warm and malleable under the lamp, cut small inci-

sions at the top and make a 1-cm-long (⅜-in.) indentation with a scissors or small pruning shears. Repeat this step, leaving approximately 2 mm (1/16 in.) between the cuts and indentation.

Cut the strip in a trapezoid shape, making the serrated side the larger, approximately 5 cm (2 in.) long. The height of the trumpet and the shorter side should be equal to each other and to the

width of the petals, approximately 3 cm (1 in.).

Quickly mold the trumpet into a cup shape around a stem (to make stems, see page 199).

Assembling the Flower

Attach three petals at the base of the trumpet by heating the ends. They should form a triangle around the base. Attach the last three petals between and under the first three.

Orchids

Orchids, fairly easy to make, can be made in a variety of colors and shapes. The orchids described and shown here are not identical to living orchids but are based on them and finished in a creative way. Orchids can be used to decorate cakes and frozen desserts.

Orchids can be made with white pulled sugar and colored with an airbrush after they are shaped, or the sugar can be separated and colored in two colors before the flower is shaped, which will produce a blending of colors.

Procedure

Pull long petals from a ball of pulled sugar, cutting them off with a scissors.

Veins can be made by pressing each petal against the top of a whisk with the palm of the hand.

Keep the petal warm and malleable under the lamp, and pinch the border of each petal between the thumb and index finger to form the wavy edge characteristic of orchids. Arch the petals upward. Each flower should have three or five petals.

The center is like a rosebud but longer, with one petal wrapped around it; each is differently colored. It is also possible to make another type of center that is attractive though also not realistic. Pull a

strand of sugar and bend it around itself to form rings, as in the photo of the green and yellow orchid on the previous page.

Assembling the Flower

Attach three petals together by heating the ends over a small flame. Fanciful orchids can be enhanced by attaching three longer petals underneath in the spaces between the first three petals.

If the flowers are to be colored with an airbrush or atomizer, they should be colored before the center is attached. Attach the center after heating the base.

Carnations

Carnations are a popular pulled-sugar flower, perhaps second only to the rose. They can be used individually to decorate a dessert or in a bouquet of pulled-sugar flowers.

Carnations are often made from white pulled sugar and colored with an airbrush, atomizer, or sponge (dipped in coloring) after the flower has been shaped.

Procedure

Pull a petal from a ball of pulled sugar as for a rose petal. Cut small incisions into the rounded, thin part with a scissors or small shears. Cut the piece off, forming a triangle, with the tip of the triangle opposite the fringed edge.

Shape the fringed side of the petal into an S. Pinch the point of the triangle, which is at the bottom.

Repeat the procedure until twenty to thirty such petals are made.

Assembling the Flower

Heat the pinched bases of each petal one by one and attach them together around a central petal.

The flower should appear round at the

top when held upside down. Held sideways, the flower should have a rounded, umbrella shape.

Carnations are often attached to a stem with a few long, slender petals around the edges.

Gladioli

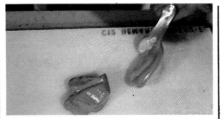

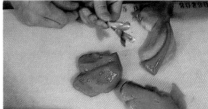

Gladioli are usually presented in a bouquet of pulled flowers. They are always attached to long stems covered with pulled sugar.

Gladioli require at least two colors of pulled sugar, green for the stem and leaves, with a second color for the petals. A third color can be used to shade the petals at the edges.

Procedure for Petals with Shaded Edges

Place a contrastingly colored strip of pulled sugar on top of a wide band of pulled sugar.

Pull a petal as for making a rose, pulling so the second color is at the edge of the petal, keeping it thin and even (see the photo above).

A two-toned edge can be made by placing a third colored strip of pulled sugar parallel and 1 cm (⅜ in.) away from the other strip.

This technique can also be used to form a border on other pulled-sugar flowers such as tulips and dahlias.

Assembling the Flowers

The first petal should be wrapped around the top of a stem dipped in pulled sugar (page 199).

Wrap a leaf around the base of the petal. The next petal should be slightly larger and more open and wrapped at the base with two leaves. Continue down the stem, making each successive petal slightly larger and more open, alternating left to right down the stem. At the base of each petal, place one, two, or three leaves before adding the next; usually the first flower is given one leaf, the larger flowers two or three.

Do not place the petals too far down the stem, as they are delicate and may break when presented with other flowers.

Lilies of the Valley

The lily of the valley is usually made in celebration of labor day in France, May 1. It is used to decorate cakes and frozen desserts or is planted in chocolate flowerpots with a cream or ganache filling.

Lilies of the valley are always made with a pulled-sugar stem, a long, wide leaf, and small cup-shaped white flowers.

Procedure

To make the flower, pinch off a small piece of white sugar as for a petal for apple blossoms (page 196). Place the tip of a lightly oiled pen, a pen cap, or large nail in the center of the piece of pulled sugar. Pinch the piece of pulled sugar around the object to form a cup shape. Cut off the pinched point at the bottom of the cup with a scissors.

Repeat the procedure, making six to ten such cups for each lily of the valley stem.

The stem is made with green-colored pulled sugar. The length of the stem is determined by how the flower will be presented, in a cake or as part of a bouquet. Pull the stem so it tapers toward the top, and bend it over like a cane at top.

Pull the leaf from the same sugar used for the stem. The leaf should be pulled wide and long, the same technique as is used for making a tulip leaf. Heat the base of the leaf and attach it by wrapping it around the stem.

Assembling the Lily of the Valley

The flowers are attached to the stem by gently heating them at the base over a low flame and placing them on the stem. Start by placing the smallest flower at the top of the stem and working down. As the flowers are very delicate, it is helpful to use a tweezers for this procedure to prevent burns or breaking flowers.

Pompon Dahlias

The pompon dahlia is very time consuming to make and is therefore not made often. It is usually presented in a bouquet with assorted pulled-sugar flowers.

The dahlia is fastened to a strong, rigid stem, as the flower is fairly heavy and would topple over on a flexible stem.

Various colors can be used for dahlias. The tips of the petals can be accented with a second color using the same technique for making gladioli with colored edges (page 193).

Procedure

To make the petals, pull a thin piece of sugar from a ball of pulled sugar and cut the petal off with a scissors to form an isosceles triangle. Roll the cut side of the petal to meet the other side, forming a cone with the point of the triangle at the bottom.

Approximately sixty such cone-shaped petals are needed to make one medium-size dahlia.

Assembling the Flower

Lightly oil the top of a can or other flat raised surface to serve as a guide for keeping the flower round and even as it is assembled. Heat the point (base) of each petal over a small flame and make the first row or base of the flower with the longer petals.

An attractive flower is achieved when all the petals fit tightly together, attached along the full length of each petal. The first row of petals will form a ring with a hollow center. Place the second row slightly farther back than the first; the third row will sit up on top of the second.

Fill the center of the flower with as many petals as needed.

Place the dahlia upside down on a flat piece of soft foam covered with a sheet of plastic to prevent breakage. Attach one last row of petals to form the bottom row, set back slightly from the previous row. This last row rounds out the flower.

Attach a stem (a wire covered with pulled sugar) securely to the base of the flower.

Violets

Violets are usually presented in a bouquet to accompany a presentation piece or decorate a buffet table. The small flowers are attached to wire stems covered in pulled sugar, made in advance. Large, heart-shaped leaves finish the bouquet.

194

Procedure

To make the petals, pull small pieces of sugar the size of a fingernail from a piece of deep-violet-colored pulled sugar. Partially fold each petal so it looks wavy, pinching the base to give it a triangular shape.

Make three to five petals for each flower.

Assembling the Flower and Bouquet

Heat the pointed bases of the petals and attach three to five petals at their bases to form a single flower. Attach

them so some flowers appear more open or closed than others.

A small piece of differently colored pulled sugar can be attached to the center of each flower to serve as the pistil and brighten up the bouquet.

Attach each flower to a stem covered with pulled sugar. The stems are connected as a bunch with a little melted pulled sugar, which can be hidden beneath a pulled-sugar ribbon (pages 201 to 203).

Place a few leaves around the bouquet, under the flowers.

Wheat Stalks

Although obviously not a flower, wheat stalks work well in a floral composition and can be used in presentation pieces.

Wheat grains are always attached to a stalk made from a wire covered with pale yellow pulled sugar.

Procedure

Pinch off a small piece of wheat-colored pulled sugar. Pinch the base of the grain with the thumb and index finger so it is slightly bulbous. With the other

hand, pull a thread from the tip of the bulb approximately 3 to 4 cm (1 to 1.5 in.) long.

Make approximately forty to sixty grains for each stalk.

Assembling

Gently heat the bases of the grains and attach them to a stalk (made from wire covered in pulled sugar) in staggered rows. This is a delicate procedure that requires a great deal of concentration.

Leaves in the same pale yellow color are attached to the base of the stalk. The leaves are pulled approximately 15 to 20 cm (6 to 8 in.) long and approximately 2 cm (¾ in.) wide at the base, tapered at the top.

Apple Blossoms

Apple blossoms represent fruitfulness and are often used on cakes or presentation pieces at engagement parties or wedding receptions.

Composition

Each flower is made with three or six petals with pistils and stamens made from spun sugar. The flowers are made in two steps: the first consists of making the petal and pistils and stamens; the second, assembling the flower.

The flowers are attached to branches that should be prepared in advance. The branches are made either from brown pulled sugar or by covering real branches with a thin coating of brown or pale green cooked sugar.

Making the Petals

Pull off a thin piece of pale pink or white pulled sugar the size of a thumbnail. White petals can be colored with an airbrush after shaping or left white for cherry blossoms.

Pinch the base of each petal to form a point.

Assembling the Blossoms

Attach three or six petals together after heating each over a small flame (al-cohol lamp). The flowers can be placed so some are more flat and others more open to achieve a natural effect.

Inside each flower place short, delicate spun-sugar pistils and stamens.

Attach the flowers to the branch in small, various-sized groups of two, three, four, or five, heating the base of each flower over a small flame.

196

Note

Leaves are not added to apple tree branches, as the blossoms usually bloom and fall before the leaves come out.

Flower Pistils and Stamens

Although it is possible to find artificial pistils and stamens that are very lifelike, using them is not recommended. Sometimes it is necessary to use nonedible materials for branches or supports. It is perhaps a matter of principle in pastry making to use edible materials when possible, even if the final result is not meant to be eaten: otherwise it would be difficult to determine whether the work is within the realm of pastry making or in another profession.

Centers Made from Spun Sugar

Composition

Colored powdered sugar
Spun sugar

Making Colored Powdered Sugar

Generally the sugar used for flower centers is made from crystallized sugar (sometimes difficult to obtain), coarse sugar, or rock sugar passed through a drum sieve, which gives a better final result than the others and stores best.

Regardless of the type of sugar chosen, it should be colored and dried in a low-temperature oven or proof box.

It is advantageous to have an assortment of differently colored sugars on hand so they are ready when needed. The most often used colors are red, yellow, and green. They should be stored in an airtight container.

Making Flower Centers

(for apple or cherry blossoms or imaginary flowers)

Make yellow or white spun sugar following the procedure on pages 174 to 175.

Pinch several threads of warm, malleable spun sugar at intervals to form olive shapes. As the sugar cools it becomes difficult to shape and breaks easily.

The bases should be pinched more tightly than the tops. With a hot knife, cut them at the bases, creating a pair of

centers attached at the tops. Again with a hot knife cut the two centers to separate them and immediately (while still warm) dip the tops into colored sugar.

Very gently heat the bases of the centers to attach them to the flowers.

The centers can be shaped longer or wider, depending on the type and size of flower decorated.

Imaginary Flowers

It is possible to make up flowers that do not really exist. Various colors and shapes can be used to create imaginary flowers. Flowers can be based on variations of real flowers, or use the photographs on this page as guide.

Leaves, stems, and branches

Pulled-sugar leaves are primarily used to adorn, accentuate, and add dimension to pulled-sugar bouquets and individual flowers.

Obviously, the form and color of the leaf is based on the type of flower it will accompany. Although most leaves are made in various shades of green, they should always be luminous.

Branches and stems are used as supports for individual flowers and bouquets.

Sometimes branches and stems are made from nonedible materials, one of the rare times this occurs in pastry making.

leaf according to the size and thickness needed. With a scissors, cut the leaf off at an angle.

Some types of leaves can be imprinted with veins. A special imprinting tool made for this purpose is used, covered

Leaves

with plastic wrap to prevent the leaf from sticking to it, as the leaf must be imprinted while it is still warm and mallea-

Autumn leaves add accents to flowers and bouquets. Two different procedures can be used to make autumn leaves.

1. Use differently colored pulled-sugar pieces, in autumn colors—for example, trimmings of a green, yellow, and red pulled-sugar ribbon.
2. Make leaves from one color (usually green) and decorate, after shaping, with a sponge, paintbrush, or airbrush to create shading and shadows.

Procedure

Pulled-sugar leaves are not very difficult to make.

From a portion of pulled sugar, pull a

ble. The cut leaf is placed over the tool and firmly pressed with the palm of the

hand until the imprint is made. Turn the imprinted leaf over, right side up, and

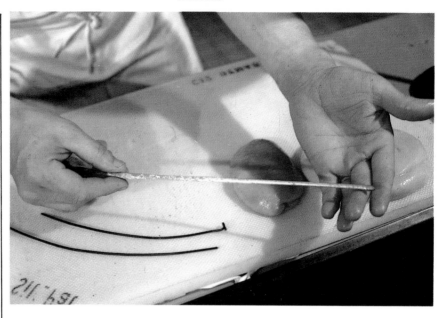

bend and arch it to create a realistic effect. This must be done while it is still malleable.

Rose and dahlia leaves are serrated and shaped like a teardrop (length and width are based on size of flower)

Tulip, lily of the valley, and gladiolus leaves are long, with wide bases, and wavy at the edges.

Carnation leaves are long, pointed, and very slender, almost needlelike.

Ivy and grape leaves are made by cutting the sides and attaching three rose leaves together. Soften the leaves under an infrared lamp (or other heat source) and join the cut sides at the same time the veins are made by pressing them together over the imprint with the palm of the hand.

Stems are often made from wires cut to length and curved.

One end can be folded into a small T to which a flat disk of pulled sugar can be

affixed after covering the stem with pulled sugar, creating a support for the flowers.

Wooden sticks or skewers are also often used to make stems. Although supple, they obviously cannot be curved like wires.

Covering Stems with Pulled Sugar

The stems (wooden or wire sticks) are gently heated. Warm a piece of green pulled sugar so it is malleable. Pinch a section approximately 1 cm (⅜ in.) thick.

Push the tip of the straight (not folded) end of the stem through the center of the

lifted pulled sugar in one even stroke, without stopping or pausing during the procedure.

Branches

Real branches chosen for their shape, size, and sturdiness are covered with cooked sugar and used for pulled-sugar flowers and presentation pieces. The

branches should be allowed to dry for several months or in a proof box for several weeks when used for presentation pieces that are to be held for a long period of time in covered, humidity-free display cases.

Dipping the Branches in Cooked Sugar

1 kg sugar (35 oz.)
150 to 200 g glucose (5 to 7 oz.)
300 ml water (10 fl. oz.)

Cook these ingredients to the hard crack stage. Lightly color the cooked sugar.

Dip the branches, previously warmed in the oven, in the cooked sugar. The pan

should be wide enough for at least the tips of all the branches to fit. With a ladle, pour the sugar over the parts of the branches sticking out of the pan.

To obtain a thin, delicate coating of sugar, it is important that the cooked sugar be hot and the branches still warm.

Careful! Work cautiously to prevent burns from the hot cooked sugar.

Branches Covered in Gelatin Syrup

It is possible to replace the cooked sugar with sugar syrup at 1260 D, lightly colored, and strongly bound with gelatin. Use 32 g (1 oz.) of gelatin for each liter (34 fl. oz.) of sugar syrup.

With a pastry brush cover the dried, cold branches with the gelatin/syrup mixture.

This method is good for achieving a very thin and less fragile, more flexible covering.

Pulled-sugar Ribbons

Although pulled-sugar ribbons are not made very often, there are many occasions for which they can be used.

Usually ribbons are made into bows and decorate the tops of cakes. However, it is also possible to encircle a cake with a flat ribbon; for example, to make a ribbon descending a frozen dessert in a spiral.

Ribbons are more attractive when made in several colors. Making thin and even pulled-sugar ribbons requires a great deal of practice.

Preparation

Prepare the equipment and work area as for making any pulled-sugar ornament (page 184).

It is best to have a large work surface under an infrared lamp, approximately 40 × 60 cm (16 × 24 in.). Cover the work surface with a nonstick paper, such as a sheet of silicone paper (oilcloth). The cloth should be lightly oiled and lie flat.

An old chef's knife or scissors, alcohol burner, and heat lamp (infrared) are all the materials needed to make the ribbon.

Recipe

The recipe for pulled sugar (using fondant, page 185) works very well for making ribbons. However, beginners are advised to add more acid, which will make stretching the sugar to obtain a thin delicate ribbon easier.

Recipe

Cook the following to 160°C (320°F):

2 g cream of tartar (¼ to ½ tsp.)
2 Tbsp. white distilled vinegar
1 kg white fondant (35 oz.)

Note

Although this recipe makes it easier to form ribbons because of the increased acid, the acid also absorbs humidity faster, causing the sugar to melt and sweat faster. It is therefore helpful to dry the ribbon as soon as it is finished by placing it in an airtight container with dehydrating packets. Store it there until needed.

Procedure

Place the assorted colors of cooked pulled sugar under the heat lamp to keep them malleable. Occasionally fold the pieces over so they heat evenly.

Pulled-sugar ribbons

Three different colors of pulled sugar (pieces left from making flowers)—gold, red, and green—are used in the example below.

Note

For the quantity of sugar used in the following procedure, it is possible to obtain a ribbon 3 meters (10 feet) long.

Beginners will find it much easier to handle smaller amounts at a time.

Procedure

A. Make a two-toned rod of pulled sugar, approximately 1.5 cm (⅝ in.) thick. This will serve as the center strip.

B. Attach a second strip that is the same thickness as the first piece and 25 to 30 cm (10 to 12 in.) long to the center piece, encircling it.

C. Pull the two attached pieces of sugar, doubling the length.

D. Fold the piece in half and line up the two ends, sticking the inside edges together. Keep the pulled sugar under the lamp during this procedure so it remains malleable. It is important not to let the sugar become too warm, so that it loses its shape, or too cold, in which case it will be difficult to pull and will crack easily.

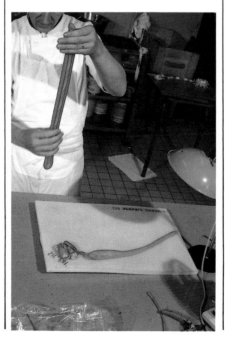

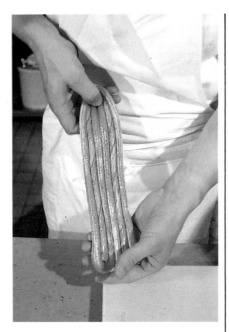

G. Pull the entire strip until it is approximately 60 cm (24 in.) long.

I. Repeat pulling, folding, and cutting the piece, which will now be more difficult to work with because of its size.

E. Cut the piece at the fold with a scissors.

H. Fold the piece in half and stick the two ends together, as in step D.

J. Cut the ends to keep them even when necessary.

K. The ribbon should be the same consistency throughout.

F. Attach the third color to one side. This last strip should be the same thickness as the first pulled piece, which will now be thinner than before it was pulled. Cut or pull the strip as needed so it is the same length as the main piece.

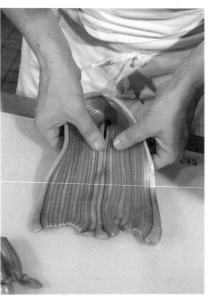

L. To ensure an even thickness throughout the ribbon, rub it back and forth over a thigh covered with an apron. A slower movement will make it adhere slightly to the apron, making evening out the thicker sections easier.

M. Once the ribbon is even in thickness and malleable throughout, it is ready to be pulled, which should be done quickly

P. Slowly heat each section (except for the two larger ones) under the lamp and gently bend each in half, into a well-rounded loop.

and in one step. It is best if a second person is available to making it easier to form a thin, even ribbon.

Q. Heat the cut ends of each loop until they are malleable. Bend them until they meet. Pinch the ends gently, making them slightly narrower and pleated. This procedure gives a more realistic look to the bow.

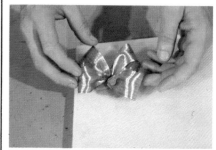

N. Once the ribbon has been pulled to the desired length and thickness, place it on a lightly oiled marble.

Assembling the Ribbon

Heat the pleated ends of the loops and attach them together on a flat piece of trimming from the ribbon.

Carefully position each loop to form an attractive bow.

Heat the two longer pieces just enough to bend them, giving them a wavy appearance. Heat each piece at one end and attach to the bow.

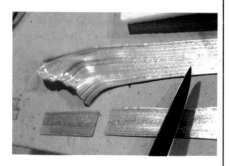

O. Heat an old knife in a flame. Cut the ribbon into sections 12 to 15 cm (4.5 to 6 in.) long. Cut two longer pieces, which will be used as the ends of the ribbon, branching out from the bow.

Weaving or basketry

Stretch the point of the teardrop of pulled sugar until it is a few mm (about ¼ in.) in diameter. Maintain this thickness throughout the weaving.

Place the tip of the strand of pulled sugar inside one of the rods of the mandrel. Hold the bulk of the pulled sugar in one hand to the side of or just under the heat lamp so it remains malleable. Baskets are often made with two pieces of

pulled sugar, making it easier to handle the sugar and maintain the proper temperature.

The fingers of the other hand should help guide the strand of sugar, keeping it even in thickness, helping the strand to weave in and out around the rods, and

Weaving with pulled sugar offers numerous possibilities for presentation pieces, such as baskets filled with decorated fruits (marzipan-stuffed fruits), blown-sugar fruits, or flowers.

All woven pulled-sugar pieces are formed on a special frame made for this purpose.

The frame, known as a mandrel, can be found in various sizes and shapes. It consists of an odd number of metal rods that fit into notches on a base. The base often has several rows of notches, making it possible to adjust the size of the basket. Check that the rods are securely in place to prevent them from slipping and breaking the basket while it is being made.

Procedure

Baskets are often made with straw-colored pulled sugar. It is possible to give the completed basket and handle an antique veneer by shading it with coffee extract or brown coloring applied with a paintbrush, a piece of sponge or foam, or an airbrush.

Form a ball of pulled sugar into a teardrop shape about the size of a pear. Do not let the pulled sugar become overly soft, or it will be less lustrous when set.

Prepare the Equipment

Lightly oil the base of the mandrel and the metal rods before inserting the rods.

turning the base of the mandrel so the pulled sugar remains under the heat lamp.

Remember, unless the pulled sugar is maintained at the proper temperature, it may become brittle and break if too cold or lose its shape and sheen if too hot.

To finish, cut off the strand of sugar and place it inside the basket.

When the desired height of the basket has been reached, carefully remove the metal rods and replace them with strands of pulled sugar, bending them over at the top inside the basket to prevent them from falling into the notches on the base.

Making a Coiled Base

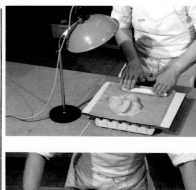

Finish the base of the basket by wrapping it with a coil of pulled sugar. The coil is started by rolling a piece of pulled sugar into a sausage shape and pulling it into a long, thin strand. The strand is then folded in half and twisted, using both hands. Hold one end in each hand and twist in opposite directions at the same time.

Place the coil of pulled sugar around the base of the basket while it is still malleable.

The Handle

To make a handle for the basket, bend a wire cord to the size needed. Starting with the same technique as for weaving, pull a strand from a teardrop-shaped piece of pulled sugar held in one hand and wrap it around the wire, guiding it with the other hand.

Once the handle is finished, place it inside the basket and affix it with a small piece of soft pulled sugar.

Small pulled-sugar figures

Small figures and subjects can be made out of pulled sugar (usually white) to decorate desserts. Examples include a ballerina on an ice-cream cake, a small swan on an individual dessert, or a rose on a serving of ice cream.

These types of pulled-sugar figures are always quite small and are made in two steps.

Step 1: Make the separate components of the piece.

Step 2: Assemble, attach, and color, usually with a paintbrush, piece of foam, or airbrush.

The photographs on these two pages can serve as a guide to examples of various pulled-sugar subjects. Finish them as desired.

It is interesting to note that the base or major support of most figures is shaped in the same way as a rosebud, one reason why it is important to learn first to make a rose with pulled sugar.

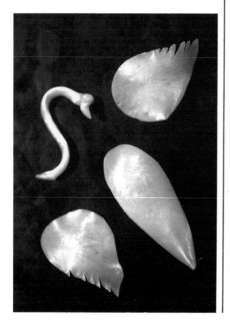

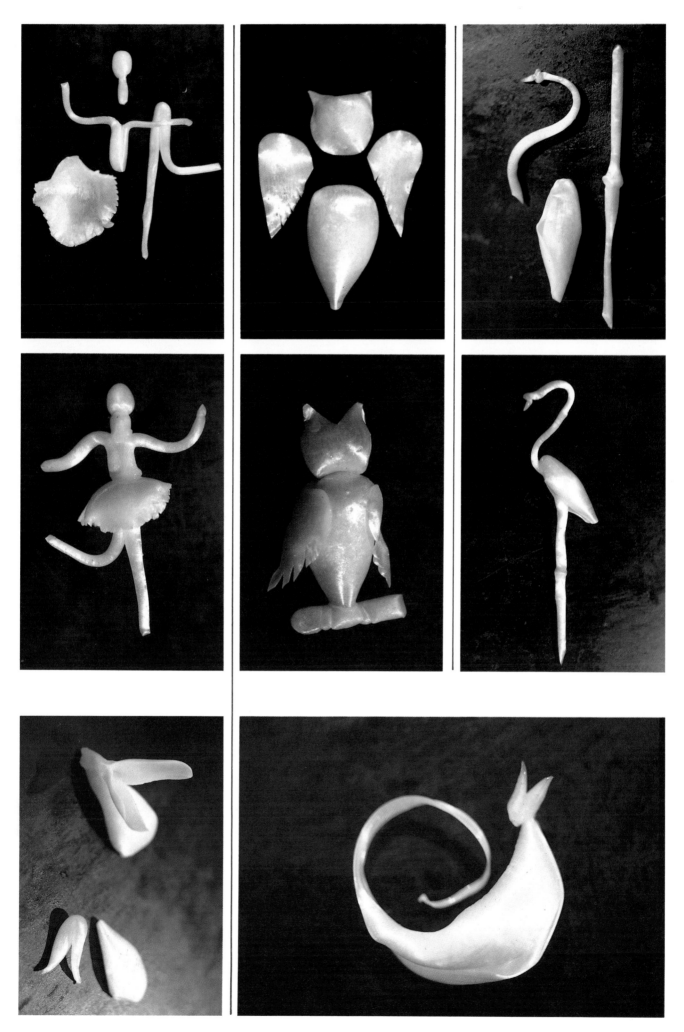

Assembling a bouquet

No two pulled-sugar floral arrangements are the same, nor should they be. The occasion for which a piece is intended will determine how it is constructed. A few key points are given on this page to help in assembling pulled-sugar bouquets.

A pulled-sugar bouquet that is to be held for a long period of time should be kept in a display case designed to absorb humidity (see page 212).

It is best to assemble pulled-sugar pieces during dry periods in an area that is well ventilated and free of steam. If possible, place a fan or dehumidifier in the area several hours before working.

Prepare all equipment and clean the work area before beginning to assemble the piece.

Sketch a scale-sized drawing of the bouquet on a piece of paper. This will make it easier to have an idea of where to place the larger pieces and how to distribute colors.

If the basket is placed on a permanent base, it can be glued to the base with some heated pulled sugar.

Although there are no hard-and-fast rules to follow for setting up a bouquet of flowers, they are often started at the back of the piece. Set the branches and flowers in place without fastening them so it is possible to make changes.

Once certain of where each piece will be positioned, glue them in place with cooked sugar high in glucose. Dip the bottoms of the stems in the cooked sugar or use the tip of a knife to bring the sugar over to the basket.

It is best to secure each piece in place at several points. Each branch or stem can be attached at the base and rein- forced halfway up by affixing it to another stem or to the edge of the basket. Branches can also be used as supports for stems. To further ensure stability, it is a good idea to attach flowers to a support, such as the handle of the basket.

Having a second person available to hold items in place before they are secured can be very helpful, making it possible to step back and see how the bouquet looks.

Finish the bouquet by covering joints with leaves. Place an attractive cloth beneath the basket.

It is advantageous to ask for constructive criticism from a third party, who may have suggestions or notice details that go unnoticed by those assembling the piece.

Constructing an artistic piece

Basic Instructions

It takes a great deal of forethought and analysis to construct an artistic piece that, when finished, is truly satisfying and rewarding.

Many hours of work are required to construct a presentation piece of high caliber, even longer for a competition piece.

The pieces presented on these two pages required roughly the following amounts of time:

- 15 hours of work to make the horizontal bouquet of roses and the painting of Beethoven
- 25 hours of work for the bouquet of flowers
- 50 hours for the piece with white roses
- 75 hours for the piece with the painting of Strauss
- 120 hours for the feast in the photograph on the opposite page. This piece was partially assembled with items made using techniques already covered in the book. How the other items are made will be discussed later in the chapter.

The Six Steps for Assembling an Artistic Piece

1. Choose a theme.
2. Sketch a diagram.
3. Decide which components are needed.
4. Decide where the individual pieces will be placed.
5. Allow for the necessary time to shape, cut, construct, and dry pieces made from pastillage. Allow 1 week to dry each mm (1/16 in.) of pastillage, to prevent enclosing a piece in a display case before it has dried thoroughly.
6. Allow enough time to construct each piece (especially a piece meant for competition), storing them in the correct way until they are assembled. It is often prudent to make two or three copies of each piece to allow for any possible mishaps and to be able to choose from more than one.

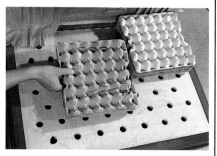

Assembling the Piece

As no two pieces are alike, it is difficult to give advice that covers all pieces; each presents different problems.

Making the display case is important for conserving the piece. Below are a few key points.

The display case should be an appropriate size: too small and the piece will seem crowded; too large and the piece will be lost; too tall or short and the proportions of the piece will be adversely affected.

The base should be solid, raised, and decorated. It should be completely waterproof and covered with a sheet of plastic or Formica. Space should be reserved for assembling a desiccator.

All pieces should be thoroughly dry.

The desiccant is set in place when the piece is ready to be assembled. Depending on the pieces made, choose an appropriate amount and type of desiccant, such as carbide, quick lime, silica gel, or calcium chloride. For the desiccant to be most effective, make numerous holes in the board that rests just above it. To get the maximum and fastest effect possible, place some of the desiccant directly under the cloth covering the base.

If the base has more than one level, attach the sugar work or pieces to be presented to the base to prevent them from slipping or breaking during transport.

Choose a cloth that is large enough to cover the entire base and supports. Sometimes it will be necessary to protect a portion of the cloth with clean towels or sheets of paper while assembling the piece.

The display glass, approximately 3 to 5 mm (⅛ to ¼ in.) thick, should be cleanly and accurately cut to the size needed. Assemble it with two or three layers of strong adhesive tape to ensure solidity and yet make it possible to store it flat.

For a display case 80 cm (32 in.) wide in front, 60 cm (24 in.) deep, and 70 cm (28 in.) tall:

- 2 panels of glass 80 × 70 cm (32 × 28 in.) for the front and back
- 2 panels of glass 59 × 70 cm (23.5 × 28 in.) for the sides
- 1 panel of glass 80 × 60 cm (32 × 24 in.) for the top

All panels should be 5 mm (¼ in.) thick.

Before attaching them together, check that each panel is perfectly clean on the inside and that the edges join neatly.

Be sure the joints are held tightly together; check for any weak points. A little putty or a strip of glucose can be used to attach the display glass to the molding around the sides.

Never expose a presentation piece to the sun.

Note

The base of the display case is often covered with a cloth and/or lace ribbon. This base is often glued to the bottom support before the piece is assembled.

Le sucre soufflé (Blown sugar)

Definition

Blown sugar is pulled sugar that is shaped into a sort of pouch into which air is blown with the aid of a hand pump. Blown sugar is similar to blown glass.

The most simple to the most complex shapes can be formed in various sizes.

Just as when learning the techniques for pulled sugar, blown sugar requires a great deal of practice.

It is not possible to describe in detail each shape that can be formed. Instead it is sufficient to master the different basic techniques, progressively acquiring the abilities necessary to make more diverse figures.

Equipment

Use the same equipment called for in cooking pulled sugar plus:

Heat lamp or other heat source

Work surface: marble, plastic, or silicone sheets (preferred)
Hand pump with attachment
Large scissors
Chef's knife
Alcohol lamp.

Preferred Recipe

1 kg sugar (35 oz.)
1 g cream of tartar (¼ tsp.)
400 g water (13.5 fl. oz.)
200 g glucose (7 oz.)

Cook the above ingredients to 153° to 155°C (307° to 311°F).

This recipe produces a dryer and firmer cooked sugar, which makes it easier to make all blown-sugar pieces.

Beginners will find making fruits easier if they use the recipe given for pulled sugar on page 185.

Preparation

One of the most common problems encountered with blown sugar involves the deforming of the piece before it has completely cooled.

There are a few ways to cool the piece quickly to prevent it from becoming misshapen.

● Fill a bucket (with a cover) two-thirds full with a strong rubbing alcohol and place it in the freezer for 24 hours before using it. The blown-sugar pieces are plunged into the cold alcohol, which cools them instantly.
● Use a fan to cool large pieces quickly.
● Place a covered container filled with granulated or confectioners' sugar in the freezer until very cold. Large pieces covered with the cold sugar cool very quickly.

Techniques for Blowing Sugar

Fruits

Before making blown-sugar fruits, it is important to know their shapes. It is helpful to have a model to work from, either real or plastic.

Basic Tips

All blown-sugar pieces are made from the same basic form. They are broken down into four groups of increasing difficulty.
1. **Fruits,** small, regularly shaped pieces that cool quickly, are the simplest forms to make with blown sugar. Learning to make them will help the beginner understand the basic techniques for blowing sugar.
2. **Large objects with simple shapes,** such as vases or horns of plenty, are not much more difficult than fruits but allow the

beginner to learn how to work with a large quantity of blown sugar.
3. **Large pieces with complex shapes** are made by joining more than one piece of blown sugar. Each piece is formed separately, in proportion to the final figure. Swans, rabbits, bears, squirrels, and doves are made in this way.
4. **Four-legged animals** are made in one piece and cut to shape. This requires a great deal of skill and practice, especially to make large figures.

From a piece of pulled sugar, which should be malleable and yet not overly soft, pull a thick piece and place a thumb

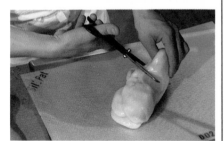

inside, forming a cavity with walls of even thickness, approximately 1 cm (⅜ in.).

Cut this section of pulled sugar off the larger piece with a scissors, maintaining the thickness.

Under the lamp, use the fingers to shape the piece and even it out.

Place the tip of the pump attachment inside the cavity and press the sides around it so no air leaks out. Pump a little air into the ball of sugar.

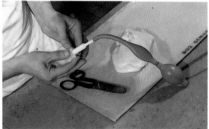

Stretch the ball of sugar away from the attachment. This makes it easier to shape the piece.

Shape the piece with one hand while pumping air slowly into it with the other. Be careful to control how much air is

pumped in; apply only as much pressure as needed.

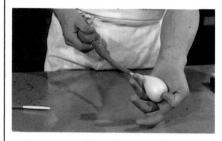

Once the fruit is shaped as desired, plunge it in cold alcohol to cool it immediately.

Caution: Never place the container of alcohol near the heat source (infrared lamp) or flame (alcohol burner). It will ignite. Also be sure to allow the alcohol to evaporate from pieces that have been cooled in it before returning them to the flame for any final shaping.

Fruits with grooves (such as peaches) are given the indentations before being cooled in alcohol. The indentations can be made with a closed scissors.

After the alcohol has completely evaporated, slowly heat the top of the fruit over a small flame, turning it around in the flame to pull it off of the pump. Once the pump is disengaged, the fruit will be malleable, making it possible to shape the top of the fruit as desired.

215

Small blown-sugar fruits

Cherries, strawberries, and grapes are grouped in a category of small blown-sugar fruits. All are made with the same fairly simple technique.

Pull a piece of pulled sugar up above the ball of sugar in the same way as when covering a stem with pulled sugar (page 199). This time, press a lightly oiled whisk handle into the ball of sugar, creating an elongated fingerlike shape, similar to the cavity for larger fruits. Gently pull out the whisk handle by rotating it.

Close the top of the cavity to enclose air inside the cavity.

Force as much air as possible into the tip of the cavity to obtain the desired-size small balls for cherries and grapes or larger ones for strawberries.

Cut off the ball of fruit with a scissors or small shears.

Assembling a Bunch of Grapes

Grapes are assembled and attached to a pulled-sugar support (made from the same color of pulled sugar used to make the grapes) with a vine shoot.

The piece is decoratively shaded after it is assembled. Amber shading can be applied to fruit and leaves with a piece of sponge or foam, paintbrush, or airbrush.

Grape bunches are usually presented with one or two grape leaves (see page 198 to 199) attached to the vine shoot.

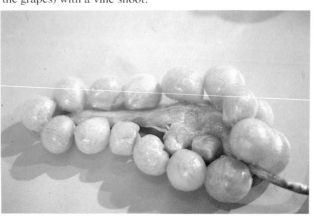

Making Large Pieces

When making large pieces, larger than 500 g (17.5 oz.), the sugar is cooked and pulled just before it is used and placed in a ball to soften under a heating lamp until the texture is homogeneous.

Place the ball of pulled sugar on the end of a lightly oiled rolling pin, shaping it to form a cavity as for smaller pieces. Make the walls even in thickness.

A Vase

The same techniques for making a vase out of blown sugar can be used to make a carafe, pitcher, horn of plenty, or teapot.

Place the piece of cup-shaped pulled sugar around the attachment for the hand pump, as described on page 215 for making large fruits.

Pull the base of the ball of sugar away from the pump so it is somewhat elongated.

Slowly pump air into the vase with one hand while the other hand pulls and shapes the piece. By placing the piece on the marble upright, a base can be formed.

A horn of plenty would be placed on its side.

Once the piece has been shaped, cool it quickly by submerging it in cold alcohol, rubbing it in cold sugar, or using a fan. Allow the alcohol to evaporate before finishing.

To form the neck of the vase, heat the top section over a small flame to soften the sugar again and shape as desired. Remove the pump as when making fruit, heat the top, and cut it with a scissors when soft. Shape the opening of the vase while the sugar is still malleable.

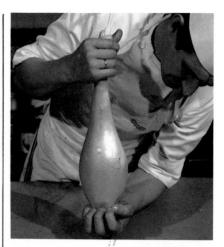

A handle can be made by twisting pulled sugar into a coil and attaching it to the vase. The vase can be colored using a piece of foam, sponge, or an airbrush. Flowers or other decorations can be painted on with a paintbrush or with a paper cone filled with royal icing.

Medium and large pieces made from several parts

A Swan

The technique for making a swan in blown sugar can also be used to make a duck, rabbit, squirrel, bear, cat, or owl.

The most challenging aspect of making blown-sugar pieces comprising more than one piece involves studying the form of each figure especially its proportions. The difficulty of this work is especially evident when the figure requires two or more identical pieces, such as the wings of the swan.

Procedure

Place half the pulled sugar on a hand pump as for large fruit. This half of the pulled sugar will be used to make the body; the other half, to make the two wings.

Stretch the ball of sugar, elongating it as when making a vase.

At the end of the piece (opposite the end attached to the pump), begin to pull and shape the head and beak of the swan gently.

Pull and shape the neck. Pump in more air to expand the body.

Cool the blown sugar quickly by rubbing it in a sheet pan of cold sugar (taken from the freezer). Heat the tail and cut off the excess to remove the pump.

Making the Wings

Each wing is made with one-quarter of the entire mass of pulled sugar, so they will be equal in size to each other and in proportion to the body.

The wing is first shaped like a pear, then curved, placed on a clean towel over the marble (to prevent it from becoming firm too quickly), and given a rounded shape while air is pumped in. Each wing will have the form of half a heart.

After the wings have completely cooled, they are attached to the body with a little cooked sugar or by warming and softening the base of the wing over a flame.

The swan can be decorated with food coloring applied with a paintbrush. The wings can be completed with feathers made of pulled sugar, by applying royal icing with a paper cone, or by covering the entire wing with pulled sugar.

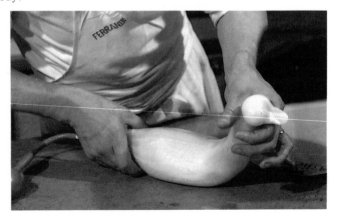

 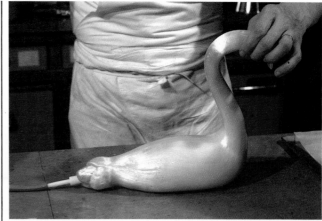

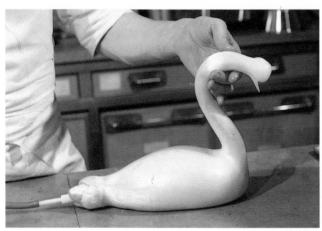 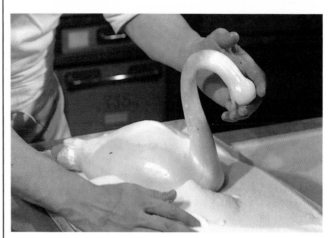

 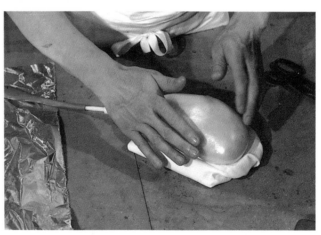

 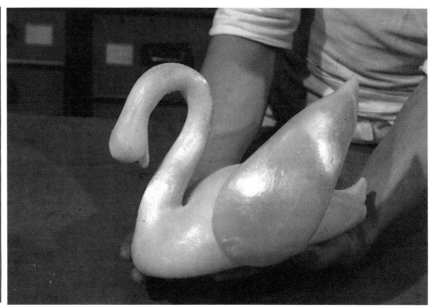

Blown-sugar figures cut to shape from one piece

This is the most difficult type of blown-sugar work. Each figure requires a great deal of practice and patience.

This technique can be used to create artistic and decorative pieces.

The technique is basically the same for all animals. It is important to study the form of the animal. Having a model to work from can be very helpful.

The techniques given on these two pages for making a fawn can be applied to other animals such as a doe, giraffe, llama, or horse.

Procedure

Place a ball of pulled sugar over the tip of the hand pump attachment, as for the preceding blown-sugar figures. Once the sugar is securely attached to the pump, pump in air and pull it to create a sort of pistol shape. The tip of the pump should be at the handle base (which will be the tail of the fawn). The barrel will become the neck and head, and the handle with be cut into quarters to form the legs.

Pull the neck and shape the head, pinching it at the tip to form the snout.

Cut the base (handle) in half with a strong scissors. Cut off the tip of each section to flatten it (forming the hooves), and cut each half in two again to create the front and hind legs.

using alcohol, allow it to evaporate before proceeding.

Warm the area where the pump is attached (the tail) and cut off the excess with a scissors to detach the pump. Shape the tail while the section is still warm and malleable.

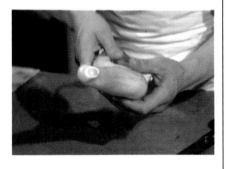

Certain animals are finished by shaping horns, ears, or a mane.

The figure can be colored after it has cooled completely with an airbrush, a paintbrush, or both.

The figures are often attached to bases made of poured sugar, which can be decorated with rocks made from rock sugar, leaves, small shrubs, or pulled-sugar flowers.

Gently pull on the legs to lengthen them, being careful not to deform the shape of the body.

Once the figure is shaped, cool it immediately in cold alcohol or sugar. If

Examples of blown-sugar pieces

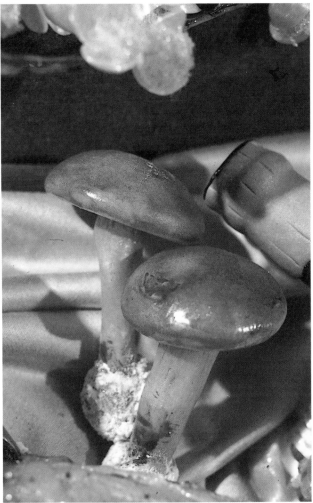

Glossary

Abaisse (sheet of dough)
A thin sheet of pastry dough that is rolled out with the aid of a rolling pin or electric rolling mill (sheeter) to the desired thickness.

Abaisse

Abaisser (to roll out)
To roll out a sheet of pastry dough to the desired thickness with a rolling mill (sheeter) or rolling pin.

Abaisser

Abricoter (to glaze or coat with jelly or preserves)
To coat a tart, a génoise, mille-feuilles, or other pastries with a thin coat of jelly or preserves using a pastry brush or metal spatula. Its purpose is to:
● give a sheen to finished pastries
● reinforce the fruit flavor already in the pastry
● protect a finished product from air (as for tart Chantilly)
● act as a base layer before glazing with other products such as fondant.
See also **napper.**

Abricoter ou napper

Alcooliser (to add liquor)
To add liquor or liqueur to syrups, sauces, creams, or doughs.

Alcooliser

Appareil (mixture)
Various ingredients that have been combined for a particular preparation but have not yet been baked, glazed, turned into ice cream, or otherwise treated. The term is used not only in pastry but in candy making, ice cream making, and other areas. Examples are "appareil a crème pâtissière" (pastry cream mixture) or "appareil à génoise" (génoise batter).

Appareil

Apprêt (final rising)
The final rising of a leavened dough from the time it is shaped or molded to the time it is baked.

Aromates (flavorings)
Refers specifically to natural flavorings that are used in sauces and other mixtures. Examples include bouquet garni and vanilla beans.

Aromates

Aromatiser (to flavor)
To add flavoring to a mixture, sauce, or cream. Examples are adding vanilla beans and bouquet garni.

Arroser or asperger (to add liquid)
To pour or sprinkle liquid such as water, liquor, or syrup, in a steady stream over a preparation to moisten, soften, or flavor it. Examples are moistening génoise or a baba with syrup.

Assaisonner (to season)
To season a preparation with pepper, salt, vinegar, nutmeg, or other spices.

Assouplir (to soften)
To soften butter or shortening to make it more malleable, using a rolling pin or the hands. To render less firm.

Bain-marie, cuisson au (cooking in a water bath)
Cooking method. See **cuire**

Battre (to whip or beat)
To beat a mixture or a preparation such as egg whites or whipped cream with a whisk or electric mixer in such a way as to incorporate air into the mixture and lighten it.

Beurrer (to butter)
To coat a mold or sheet pan with melted or softened butter with a pastry brush, in order to prevent a preparation from sticking during baking. To coat the inside of tart rings with butter, with the fingers, to help line them with dough and to prevent it from sticking. This facilitates removal of the tart after baking. To add butter to a dough or batter such as feuilletage or croissant dough.

Beurre (butter)
Clarified. See **clarifier**
Manié. See **manier**
Pommade. See **pommade**
Malaxé. See **malaxer**

Beurre noisette (brown butter)
Butter that has been cooked in a saucepan until the milk solids caramelize slightly. Characterized by a hazelnut-like odor.

Aromatiser

Assaisonner

Assouplir

Battre

Beurrer

Beurre noisette

Blanchir (to blanch)
1. To beat together egg yolks and sugar with a whisk until the mixture is white and frothy.
2. To cook a product, starting in cold water, bringing the water slowly to a boil. The length of time depends on the product being blanched.
3. To plunge fruits in boiling water. Certain dried fruits, vegetables, and even meats are blanched in order to soften them before the final cooking.

Certain foods, such as almonds and apricots, are blanched so that their skins can be removed more easily.

Blanchir

Bloquer/débloquer (to stiffen/to loosen)
Often used to describe the various stages in tempering chocolate. Chocolate is said to *bloque* when it sets up after being melted and then congeals. It is said to *débloque* when it is slightly overheated and becomes liquid. If it reaches this stage, chocolate must be tempered again before it can be used for molding or dipping. Certain mixtures are loosened by adding liquids before mixing with other, lighter ingredients, as in soufflés and ladyfingers.

Bloquer/débloquer

Bouler (to roll into balls)
Method of working dough with the palm of the hand, using a circular motion, to obtain even balls used for a variety of preparations.

Bouler

Bouquet garni
A packet of herbs, such as parsley, thyme, and bay leaf, that are tied together and used to flavor stocks, soups, and the like.

Brosser (to brush)
To brush the excess flour or sugar from a sheet of rolled-out pastry. To brush liqueur-flavored candies or fondant to remove cornstarch. To clean the work area with a brush.

Bouquet garni

Broyer (to grind)
To grind nuts with the use of a special grinder in order to obtain a fine powder or paste.

Broyer

Brûler (to burn)
To burn or overcook. Used also to describe egg yolks that have been allowed to sit too long with sugar or a boiling liquid such as milk. Also said of a dough that is too dry and tends to break apart and remain brittle.

Buée (water vapor)
Water vapor released by baking pastries or boiling liquids. Steam specially introduced into the oven before baking certain leavened doughs, sometimes in an oven specially designed for this purpose.

Brûler

Candir (to sugar-coat)
To submerge certain candies (for example, fruit-based or almond paste) in a concentrated sugar syrup called *sucre candi* to coat them with a shiny protective layer of crystallized sugar.

Candir

Canneler (to groove decoratively)
To cut decorative grooves in lemon and orange skins using a special tool called a *canneleur*. To decorate almond paste with a special grooved roller.

Canneler

Caraméliser (to caramelize)
To coat the interior of a mold with a thin layer of caramel.

To add caramel, cooked sugar, or diluted caramel to a cream, sauce, or mixture.

To coat the surface of certain pastries (mille-feuilles, polkas, puits d'amour) with confectioners' sugar and to burn or caramelize the surface with a heating element (caramélisateur) designed for this purpose.

To coat almonds or hazelnuts with cooked sugar or caramel.

Casser un oeuf (to break eggs)
See *Breaking and Separating Eggs* in the text.

Chapelure (cake crumbs or breadcrumbs)
Breadcrumbs or génoise crumbs that have been dried in the oven and passed through a drum sieve.

Charger/décharger (to weight/to remove weights)
To place weights (cherry pits, dried beans) on unfilled pastry dough covered with parchment paper to hold it down during a preliminary baking, referred to as baking blind (à blanc).

Décharger: to remove weights after baking.

Caraméliser

Casser un œuf

Charger/décharger

Chemiser (to line, coat)
To line a chilled mold with ice cream. To line a mold or sheet pan with parchment paper or flour. To line the sides and bottom of a mold with cooked sugar or jelly.

Chemiser

Chinoiser (to strain)
To strain liquids through a fine strainer (china cap) to eliminate certain substances (egg shells or lumps, for example).

Chinoiser

225

Chiqueter (to flute)
To make indentations or incisions on the side of certain uncooked pâte feuilletée preparations with the back of a knife. This is decorative and facilitates even rising of the pastry.

Chiqueter

Ciseler (to incise)
To make light incisions on certain pastries with the tip of a knife to help heat penetrate the interior and to prevent them from bursting open. Also, to dice parsley, lettuce, chervil, or other herbs finely.

Clarifier (to separate/to clarify)
To separate eggs.

To melt butter slowly so that it separates into whey (skimmed off the top), butter fat (stays in the middle), and milk solids (fall to the bottom). Remove the butter fat (which is the clarified butter).

To clarify a syrup, stock, or jelly by adding beaten egg whites to the liquid and bringing the mixture slowly to a boil for several minutes. Once the whites have floated to the surface, the liquid should be completely clear. The eggs can then simply be strained or skimmed off.

Clarifier

Coller (to thicken)
To add gelatin that has been softened in cold water and drained, to give a mixture added consistency. See also **gommer.**

Coller

Colorer or teinter (to color/to dye)
To color a mixture (sauce, cream, dough, cooked sugar) with either an authorized artificial food coloring or a natural ingredient: To color certain pastries in a hot oven.

Colorer ou teinter

Concasser (to chop coarsely)
To crush or chop coarsely, as for walnuts, hazelnuts, and coffee beans.

Concher (to smooth)
To work chocolate to make it smooth and homogeneous.

Confire (to preserve in sugar)
To submerge fruits in sugar syrup to preserve them or for the preparation of fruits confits (candied fruits).

Concasser

Congélation and surgélation (to freeze and deep-freeze)
To freeze at an extremely low temperature to preserve and solidify foods.

Corner (to scrape)
To scrape the sides of a mixing bowl or other container with a rubber spatula or pastry scraper so as to prevent waste. A well-scraped container should have no remaining matter.

Corner

Corps (body)
A dough is said to have developed body when it has become elastic after successful kneading. Working a dough develops its body by activating the gluten to obtain elasticity, smoothness, and malleability.

Corps

Coucher or dresser (to pipe out)
To place batter on a sheet pan or in a mold using a pastry bag with a plain or fluted tip. Examples are *coucher des éclairs* or *dresser des choux*. Piping batter with the pastry bag at an angle is called *coucher*. If the bag is held straight up and down, piping is *dresser*.

Coucher ou dresser

Couler (to mold liquids)
To fill molds or embossed sheets with a liquid or semisolid either with a special funnel designed for this purpose (fondant) or mechanically for candy making.

couler

Couper or découper (to cut)
To slice a génoise or other cake in two or three layers with a serrated knife in order to fill it. This is done as follows :
● Mark the sides of the cake with the knife in order to cut it evenly.
● Cut around the sides of the cake in order to obtain even slices.

Also, to cut pastries such as cakes, tarts, or ice creams with a knife.

Couper ou découper

Couvrir (to cover)
To protect a preparation from air by covering with plastic wrap, aluminum foil, a wet towel, etc. To cover a preparation during baking to prevent it from browning excessively.

Cracher (to split open)
1. The splitting open of a decorative incision made in a pastry in an appealing way when baked. Examples are Pithiviers, turnovers, and other feuilletée pastries.
2. The opening of an incision of any type because of heat.

Crémer (to cream)
To work a mixture so that it has a creamy consistency. To combine butter with sugar and eggs until it has a creamy consistency, either by hand or in the electric mixer.

Couvrir

Cribler (to roll)
To roll a mixture or substance inside a drum sieve, in order to separate particles. Hazelnuts are treated in this way to remove their skins.

Cristalliser (to crystallize)
To roll pastry or candy (fruits and fruit pastes) in crystallized sugar to coat them. To cook certain syrups to the stage where they crystallize. See also **candir.**

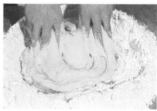

Crémer

Croûter (to crust)
To form a crust through exposure to air. Used to describe dough or creams that have been exposed to air and have dried and formed a thick, dry crust. The formation of a crust is caused by too low a humidity or a sudden change in temperature. To avoid this, doughs and creams should be covered at all times with plastic wrap or aluminum foil. The humidity can also be increased (for example, by putting water in a proofing oven).

Cribler

Croûter

Cuire (to cook)
Different cooking methods :

au four (in the oven) : The temperature of the oven and the baking time are both functions of the size of the pastry being cooked.

sur le feu (on the stove) : To cook in a saucepan, crêpe pan, frying pan, or other vesicle in direct contact with the flame. Used, for example, for cooked sugar, creams, and crêpes.

au bain-marie (in a water bath) : To cook in a container (bain-marie) half-filled with hot water maintained at a temperature of 80° to 95° C (175° to 200° F). The water in the water bath must never boil. For certain delicate preparations, such as custards, diplomates, and terrines, the bain-marie is used directly on the stove.

Cuire   au four

au bain-marie

à blanc (baking blind): Method of pre-baking tart and pie shells for which the fruit or cream used in the filling cannot be baked (crème Chantilly, raspberries, red currants). The method consists of first lining the raw dough with parchment paper, filling it with something to weigh it down (such as cherry pits or dried beans) and baking it ahead of time. The weights prevent the dough from swelling during this initial baking. If the procedure is performed correctly, the tart or pie shell should be an even, pale brown color. For best results, the weights should be removed about 5 to 8 minutes before baking is finished.

à blanc

pre-cuisson à blanc (half-baking blind): This method is the same as for full à blanc baking, but as the name implies, it consists of cooking the tart or pie shells only halfway. The weights should be removed 5 to 10 minutes into the baking. The shell should then be filled with the appropriate mixture and the baking continued. Examples of preparations requiring this method are tart alsacienne and quiche.

Culotter (to scald)
To scald a mixture in a saucepan by cooking on too high a heat in such a way that the mixture adheres to the sides of the pan and burns.

Culotter

Décanter (to pour off)
To pour liquids carefully to separate liquids from solids. Melted butter is clarified using this technique. When decanting liquids, pour into another container with great care in order to separate the elements.

Décanter

Décercler (to remove tart rings)
To remove a ring from a tart, either during baking or as soon as the tart has been placed on a cake rack to cool. The term is also applied to miniature cakes and mousses.

Décercler

Décorer (to decorate)
To decorate with a variety of ingredients (including cocoa powder, royal icing, chocolate nougatine, sugar, or almond paste) to make the appearance of a preparation more appealing. Decorating requires good taste, dexterity, cleanliness, and professional experience. In this area the professional may freely use his or her imagination.

Décortiquer (to shell/to shuck)
To remove the shell or peel from a fruit, nut, etc.

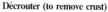
Décorer

Décrouter (to remove crust)
To place warm water over the surface of fondant to eliminate the crust that has formed. This operation should precede the working and tempering of the fondant.

Décuire (to reverse cooking)
To add a certain amount of water to a cooking sugar syrup or fruit jelly to lower its temperature. To bring down the temperature once the optimum temperature has been exceeded.

Défourner (to remove from the oven)
To take from the oven, sometimes using a special paddle designed for this purpose.

Déglacer (to deglaze)
In French pastry, this term refers specifically to the removal of caked-on sugar from a copper sugar pan by dissolving it with boiling water. It is also possible to deglaze a hot sugar pan by brushing it with water and a pastry brush.

Dégourdir (to warm)
To warm a liquid, such as water, eggs or a syrup, gently. To temper a liquid, at 37° to 40° C (98° to 104° F).

Déguiser (to fill fruits with marzipan)
To fill certain types of petits fours, made with fruits, with marzipan.

Délayer (to mix with liquid)
To combine dry ingredients with liquids. Examples are powdered milk and water or flour and milk for soufflés.

Décorer

Décrouter

Décuire

Déglacer

Dégourdir

Déguiser

Délayer

Démouler (to unmold)
To remove a hot or cold preparation carefully from a mold. Examples are génoise, savarin, and molded ice creams.

Démouler

Dénoyauter (to pit)
To remove the pits from certain fruits using a special pitter. Examples are plums, cherries, and olives. Also, to remove the pits from certain fruits such as prunes and dates by opening them with a paring knife.

Dénoyauter

Denteler (to indent or scallop)
To cut the edge of a Pithiviers in a decorative scallop shape using a paring knife.

Denteler

Dessécher (to dry)
To dry a mixture by working it over the stove with a spatula to cause the moisture to evaporate. Pâte à choux (cream puff pastry batter) is an example. It is dried out over the stove before the eggs are added. To place certain preparations in an oven or proofing oven to dehydrate them.

Dessécher

Détailler (to section)
To divide dough into several chunks or pieces; for example, dividing a 500-g (17.5-oz.) piece of dough into 14 small balls, rolling out dough and cutting out turnovers, Pithiviers, or other pastries using a pastry cutter. Also, to cut a sheet of pastry dough using a knife; for example, cutting a strip of rolled-out pastry dough to form croissants.

Détailler

Détendre (to thin)
To thin a mixture (a dough, cream, batter, or other liquid or semiliquid) by adding liquid; for example, thinning heavy cream by adding milk.

Détendre

Détrempe
A mixture of flour, water, salt, butter, and sometimes sugar or yeast used in the preparation of pâte feuilletée (puff pastry dough) or croissants.

Détrempe

Développer (to rise)
The rising of a dough or mixture caused either by heat or fermentation.

Développer

Dissoudre (to dissolve)
To dissolve ingredients such as salt and sugar in a liquid such as water or milk.

Dorer (to glaze)
To brush the surface of certain pastries with glaze (such as egg wash), to prevent the formation of a crust, to give a sheen, to help form a finer crust, or to develop an appealing brown appearance. Glazing is also used to attach two pieces of pastry dough during baking and to avoid the misshaping of certain preparations in the oven.

Dorure (glaze)
Mixture of beaten eggs that have been strained. Different types of glazes are used for different preparations : whole beaten eggs that have been salted and strained, whole eggs combined with yolks and milk or water, egg yolks combined with milk or water. Also, a mixture of milk and sugar or salt. A colored glaze contains caramel or coffee extract (as for sablées).

Doubler/tripler (to double or triple sheet pans)
To bake on a doubled or tripled sheet pan to help prevent the bottom of a pastry from browning too rapidly. This protects the pastries from the heat of the oven floor.

Dresser (to plate)
To place a preparation on a platter or plate for final presentation to the customer. Also, to arrange raw pastries such as croissants on a sheet pan in an orderly way. See also **coucher.**

Ebarder (to trim)
To trim the edges of cooked sugar preparations or molded chocolates with scissors or a paring knife.

Ebouillanter or échauder (to plunge in boiling water)
To plunge nuts or fruits in boiling water to facilitate the removal of the skin or shell. Examples are almonds and tomatoes.

Ecaler (to shell)
To remove the shell or skin from fruits and nuts such as walnuts and hazelnuts. To remove the shell from hard-cooked eggs.

Ecraser (to crush/to smash)
To force fruits (peeled and blanched if appropriate) through a drum sieve with a pastry scraper to turn them into pulp or puree.

Ecumer (to skim)
To remove froth and scum from the surface of a simmering liquid such as syrup or jelly, using a skimmer or spoon.

Effiler (to slice thinly)
To cut almonds, pistachios, or other nuts into thin slices using a paring knife or a special machine designed for this purpose (*effileuse* or *râpe à effiler*).

Egaliser (to trim/to smooth)
To trim certain pastries before their final assembly so the surfaces are even and flat. Used for génoises and meringues.

Egoutter (to drain)
To put a substance in a colander, strainer, china cap, drum sieve, etc., to drain off excess liquid.

Dissoudre

Dorer

Ebarder

Ebouillanter ou échauder

Ecaler

Ecraser

Ecumer

Egaliser

Emincer (to slice)
To slice pears, apples, peaches, onions, mushrooms, and other fruits and vegetables thinly.

Emincer

Emulsionner (to prepare an emulsion)
To make a mixture of butter, oil, or other fats and egg yolks. The particles of fat are held in suspension by forming a liaison with the egg yolk (as in mayonnaise).

Enfourner (to put into the oven)
To place in the oven, sometimes using a special paddle designed for this purpose.

Emulsionner

Enrober (to coat)
To cover a preparation completely with a protective and decorative layer of chocolate, cooked sugar, fondant, or other coating.

Enrober

Envelopper (to seal)
To enclose butter or shortening within a détrempe for the preparation of croissants or pâte feuilletée (puff pastry dough).

Epaissir (to thicken)
To thicken a cream or other mixture by adding a thickener such as starch or flour.

Eplucher (to peel/to trim)
To remove the peel from a fruit or vegetable. To remove what is spoiled or unusable.

Envelopper

Equeuter (to stem)
To remove the stem from washed and drained fruits.

Etaminer (to filter)
To filter a liquid through a fine-mesh strainer or through cheesecloth.

Equeuter

Etuver (to warm or to cook covered)
To place certain preparations in a warm oven or proofing oven to dry them or protect them from humidity. Examples are fruit pastes, liqueur candies, and nougatine. Also, to place certain types of dough in a proofing oven in order to encourage rapid fermentation. Also, to cook certain ingredients slowly in a covered pot or saucepan.

Etuver

Evider (to hollow)
To remove the cores of apples, pears, and other fruits. To remove the inside pulp of a fruit while leaving the outer peel intact, as for oranges and lemons.

Evider

Façon (preserving fruit)
Method of preparing preserved fruits (fruits confits) by submerging them in sugar syrups whose density is increased every 24 hours.

Façonner (to shape/to form)
The process of shaping a dough or preparation. An example is the shaping of dough into individual breads or braided breads. Also, to carve a block of ice or shape pastillage.

Façonner

Farcir (to stuff)
To fill the inside of a fruit, pâté, fowl, meat, etc., with a stuffing.

Farcir

Farder (to tint/to dye)
To tint lightly the surface of a substance, such as almond paste, cooked sugar, or pastillage, with food coloring.

Farder

Fariner (to flour)
To flour the work surface (table, marble) or dough lightly to prevent dough from sticking. To flour a mold or sheet pan that has been buttered. This leaves a film, which prevents batters and dough from running over the surface of the mold or sheet pan and also prevents them from sticking.

Fariner

Ferrer (to burn and stick)
A preparation that has accidentally burned on the bottom and thus sticks to the mold or sheet pan. An example is a génoise that has burned and is sticking to the cake pan. Bread that is burned on the bottom and sticks to the floor of the oven is also referred to as being ferré.

Feuilleter (to make into leaves)
To prepare a pastry by enclosing butter or shortening in a layer of dough and folding and rolling the dough to form thin layers or "leaves." Examples are pâte feuilletée (puff pastry dough) and croissants.

Feuilleter

Filtrer (to filter)
To strain a liquid through a fine-mesh china cap, cheesecloth, fabric, or filter paper in order to separate solid particles held in suspension in a liquid. Examples are to filter sugar syrup for babas and savarins and to filter coffee extract.

Filtrer

Flamber (to flambé/flame)
To coat a preparation with liquor that has been preheated to ignite the alcohol vapors. This technique is used for bananas, crêpes, baked alaska (omelettes norvégiennes), and other preparations.

Fleurer (to flour)
See **Fariner.**

Flamber

Foisonner (to whip)
To beat a mixture vigorously with a whisk so that it expands in volume, as in the whipping of cream mixtures.

Foisonner

Foncer (to line with pastry)
To line a tart mold, ring, or baking sheet with a layer of dough so that it holds firmly in the mold.

Foncer

Fonds (pastry bases or stocks)
1. Layers or rings composed of a wide variety of batters and dough, which enter into the final composition of a finished pastry. Examples are fonds de succès, fonds de génoise, meringues, and fonds de tart.
2. Stocks—veal stock, chicken stock, fish stock, etc.—used for the making of sauces and soups. See also **aromatiser**.
3. Roux.

Fonds

Fontaine (flour well)
A hollow space made in the center of flour which has been measured out for the preparation of a dough. The well in the middle is used to hold the liquid ingredients, which are gradually mixed with the flour using the fingertips.

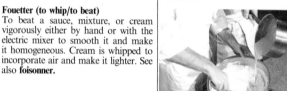

Fontaine

Fouetter (to whip/to beat)
To beat a sauce, mixture, or cream vigorously either by hand or with the electric mixer to smooth it and make it homogeneous. Cream is whipped to incorporate air and make it lighter. See also **foisonner**.

Fouetter

Fournée (pastries for the day)
All of the pastries to be prepared for a particular day. Also, a particular batch of pastries that go into the oven at the same time.

Fourrer (to fill/to stuff)
To fill the inside of certain preparations with creams, mousses, or other mixtures, as for fond de succès (succès base), génoise, meringue, fond de tart (a tart base), and pâte à choux (cream puffs, eclairs).

Fourrer

Fraiser or fraser (to crush dough)
To crush a dough against the work surface or in a mixing bowl to make it smooth and homogeneous without overworking it. It is important that the different components in a dough be well incorporated at this point. To do this, the dough is broken up into sections and either pushed or pulled with the palm of the hand or with a pastry cutter. This method is used for pâte à foncer, sablée, sucrée, and other preparations.

Fraiser ou fraser

Frapper (to chill suddenly)
To cool liquids rapidly by placing them in a freezer or deep-freeze or by plunging them in crushed ice.

Frapper

Frémir (to simmer)
To heat liquid so that its surface trembles, barely simmering, not boiling. Simmering liquid is used for poaching. This simmering stage can be maintained with the help of a bain-marie (water bath).

Frémir

Frire (to deep-fry)
To cook submerged in hot fat or oil. This method is used for beignets and bugnes.

Frire

Garnir (to garnish/to fill)
To fill a tart shell with filling or garniture such as creams or fruits. To fill pâte a choux (eclairs, cream puffs). To fill a mold or a pastry bag.

Garnir

Givrer (to frost)
To produce frost, for decoration, on the surfaces of pastries, fruits, etc., that have been placed in the freezer. Frost sometimes resembles confectioners' sugar. The term is also applied to fruits such as lemons and oranges that have been filled with sorbet.

Givrer

Glacer (to glaze)
To give a sheen or glaze to the surface of a pâte feuilletée (puff) pastry by first sprinkling it with confectioners' sugar and then placing it in a very hot oven long enough for the sugar to caramelize. The Pithiviers is an example of this.

To coat the surface of pâte feuilletée with sugar syrup (density 1260), using a pastry brush, as soon as it comes out of the oven, to give it an appealing sheen.

To cover certain pastries such as pâte à choux (eclairs, religieuses, glands) and petits fours with fondant, confectioners' sugar, or chocolate.

Glacer

Glucoser (to add glucose)
To add glucose to a sugar syrup, fruit preserves, or other mixtures.

Gommer (to thicken)
To put a gelatinous substance into a preparation to thicken it. Examples are gelatin added to a crème anglaise or pastillage or pectin added to fruit preserves. See also **coller**.

Glucoser

Grainer or grener (to become grainy)
To produce a grainy texture in incorrectly beaten egg whites, in a sugar syrup that crystallizes, in a fondant that has been overheated and the crust not removed before cooling, or in a crème anglaise that has been overcooked.

Grainer ou grener

Gratiner (to prepare au gratin)
To form a light crust on the surface of a preparation by placing it in an oven or under a salamander. An example is the croque-monsieur.

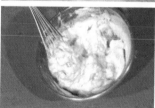

Gratiner

Griller (to grill/to toast)
To color almonds, hazelnuts, or other nuts by roasting in the oven. The nuts are placed in a mold on the floor of the oven, directly on a sheet pan, or in a tart mold placed on a sheet pan.

Griller

Hacher (to chop)
To chop into small pieces, sometimes using a chef's knife (*couteau de tour*) designed for this purpose. In French pastry the term is usually applied to chopping preserved fruits, almonds, pistachios, and other nuts.

Hacher

Homogénéisation (to homogenize)
Method of breaking up minute particles of fat contained in certain mixtures to work the fat evenly throughout (milk, ice cream mixtures). This operation is performed either mechanically using pressure or with a centrifuge. To make homogeneous.

Huiler (to oil)
1. To coat with a fine film of oil to prevent substances from sticking.
2. Badly worked almond paste or praline that has an oily feel and appearance.
3. A leavened dough that is too warm and has taken on an oily appearance.
4. A pâte à choux (cream puff pastry) that has been incorrectly dried.

Huiler

Hydrater (to moisten)
To add liquid to a solid ingredient in order to combine them. An example is water or egg being absorbed by flour.

Imbiber (to moisten)
To moisten with a liquor and/or sugar syrup to give a moist texture and provide flavoring. An example is to moisten a génoise with liquor-flavored sugar syrup.

Imbiber

Inciser (to cut/to make an incision)
To make a cut in a pastry with a sharp knife. An example is to make a cut in a puff pastry galette to put in a dried bean (for children to find during holidays).

Inciser

Incorporer (to incorporate)
To combine two mixtures to lighten such as folding beaten egg whites into a soufflé, or to carefully fold one mixture into another in order to maintain airyness such as flour into beaten egg and sugar to prepare génoise.

Incorporer

Infuser

Infuser (to infuse)
To cook a substance in a liquid to add its aroma and flavor to the liquid. An example is heating milk with vanilla, coffee beans, cinnamon, or lemon zest.

Intérieur (inside)
The inside of a pastry or mixture, which may contain a cream or other filling. Sometimes the interior is glazed with covering chocolate, fondant, etc. Frequently used to describe a wide variety of candies.

Intérieur

Inverti or intervertir (to invert)
To break down complex sugars into simple ones through hydrolysis. An example is turning sucrose into trimoline (invert sugar).

Laminer (to roll out with a machine)
To roll out dough using a machine called a sheeter, designed for this purpose. The machine has two cylinders that roll the pastry.

Laminer

Laver (to wash)
Refers specifically to washing the inside of a copper sugar pan using clean water and a pastry brush. Also cleaning sugar by dissolving it, bringing it to a boil, and skimming off the impurities that rise to the surface with a skimmer. To brush the walls of the sugar pan continually with a pastry brush during the cooking of a sugar syrup to prevent the formation of crystals.

Laver

Levain (a sponge or yeast starter)
A mixture of flour and water that contains either wild or manufactured yeasts and is used to inoculate and initiate the fermentation of leavened dough.

Lever (to rise)
The rising of a leavened dough as a result of fermentation.

Levain

Lier (to bind/to thicken)
To bind a substance with thickeners such as flour, egg yolks, or cornstarch. When using egg yolks, the temperature must never exceed 90° C (195° F), unless flour or starch has been added, or the mixture will coagulate.

Lier

Lisser (to smooth)
To beat a cream or a sauce with a whisk to smooth its texture.
    To make the surface of a cake or pastry smooth or flat using a metal spatula or palette.
    To sand the surface of a piece of pastillage or almond paste.
    To smooth out starch in a high-sided pan in order to make imprints for liquor candies.

Lyophiliser (to freeze-dry)
Method of dehydrating frozen products by evaporating the crystallized moisture in a vacuum.

Lisser

Macérer (to macerate)
To soak fresh or preserved fruits in a liquid (syrup, liquor, liqueur) to flavor or preserve them. During the maceration, the fruit becomes saturated with the liquid.

Macérer

Malaxer (to work/to mix)
To work or knead butter or shortening to soften and give it an even consistency. To work fondant between the hands to soften and warm it. To work a marzipan to make it soft and malleable.

Malaxer

Manier (to work)
To work together butter or shortening either by hand or in an electric mixer to form a smooth mixture.

Marbrer (to marble)
To give a cake or pastry that has been glazed with fondant the appearance of marble. To obtain this effect, lines of different-colored fondants are applied to the surface of the glazed pastry using a paper cone. The lines are then immediately streaked with a small knife so that they merge with the glazed surface. It is important that this be done rapidly so that the fondant does not have time to form a crust.

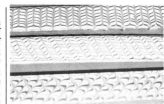
Marbrer

Mariner (to marinate)
To place pieces of fish or meat in a flavored liquid to preserve and flavor them. See also **aromatiser.**

Masquer (to mask/to coat)
To coat a preparation with a cream, a sauce, marzipan or jam using a pastry brush or a spatula in order to form a preliminary coating that will serve as a base for the final decoration. This preliminary coating is often applied before the final glazing of a pastry. A sheet of marzipan can be rolled out and placed over a cake to mask and decorate it. Masking a pastry also helps keep its texture and flavor intact.

Masquer

Masse (mixture)
A combination of several ingredients that form the basis for a finished product. See also **appareil.** The insides of candies are often referred to as the masse.

Masse

Masser (to form/to solidify)
The crystallization of a sugar syrup. Also, the cooked sugar that recrystallizes during or after cooking and becomes cloudy. To work cooked sugar from a liquid and transparent state to a solid, opaque paste (fondant). This may be done in the electric mixer or on a marble by hand.

Masser

Maturation (to ripen/to develop)
Technique used in ice cream making in which a pasteurized dairy product is allowed to ripen at a low temperature so that it develops a better flavor. This process may continue for up to 72 hours.

Meringuer (to stiffen egg whites)
To add a small quantity of sugar to egg whites near the end of beating to stiffen them and prevent them from becoming grainy. To coat a preparation with meringue and glaze it in a hot oven.

Mesurer (to measure)
To measure a liquid using a measuring cup.

Meringuer

Mix (mixture)
Primarily in ice cream making, a mixture to be used in a final preparation.

Modeler (to shape/to form)
To work or knead a substance, such as marzipan, nougatine, or pastillage, to give it texture and eventually a shape. To work one of these materials into a decorative shape.

Modeler

Monder (to peel)
To plunge fruits and nuts into boiling water and then rinse them so that the peel can be more easily removed.

Monder

Monter (to beat/to construct)
To beat egg whites with a whisk or electric mixer to increase their volume. Also, assembling a finished cake, such as a moka, in preparation for its final decoration. Also, to construct a finished pastry such as presentation pieces or croquembouche.

Monter

Mouiller (to moisten)
To moisten a sheet pan before placing a preparation on it to be baked. To add liquid (eggs, milk, water) to a mixture. To add water to sugar in order to prepare a sugar syrup or cooked sugar.

Mouler (to mold)
To place a batter or other mixture in a mold so that it takes on the desired form when baked, as for génoise, pâte à cake, nougatine, pastillage, or chocolate. Frozen mixtures such as sorbets, parfait, and ice cream can also be molded.

Mouler

Mousser (to froth/to foam)
To work a sauce or mixture too much, so that it becomes frothy or covered with foam.

Napper (to coat)
To coat a spoon with crème anglaise to check its doneness. To coat a finished preparation with either a cold or hot sauce using a spoon, ladle, or metal spatula. To put the final coating on a cake or tart using a pastry brush or metal spatula. See also **abricoter.**

Napper

Paner (to bread)
To coat a preparation with breadcrumbs after first dipping it in egg glaze (beaten eggs).

Parer

Parer (to trim)
To trim the edges of cakes, cookies, génoise, or mille-feuilles before applying the final coating of glaze or before assembling a finished cake.

Parfumer (to flavor)
To add a flavoring to a preparation. See also **aromatiser.**

Parfumer

232

Pasteuriser (to pasteurize)
To heat a mixture to a certain température :
● for low-temperature pasteurization, the mixture should be heated to between 60° and 65° C (140° and 150° F) for 30 minutes and then quickly cooled to 6° C (43° F).
● for high-temperature pasteurization, the mixture should be heated to between 80° and 85° C (175° and 185° F) for 3 minutes and then quickly cooled to 6° C (43° F).
Pasteurization is used to kill harmful bacteria without altering the flavor or destroying the nutrients in a mixture.

Pasteuriser

Pâton (block of puff pastry dough)
A block of puff pastry dough or croissant dough after the butter has been folded into the détrempe to form an envelope. Section or piece of dough cut to the size of a piece of pastry to be prepared.

Pâton

Peser (to weigh)
To weigh the raw ingredients called for in a preparation. It is important to weigh all needed materials carefully before beginning to work. Also, to measure the density of a sugar syrup using a hygrometer.

Pétrir (to knead)
To work or knead a dough either to work together the various ingredients or to activate the gluten for leavened dough.

Pétrir

Piler (to grind/to crush)
To grind to a powder or paste with a mortar and pestle, as for almonds, hazelnuts, and walnuts.

Pincer (to pinch)
To pinch the edges of a tart or pâté with a pair of pastry pinchers or with the fingers to create a decorative border.

Pincer

Piquer (to prick)
To poke a sheet of dough (such as pâte feuilletée, pâte à foncer) with a fork or a roller docker to produce small holes. The purpose is to prevent dough from puffing irregularly or from shrinking during baking.

Piquer

Pocher (to poach)
To cook in a simmering (not boiling liquid) so that the substances being cooked hold their shape. Examples are fruits (poached in syrup), eggs, and quenelles. Also, a method of cooking certain fragile preparations that must not come into contact with direct heat, such as lemon curd or egg custard.

Pocher

Pointage (rising/fermentation)
The rising of a fermented dough, which occurs between the kneading and the final shaping and molding of the dough.

Pommade (creamed butter or shortening)
Butter, shortening, or a cream that has been creamed to the consistency of a pomade or ointment. Examples are pâte à cake, pâte à quartre-quarts, and creamed butter used for. buttering molds and sheet pans.

Pommade

Pousse (rising/expansion)
The expansion of a fermented dough caused by yeast during rising. Also, the puffing of a whipped rising batter caused by baking powder during baking.

Praliner (to coat with cooked sugar)
To coat pieces or whole almonds or hazelnuts with cooked sugar.

Presser (to squeeze/to press)
To squeeze a mixture or fruit to extract liquid. Often a special squeezer or juicer is used especially for fruits.

Puncher (to soak)
To soak sections of cake, biscuit, or other baked products with a liquor-flavored syrup.

Quinconce (to stagger rows)
To place batter on baking sheets in staggered rows. Each new row is started one-half space after the one preceding it. This helps the pieces of batter to cook evenly. The spaces between the pastries must be determined based on the anticipated expansion of the batter during baking.

Rabattre (to fold over)
To fold a risen leavened dough over itself in such a way as to force out the accumulated carbon dioxide. See also **rompre.**

Raffermir (to stiffen)
To solidify a dough or other preparation by placing in a cold place (refrigerator or freezer), as when placing a cake in a cold place before the final glazing.
    Also to stiffen a mixture by adding a solid ingredient. An example is adding confectioners' sugar to a glace royale (royal icing).

Rafraîchir (to cool/to refresh)
To add fresh fondant to fondant that has already been used and the crust removed. This is done each time the fondant is to be used. Also, to chill a preparation by placing it in the freezer or refrigerator.

Râper (to grate)
To grate certain substances, such as lemon, orange, nutmeg, or cheese, using a grater.

Rayer (to score)
To make decorative indentations or lines in pastry using a paring knife. This should be done after glazing with egg wash but before baking. This method is used for Pithiviers and chaussons (turnovers).

Réduire (to reduce)
To reduce a mixture by cooking it down to eliminate excess liquid through evaporation. Used to concentrate the flavor and at times to thicken a final preparation.

Praliner

Quinconce

Rabattre

Rafraîchir

Rayer

Réduire

Relâcher (to soften or liquefy excessively)
Refers to a dough, sauce, or cream that loses its texture by liquefying or softening abnormally. This sometimes happens after kneading or during baking.

Repérer (to mark)
Method of marking the pieces used in the assembly of a final preparation in order to fit them together evenly. This method is used to mark the edges of cakes such as génoise so that they can be reconstructed evenly.

Retomber (to fall)
A preparation that falls in the oven after rising because of a sudden drop in oven temperature, excessive beating, or incorrect baking. Examples are a génoise that falls if the oven is opened prematurely or egg whites that fall if they have been overbeaten. Pâte à choux may also fall if it is taken out of the oven too soon.

Rioler (to decorate with strips of dough)
Method of decorating tarts or pies by placing strips of dough over the surface in a diagonal, lozenge pattern. Refers also to a similar pattern made from jelly piped from a paper cone on such preparations as tarts and tartlets.

Rognures (trimmings)
Trimmings of pâte feuilletée that are left after cutting the pastry for particular preparations. These trimmings may be used for other preparations such as napoleons or tarts. Trimmings that result from preparations made from the rognures are called second rognures. Also, sometimes used to refer to trimmings from cakes and meringues.

Rompre (to push down)
To push down a leavened dough to its original volume after it has risen, by folding it several times over itself. This technique eliminates carbon dioxide that has accumulated in the dough. It also helps stimulate the yeast cells by working additional oxygen into the dough, and it contributes to the final consistency of the dough.

Ruban (ribbon)
Method of measuring the consistency of a batter or preparation by seeing how it falls when lifted with a wooden spoon or whisk. A mixture is said to form a ribbon when it flows evenly off the whisk or spoon and folds over itself and also rests on the surface of the remaining batter. This technique is used most frequently in the preparation of génoise.

Sabler (to break up)
Method used in the preparation of pâte brisée, pâte à foncer, and pâte sucrée, in which the butter and flour are worked together with only the tips of the fingers or by rolling them in between the palms of the hands in such a way as to cause the mixture to break up into little beads or chunks. Also, to recrystallize sugar used in the preparation of praline almonds.

Saisir (to seize/to heat)
To expose certain preparations to intense heat either on the stove or in the oven for short periods of time. This method is usually used at the beginning of baking, before the final baking at a lower temperature.

Retomber

Rioler

Rognures

Rompre

Ruban

Sabler

Salpicon (chopped fruit filling)
A mixture of several types of fresh, preserved, or canned fruits that are cut into even cubes and added to certain preparations such as fruit cakes or diplomates. Also, any preparation that contains a mixture of elements that have been cubed and bound together with a sauce.

Sangler (to freeze)
Freezing ice creams and sorbets by placing crushed ice and salt around a mold filled with the preparation in a container or ice cream machine in order to freeze it. Crème anglaise, cream, and fruit syrups are converted into ice cream or sorbets by using an ice cream machine or sorbetière.

Also, to place a mold in the freezer before coating the inside with ice cream or sorbet.

Sauce (sauce)
A flavored liquid that can be made from a variety of bases. Many different sauces are used in French pastry, usually as accompaniments to finished pastries, ice creams, etc.

Saupoudrer (to powder/to sprinkle)
To cover the surface of a preparation or work surface with a powder such as chocolate, confectioners' sugar, or flour, to decorate finished pastries or (on work surfaces) to prevent sticking.

Sentir (to smell)
To recognize, appreciate, or judge the quality of a raw ingredient or finished product through smell.

Serrer (to stiffen/to tighten)
To beat certain preparations quickly by making a circular motion with a whisk to obtain a perfectly smooth mixture, as for crème Chantilly and light cream. To stiffen egg whites through a final beating with sugar.

Singer (to flour/to bind)
To add flour to a mixture during cooking in order to thicken or bind the final sauce. It is important to avoid the formation of lumps.

Siroper (to soak in syrup)
To add flavored syrup to a preparation in order to soften, moisten, or flavor it.

Souder (to attach)
Method of attaching two sheets of dough with either water or egg wash. The first sheet of pastry is brushed with a thin layer of egg wash. The second sheet is placed over the first and the two are pressed gently on the outer edges with the fingers.

Stériliser (to sterilize)
To eliminate bacteria from a substance or material by killing them using heat, ultraviolet radiation, or an antiseptic such as household bleach or alcohol.

Salpicon

Sangler

Saupoudrer

Serrer

Souder

Suinter (to sweat/to ooze)
A dough or other preparation in which fat or liquid works out from the inside and coats its surface.

Tabler or mettre au point (to temper)
Method of working melted couverture (covering) chocolate to cool it, using a metal spatula or a triangle. This process is best carried out on a refrigerated pastry marble or other cool surface until the chocolate begins to thicken but not harden or set, before it is brought to the correct temperature for use (such as for molding and dipping).

Tamiser (to sift)
To sift a powder or mixture, usually through a drum sieve, to remove lumps and impurities. This method is most often used for flour, confectioners' sugar, and nut powders. Also, to crush or grind mixtures and to strain them in order to separate different-sized grains. To strain fruits to obtain purees.

Tamponner (to press/to tamp)
To tamp down the surface of a dough-lined mold with a piece of dough in order to press the dough firmly against the inside surface of the mold.

Tempérer or tiédir (to temper/to warm)
To warm a mixture gently without overheating. To warm a mixture to the same temperature as the preparation or mixture to which it is to be added.

Tirer (to pull)
To pull and refold sugar over itself. This operation is repeated until the sugar has a satinlike texture and appearance.

Tolérance (tolerance)
The ability of a certain preparation, especially a leavened dough, to tolerate errors in its preparation, such as insufficient fermentation or overrising.

Tourer (to turn)
To give turns to pâte feuilletée or croissant dough by rolling the dough into a strip three times as long as it is wide and folding it in thirds or quarters.

Tourner (to turn/to shape)
To give the final shape to leavened dough before baking. Used most often with breads such as pain de mie (white bread) and pain de campagne (country-style bread).

Tabler ou mettre au point

Tamiser

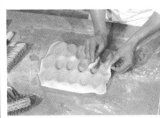
Tamponner

Tirer

Tourner

Travailler (to work)
To work or beat a mixture energetically, either by hand or in the electric mixer, to make it smooth, light, and homogeneous.

Tremper (to soak)
To soak pastries such as babas or savarins in sugar syrup. Also, to coat certain types of candies with a thin layer of couverture (covering) chocolate, fondant, or cooked sugar.

Turbiner (to churn/to turn)
To turn a liquid mixture in an ice-cream maker to convert it into ice cream or sorbet.

Upériser (to sterilize)
To sterilize (not pasteurize) milk by heating it to a very high temperature, 140° to 150° C (285° to 300° F) for 2 seconds, followed by immediate cooling.

Vanner (to stir/to whisk)
To stir a cream, sauce, or other mixture with a wooden spatula or whisk to keep it smooth and to prevent the formation of a film or skin on the surface during cooling.

Venue (raw ingredients)
The specific types and quantities of raw ingredients needed for a particular preparation.

Videler (to form a border)
To form a border on a tart or pie by folding the dough over itself on the edge with the fingers. This adds a decorative effect and also helps hold the filling within the borders.

Viennoiserie (Viennese pastries)
Richer leavened pastries. In France, these are usually eaten at breakfast or served at teas. Examples are pâte à brioche, croissants, pâte à pain au lait (milk bread), chaussons (turnovers), and carrés feuilletés (filled puff pastry squares).

Voiler (to veil)
To surround a finished pastry or ice cream with a net or veil of spun or pulled sugar. The technique is used for presentation pieces.

Zester (to zest)
To remove the thin, colored zest from a citrus fruit, using either a zester, a tool especially designed for this purpose, or a small paring knife. It is important to remove only the zest and none of the white pith, which tends to be bitter. The purpose of zesting is to extract the flavor from the zest. Also, to grate the zest of a citrus fruit with a small grater.

Travailler

Tremper

Venue

Videler

Viennoiserie

Zester

Glossary cross references: English / French

add decorative strips : rioler
add glucose : glucoser
add liquid : arroser/asperger
add liquor : alcooliser
attach : souder
bake : cuire, au four
bake blind : cuire, à blanc
balls, to roll into : bouler
beat : battre ; fouetter ; monter
bind : lier ; singer
blanch : blanchir
body : corps
boiling water, to plunge into :
   ébouillanter/échauder
borders, to form : videler
bread : paner
breadcrumbs : chapelure
break eggs : casser un œuf
break up : sabler
brush : brosser
burn : brûler
burn and stick : ferrer
butter (v) : beurrer
butter (n) : beurre
butter, brown : beurre noisette
butter, creamed : pommade
cake crumbs : chapelure
caramelize : caraméliser
chill suddenly : frapper
chop : hacher
chop coarsely : concasser
churn : turbiner
clarify : clarifier
coat : chemiser ; enrober ;
   masquer ; napper
coat with cooked suger : praliner
coat with jelly or preserves :
   abricoter
coat with sugar : candir
color : colorer/teinter
construct : monter
cook : cuire
cook covered : étuver
cool : refraîchir
cover : couvrir
cream : crémer
crumbs, cake or bread :
   chapelure
crush : écraser ; piler
crush dough : fraiser
crust : croûter
crust, remove : décrouter
crystallize : candir ; cristalliser
cut : couper/découper ; inciser
decorate : décorer
decorate with dough strips :
   rioler
decorate with grooves : canneler
deep-freeze :
   congélation/surgélation
deep-fry : frire
deglaze : déglacer
develop : maturation
dissolve : dissoudre

double/triple sheet pans :
   doubler/tripler
dough sheet : abaisse
drain : égoutter
dry : dessécher
dye : colorer/teinter ; farder
eggs, to break : casser un œuf
emulsion, to prepare :
   emulsionner
expansion : pousse
fall : retomber
fermentation : pointage
fill : fourrer ; garnir
fill fruit with marzipan :
   déguisser
filter : étaminer ; filtrer
final rising : apprêt
flambé : flamber
flavor : aromatiser ; parfumer
flavorings : aromates
flour : fariner ; fleurer ; singer
flour well : fontaine
flute : chiqueter
foam : mousser
fold over : rabattre
form : façonner ; masser ;
   modeler
freeze : sangler
freeze-dry : lyophiliser
frost : givrer
froth : mousser
fruit filling, chopped : salpicon
fruit preserve technique : façon
garnish : garnir
glaze (v) : dorer ; glacer
glaze (n) : dorure
glaze with jelly or preserves :
   abricoter
glucose, to add : glucoser
grainy, to make : grainer/grener
grate : râper
grill : griller
grind : broyer ; piler
groove decoratively : canneler
hollow : évider
homogenize : homogénéïsation
incise : ciseler ; inciser
incorporate : incorporer
indent : denteler
infuse : infuser
inside : intérieur
invert : inverti/inverterir
jelly, to glaze with : abricoter
knead : petrir
leaves, to make into : feuilleter
line : chemiser
line with pastry : foncer
liquefy excessively : relâcher
liquid, to add : arroser/asperger
liquid, to mix with : délayer
liquid, to mold : couler
liquor, to add : alcooliser
loosen : bluquer/débloquer
macerate : macérer

marble : marbrer
marinate : mariner
mark : repérer
mask : masquer
measure : mesurer
mix : malaxer
mix with liquid : délayer
mixture : appareil ; masse ; mix
moisten : hydrater ; imbiber ;
   mouiller
mold : mouler
mold liquids : couler
oil : huiler
ooze : suinter
oven, put into : enfourner
oven, remove from : défourner
pasteurize : pasteuriser
pastries for the day : fournée
pastry, to line with : foncer
pastry bases : fonds
peel : éplucher ; monder
pinch : pincer
pipe out : coucher/dresser
pit : dénoyauter
plate : dresser
plunge in boiling water :
   ébouillanter/échauder
poach : pocher
pour off : décanter
powder : soupoudrer
preserve in sugar : confire
preserved fruit technique :
   façon
preserves, glaze with : abricoter
press : presser ; tamponner
prick : piquer
puff pastry dough block : pâton
pull : tirer
push down : rompre
raw ingredients : venue
reduce : réduire
refresh : refraîchir
remove crust from : décrouter
remove from oven : défourner
remove tart rings : décercler
reverse cooking : décuire
ribbon : ruban
ripen : maturation
rise : développer ; lever
rising : pointage ; pousse
rising, final : apprêt
roll : cribler
roll into balls : bouler
roll out : abaisser
roll out with a sheeter : laminer
sauce : sauce
scald : culotter
scallop : denteler
score : rayer
scrape : corner
seal : envelopper
season : assaisonner
section : détailler
seize : saisir
separate : clarifier
shape : façonner ; modeler ;
   tourner
sheet of dough : abaisse
sheet pans, to double or triple :
   doubler/tripler
shell : décortiquer ; écaler

shortening, creamed : pommade
shuck : décortiquer
sift : tamiser
simmer : frémir
skim : écumer
slice : émincer
slice thinly : effiler
smash : écraser
smell : sentir
smooth : concher ; égaliser ;
   lisser
soak : puncher ; tremper
soak in syrup : siroper
soften : assouplir
soften excessively : relâcher
solidify : masser
split open : cracher
sprinkle : saupoudrer
squeeze ; presser
stagger rows : quinconce
stem : équeter
sterilize : stériliser ; upériser
stiffen : bloquer ; raffermir ;
   serrer
stiffen egg whites : meringuer
stir : vanner
stocks : fonds
strain : chinoiser
streak : rayer
strike with heat : saiser
stuff : farcir ; fourrer
sugar, to preserve in : confire
sugar, cooked, to coat with :
   praliner
sweat : suinter
tamp : tamponner
tart rings, to remove : décercler
temper : tabler/mettre au point;
   tempérer/tiédir
thicken : coller ; épaissir ;
   gommer ; lier
thin : détendre
tighten : serrer
tint : farder
toast : griller
tolerance : tolérance
trim : ébarder ; égaliser ;
   éplucher ; parer
trimmings : rognure
turn : tourer ; tourner ; turbiner
unmold : démouler
veil : voiler
Viennese pastries : viennoiserie
warm : dégourdir ; étuver ;
   tempérer/tiédir
wash : laver
water bath, to cook in : cuire,
   au bain-marie
water vapor : buée
weigh : peser
weight/remove weights :
   charger/décharger
whip : battre ; foisonner ;
   fouetter
whisk : fouetter
whiten : blanchir
work : malaxer ; manier ;
   travailler
yeast starter : levain
zest : zester

Translators' Notes

Because these volumes were originally written for a French audience, some changes had to be made in the instructions to make them applicable to American practice. The following notes explain changes that were made, as well as some of the ingredients used in the recipes.

Butter and shortening: Most recipes call for butter because of its superior flavor. Other shortenings may be substituted in part or entirely, according to taste.

Chocolate: The French government strictly controls the quality and appelations of chocolate. The percentage of cocoa butter, cocoa liquor, and sugar are closely controlled. In France, there are various types and qualities of chocolate, which are discussed in detail in volume 3 of this series. Couverture chocolates (the better-quality chocolates) are made with a minimum of 31 percent cocoa butter; no other fats are allowed.

In the United States, what is referred to in this series as white chocolate is actually called white or confectionary coating, as it contains no chocolate, only cocoa butter, sugar, lecithin, and vanilla or other flavoring.

Crème fraîche: Recipes in this series often include crème fraîche. Crème fraîche is thicker than heavy cream but contains the same amount of butter fat. For most recipes, heavy cream can be substituted for crème fraîche.

Flour: Two types of flour are primarily used in the recipes in this series. In general, when products are to be light, such as cake batters, pure cake flour (without baking powder) is called for. When a batter requires more body, all-purpose flour is used. Breads usually require a strong, high-gluten flour, commonly called bread or patent flour. Many of the recipes requiring flour have been tested in the United States by the translators and have been proven to work. As the qualities of flours, as well as the conditions under which they are used (such as humidity and altitude) vary throughout the United States, the amount specified in a recipe may need to be adjusted slightly.

French products: As this series is based on French pastry-making practices, some of the products in it may be unfamiliar. All the products mentioned are available in the United States. Substitutes are given for products that may be difficult to find. All the French products (such as chocolate) can be obtained through wholesale companies that import such products.

Gelatin: In France, gelatin is marketed in 2-gram sheets, whereas in the United States, it is also sold in powdered form. Gelatin sheets vary in weight in the United States, so it is important to weigh them. The equivalent weight of powdered gelatin can be used to replace the gelatin sheets called for in the recipes. Gelatin sheets should always be softened before using them in a recipe by soaking them in cold water for several minutes and then squeezing them to remove the excess water.

Measurements: French professional pastry chefs customarily weigh their ingredients. For this reason, volume measurements are used only for liquids; dry ingredients are difficult to measure accurately by volume. Both metric and U.S. units of measure are given in the text. It is recommended that those who are serious about the profession of pastry making familiarize themselves with the metric system. Because metric measurement is based on units of ten, it is more accurate and easier to use. The metric system is also the most widely used system of measurement, standard almost everywhere but the United States.

Most U.S. conversions have been rounded off to the nearest half unit of measure, except for smaller quantities, when accuracy was important. Quantities less than 15 grams (½ ounce) are given in teaspoons and tablespoons.

Pastry tips: Pastry tip sizes are always indicated by a number. Unfortunately, each manufacturer numbers its tips differently. In this series, the pastry tip numbers are those most commonly used in France. These numbers often correspond to the diameter of the tip in millimeters. French pastry tips are available in the United States.

Sheet pans: Yields given in this series are based on the use of French equipment of standard dimensions. Professional-quality French sheet pans measure 40 x 60 cm (16 x 24 in.) and are made of heavy blue steel. It is always preferable to use the heaviest sheet pans available. If using different-sized sheet pans, be sure to take this into consideration when calculating the number of pastries to place on a pan.

Sugars: Various types of sugars are used in French pastry, each serving a different purpose. Use granulated sugar when no other indication is given.

Confectioners' sugar is sugar that has been finely ground into a powder. It often contains approximately 3 percent cornstarch to prevent caking.

Glucose, also called dextrose, is used along with granulated or cubed sugar when cooking sugar to prevent crystallization. It is also often used for sugar work such as pulled sugar or blown sugar. Corn syrup can be substituted for glucose in the recipes. It is somewhat lighter, however, and so more of it may be required.

Invert sugar, also called trimoline, is 25 to 30 percent sweeter than granulated sugar. It is made by breaking down sucrose into its components, glucose and fructose. Trimoline helps baked goods stay fresher longer because it holds moisture better than granulated sugar does. It is also used in sorbets, as it imparts a smoother texture than granulated sugar alone. Honey is an invert sugar and can be substituted for trimoline in small quantities. Of course, honey is not neutral in flavor, as trimoline is, and can impart an unwanted flavor to the product.

Yeast: The yeast called for in this series is always compressed fresh yeast, not the dry variety. If dry yeast must be substituted, it must be activated at a somewhat higher temperature than fresh yeast. Activate the dry yeast by first moistening it with 43° C (110° F) water. When substituting dry yeast for fresh, use 10 grams or 2 teaspoons of dry yeast for every 20 grams or 2/3 ounce of fresh yeast specified.

Acknowledgments

Translators Rhona Poritzky-Lauvand and Jim Peterson would like to thank the following people: Pastry chef, consultant, and friend Jean-Noel Bechamps and pastry chef Jean-Marie Guichard, for answering many questions; Paula Borden for small conversions and enormous support; Monica Yates; Rémi Lauvand and Tibi Fish for immeasurable encouragement and love.

Much gratitude to our meticulous editor, Linda Venator, and conscientious associate editor, Cindy Zigmund, and to Judith Joseph, Executive Editor, and the rest of the staff at VNR, who appreciate how special this series is.

We would also like to thank the students who helped test recipes, and we dedicate this series to all those who make this work rewarding.

About the Translators

Rhona Poritzky-Lauvand trained professionally in the culinary arts in Paris, France, working as apprentice in such restaurants as the Michelin two-star Jacque Cagna and Gerard Panguad.

Ms. Lauvand returned to New York and worked in several restaurants, where her talent for instruction became evident. In 1986 she joined the staff of the French Culinary Institute in New York City, the sister school to Le Ferrandi in Paris. Ms. Lauvand currently heads up the pastry department at the French Culinary Institute and has contributed significantly to the development of the pastry curriculum there. In addition to her own professional activities as a pastry chef and free-lance pastry specialist, Ms. Lauvand seriously studies music in New York City.

Jim Peterson trained in the culinary arts as an apprentice in several restaurants in Paris and the French countryside, including Le Vivarois in Paris and Chez La Mère Blanc in Vonnas, both three-star Michelin restaurants.

In 1979, Mr. Peterson returned to the United States where he opened Le Petit Robert in New York to critical acclaim.

Since 1984, Mr. Peterson has taught French cooking for the French Culinary Institute, where he is also writing a comprehensive curriculum for the school. Mr. Peterson also writes professionally and consults. He has a bachelor's degree in chemistry from the University of California at Berkeley.

Index